THE PERSONAL INJURY LIBRARY FROM WILEY LAW PUBLICATIONS

AUTOMOTIVE ENGINEERING AND LITIGATION (FOUR VOLUMES)
George A. Peters and Barbara J. Peters

CONSTRUCTION ACCIDENT PLEADING AND PRACTICE
Turner W. Branch

EVALUATING AND SETTLING PERSONAL INJURY CLAIMS
George M. Gold, Editor

EVALUATING TMJ INJURIES
Reda A. Abdel-Fattah

FIRE LITIGATION SOURCEBOOK: TECHNICAL, MEDICAL, AND LEGAL ASPECTS
Alexander J. Patton and John C. Russell

LITIGATING HEAD TRAUMA CASES
Arthur C. Roberts

MODERN TORT LIABILITY: RECOVERY IN THE '90S
Terrence F. Kiely

PERSONAL INJURY DAMAGES LAW AND PRACTICE
Edward C. Martin

PERSONAL INJURY TRIAL HANDBOOK
John A. Tarantino and David J. Oliveira

THERMOGRAPHY AND PERSONAL INJURY LITIGATION
Samuel D. Hodge, Jr.

UNDERSTANDING & HANDLING THE BACK & NECK INJURY CASE
Thomas J. Murray, Jr., and Donald W. Robertson

WHAT YOU NEED TO KNOW TO SETTLE WITH INSURANCE COMPANIES
Thomas H. Veitch

EVALUATING TMJ INJURIES

SUBSCRIPTION NOTICE

This Wiley product is updated on a periodic basis with supplements to reflect important changes in the subject matter. If you purchased this product directly from John Wiley & Sons, we have already recorded your subscription for this update service.

If, however, you purchased this product from a bookstore and wish to receive (1) the current update at no additional charge, and (2) future updates and revised or related volumes billed separately with a 30-day examination review, please send your name, company name (if applicable), address, and the title of the product to:

Supplement Department
John Wiley & Sons, Inc.
One Wiley Drive
Somerset, NJ 08875
1 800 225 5945

EVALUATING TMJ INJURIES

REDA A. ABDEL-FATTAH
B.D.S., M.S., F.A.H.N.P., F.I.C.C.M.O.

Boca Raton, Florida

Wiley Law Publications
JOHN WILEY & SONS, INC.
New York • Chichester • Brisbane • Toronto • Singapore

Library of Congress Cataloging-in-Publication Data

Abdel-Fattah, Reda.
Evaluating TMJ injuries / Reda Abdel-Fattah.
p. cm. — (Personal injury library)
Includes bibliographical references and index.
ISBN 0-471-57237-3 (cloth: alk. paper)
1. Temporomandibular joint—Wounds and injuries. 2. Personal injuries—United States—Trail practice. I. Title. II. Series,
[DNLM: 1. Defensive Medicine. 2. Jurisprudence—United States.
3. Temporomandibular Joint—injuries. 4. Temporomandibular Joint Diseases. WU 140 A135al
RK470.A24 1992
617.5′22—dc20
DNLM/DLC 92-30
for Library of Congress CIP

Printed in the United States of America

10 9 8 7 6 5 4 3 2

This book is dedicated to my wife,
Dr. Mervat M. Alattar,
and my children,
Kareem, Sarah, Magda, and Sharif

PREFACE

Evaluating TMJ Injuries provides a comprehensive and detailed examination of the temporomandibular joint and odontostomatognathic system injuries. It presents a thorough coverage of this field. The objective of this book is to provide plaintiff or defense lawyers, insurance adjustors, and health care providers with the essential knowledge of TMJ-OSGS injuries. It provides terminology, functional anatomy, biomechanics, mechanism of injury, etiology, and classifications of temporomandibular joint and odontostomatognathic disorder or injury.

In addition current diagnostic modalities, as well as their values in proving the injury, and the available treatment modalities are thoroughly explained. To assist the plaintiff and the defendant attorneys in case evaluation, the book provides chapters on causation, maximum medical improvement, expert witness selection, as well as handling, permanent impairment rating, and case reporting.

It is the author's opinion that the attorneys for the plaintiff or defense should be held accountable for prevention of fraudulent claims or the improper compensation of an injured person. The lawyer should engage expert witnesses of high caliber. The key is presenting the knowledge provided by the expert witness wisely. This book, when used carefully and judiciously in preparing cases, will enhance the complete presentation of and a fair outcome for the clients.

Boca Raton, Florida
January 1992

REDA A. ABDEL-FATTAH

ACKNOWLEDGMENTS

I would like to express my appreciation to Mrs. Kim Kennedy for typing the original draft, to Ms. Anita Hetzler and Mr. Jim Houston for the many hours of hard work they contributed to making this book a reality, and to Mrs. Jacqueline M. Santoro for allowing me to use her photographs.

R.A.A.

ABOUT THE AUTHOR

Reda A. Abdel-Fattah is a practicing dentist in Boca Raton, Florida. He is a graduate of the Faculty of Dentistry, Cairo University, Egypt, obtaining a degree of honor in 1973. In 1978 he earned his Master of Science in biomaterials and engineering from the University of Florida. He then completed a special program in Oral-Facial Pain and TMJ Disorders at the University of Medicine and Dentistry of New Jersey. Dr. Abdel-Fattah is a member of the American, Florida, and Atlantic Coast Dental Associations, the South Palm Beach Dental Society, University of Medicine and Dentistry of New Jersey — TMJ Alumni Society, the International Association of Orthodontics, and the American Association for Functional Orthodontics. He is a fellow of the American Academy of Head, Neck, and Facial Pain, and TMJ Orthopedics as well as the International College of Craniomandibular Orthopedics. He has delivered a number of lectures to lawyers, physicians, and dentists and has published professional articles in the field of TMJ-OSGS disorders. In Florida he acts as a consultant and expert witness to numerous law firms and insurance companies.

SUMMARY CONTENTS

DETAILED CONTENTS

DETAILED CONTENTS

EVALUATING TMJ INJURIES

CHAPTER 1

INTRODUCTION TO TMJ-OSGS

§ 1.1 Overview

TMJ, or the temporomandibular joint, is the jaw joint that articulates the lower jaw to the skull. The TMJ is located in front of the ears on each side of the skull and moves when the mouth is opening or closing. TMJ is the freely movable articulation (joint) between the condylar process of the mandible (condyles) and the glenoid fossa of the squamous portion of the temporal bone.[1] This joint consists of bone parts, condyle, fossa, an articulating eminence and an articulating disc separating the joints into upper and lower compartments. The two compartments are lined with a synovial membrane that is usually filled with a synovial fluid.[2]

The muscle attached to the TMJ is the lateral pterygoid muscle. The superior and inferior bellies of the lateral pterygoid muscle are attached to the articulating disc and condylar process, respectively.[3]

TMJ is part of a larger system called the odontostomatognathic system, or *OSGS*. It consists of a complex apparatus of teeth, two TMJs, two maxillae, a mandible, and the functional matrix of soft tissues. The OSGS must be in a state of balance in order to perform the necessary functions of mastication, deglutition, respiration, speech, head posture, etc. A disturbance of the TMJ can disturb the whole OSGS, and subsequently, the body. Disorders in the TMJ and OSGS can manifest both physically and psychologically.

TMJ-OSGS disorder is misunderstood and misdiagnosed in many head and neck pain patients. Some visit a multitude of physicians complaining of a

[1] E.L. DuBrul, *The Craniomandibular Articulation, in* Sicher's Oral Anatomy (7th ed. 1980).

[2] A. Greider & W.R. Cinotti, Periodontal Prosthesis 198 (1968).

[3] P.E. Mahan, *Anatomic, Histologic and Physiologic Features of TMJ, in* Current Advances in Oral Surgery (W.B. Irby ed. 1980).

host of seemingly unrelated symptoms, including headache, neckache, facial pain, earache, sinus pain, jaw pain, jaw joint clicking, pain during or after eating, difficulty in swallowing, inability to open the mouth wide, toothache, visual disturbances, tinnitus (ringing in the ears), dizziness, and disequilibrium,[4] perhaps gaining little relief from one or all professionals consulted.

Of the numerous causes of TMJ-OSGS disorders, direct or indirect trauma to the human body is of most interest to lawyers. The effects of trauma vary among individuals due to biological and other contributing factors, including but not exclusively the patient's tolerance to pain and systemic conditions. In some, minor trauma can result in a layering of injuries, and in others, the effects of major trauma may be negligible.

Nonsurgical treatment for TMJ-OSGS disorders consists of the fabrication and insertion of a plastic, metal, or combination mouthpiece (oral appliance, or retainer, as popularly known to those readers who wore orthodontic braces during adolescence) or splint to be placed over the lower or upper teeth, physical therapy for facial and postural muscles, and the stabilization of occlusion (bite) through the use of teeth equilibration (reshaping), dental crowns (caps) and bridges, orthodontics (braces), removable partial denture overlays, or reconstruction of dentures.[5]

§ 1.2 Functions of OSGS

The odontostomatognathic system or *OSGS* consists of bone, teeth, muscles, nerves, ligaments, blood and lymph vessels, fascia, and the skin. These tissues, coordinated by the central nervous system, perform several important functions: mastication, deglutition, salivation, taste, digestion, speech, facial expressions, sexual activity, respiration, posture, physical beauty or aesthetics, and help provide self-confidence.[6]

Mastication is the first procedure in the process of the breakdown of food products. Employing the teeth, tongue, lips, cheeks, and palate, the individual prepares food for deglutition. The incisors cut the food, the canines tear it, and the bicuspids and molars grind the food into a finer, smaller size. The tongue, cheeks, and lips press the food against the palate and combine saliva with the food to prepare it for swallowing. The parotid, submandibular, sublingual, and minor salivary glands secrete saliva, which contains

---

[4] D. Morgan, *The Great Imposter: Diseases of the Temporomandibular Joint*, 235 J. Am. Medical Assoc. (May 31, 1976).

[5] C. McNeill, W.M. Dawing, W. Farrar, H. Gelb, M. Lerman, B. Moffett, R. Pertes, W. Solberg, & L. Weinberg, *Craniomandibular (TMJ) Disorders—The State of the Art*, 44 J. Prosthetic Dentistry 434 (1980).

[6] S.I. Silverman, Oral Physiology (1961); L.L. Furstman, Neuroanatomy for the Dental Student and Clinician (1987).

a starch-digesting enzyme. Saliva also lubricates the bolus of food in order to facilitate swallowing.

Swallowing begins with the motion of the lips contracting, or pressing, against the teeth. The upper teeth come in contact with the lower teeth, and the tip of the tongue pushes against the front of the hard palate. The floor of the mouth pulls the tongue forward. The epiglottises cover the trachea and the bolus of food is pushed past the dorsum of the tongue to the pharynx and then on to the stomach, where the food begins to digest.

Taste is detected by the taste buds, a cluster of cells located on the outer surface of the tongue. The number of possible tastes is believed to be only four: salt, sweet, sour, and bitter.

The human animal is set apart from the other members of the animal kingdom by his linguistic ability. Speech is the production of sounds: an integration of respiration, phonation, resonance, articulation, and neurologic processes. A stream of air is pushed up from the lungs (respiration) and passed through the larynx, where the true vocal folds (vocal cords) modify the air stream (phonation) by creating resistance to that air. The pharynx, oral and nasal cavities, and chest wall work together to create the resonance of the voice. The air then moves to the oral cavity, where the lips, cheeks, teeth, tongue, and palate work in concert to produce sound (articulation). Damage to the oral structures may affect articulation and resonance of the vocalization.

The mandible and face are attached to a large number of muscles, many of which are responsible for facial expression. Muscle dysfunction in the OSGS, such as Bell's palsy, can affect a person's ability to smile or express themselves. Although Bell's palsy has overlapping symptoms with TMJ disorders, it is a cranial nerve disorder.

Human beings use their mouths in expressing love for one another. Oral contact between individuals is an essential part of sexual pleasure. The oral-maxillofacial musculature is in continuous motion, and when at rest, it maintains the patency of the airway, aiding in the respiratory process.

The dental occlusion has evolved to function when the head is held in an erect position. Postural changes—scoliosis, being bedridden, or during surgical intervention—can alter the body's center of gravity and cause occlusal changes. When these changes such as losing teeth on one side of the mouth, occur the TMJ on the that side will deviate, causing a compensatory change in the spine, and thus disturb posture.

Well proportioned mandible and maxilla in relation to the rest of the face and head are seen often in paintings or photographs of famous individuals—actors, fashion models, politicians—and in classical sculpture—Michaelangelo's David. It is popularly thought that a nicely sized jaw (contributing to some level of physical aesthetics) may affect a person's self-confidence and general psychological condition.

These different functions of the OSGS reveal TMJ disorders according to their function. Masticatory disturbances are common and are the first to be noticed if a TMJ disorder exists. Swallowing may be second. Difficulty in speaking for a length of time may be another common problem. After that, the next important symptom is difficulty in performing oral activities such as smiling and kissing. Taste impairment occurs when the chorda tympani nerve is affected and this is very rare. Psychological disturbances and decrease of self-esteem usually happen when a disfiguring factor disturbs the maxilla to mandible relation as in growth disturbances or major trauma.

§ 1.3 Terminology of TMJ-OSG Disorders

The disturbances of the TMJ have been called TMJ dysfunction, TMJ syndrome and TMJ disorders. These disturbances may be due to pain, limitation of function, and/or pathologic changes in the histology of the joint;[7] therefore, the word dysfunction, by itself, is an inadequate term, especially when pathological changes occur. *Syndrome* is defined as a group of symptoms commonly found in association with one another so as to constitute a distinct clinical entity.[8] Because TMJ problems manifest in different clinical forms and with combinations of signs (objective findings) and symptoms (subjective complaints),[9] the use of syndrome is inappropriate in describing TMJ disturbances. The definition of a *disorder* is an abnormality or derangement of physical or mental health.[10] It can indicate a functional disturbance and/or structural change, and more broadly describes the TMJ malady. These characteristics make it appropriate to use the term TMJ disorder to explain TMJ disturbances; however, in other instances where there are cranial or cervical symptoms, one would more accurately employ the terms craniomandibular disorder, *CMD*, or craniomandibular cervical disorder, *CMCD*.

Myofascial pain dysfunction, *MPD*, is reserved for conditions in which there is muscular involvement.[11] When signs and symptoms include more than the skeletal-muscular articulation of the mandible to the cranium, i.e., involving TMJ, dental occlusion, and the muscles of mastication, stomatognathic disorder, *SGD*, is a more inclusive nomenclature.[12] The stomatognathic system consists of TMJs, the dental periodontal complex, masticatory

---

[7] W.B. Farrar & W. McCarty, A Clinical Outline of TMJ Diagnosis and Treatment (1983).

[8] Dorland's Pocket Medical Dictionary (21st ed. 1969).

[9] D. Morgan, *The Great Imposter: Diseases of the Temporomandibular Joint*, 235 J. Am. Medical Assoc. (May 31, 1976).

[10] Dorland's Pocket Medical Dictionary (21st ed. 1969).

[11] D.M. Laskin, *Etiology of the Pain Dysfunction Syndrome* 79 J. Am. Dental Assoc. 247 (1969).

[12] F. Mongini, The Stomatognathic System: Function, Dysfunction and Rehabilitation (1984).

muscles, the mandible and maxillae, and the surrounding functional matrix. Because dental occlusion plays a major role in the stability of the TMJ,[13] odontostomatognathic disorder, or *OSGD*, more comprehensively describes this anomaly of the teeth, mouth, and jaws, and should be named with reference to the anatomical site of its signs and symptoms.

§ 1.4 Prevalence of Signs and Symptoms

TMJ and OSGS disorders have their genesis in diverse diagnostic entities; therefore symptoms and signs vary from case to case.

Symptoms. The patient usually presents to the physician with onc or more complaints or deviations from a normal, healthy condition. The complaints could be one or more of the following:

1. Pain or discomfort in front of the ears, in the ears, in or behind the eyes, at the base of the skull, in the temporal areas, at the back of the neck, at the top of the head, or at the cheekbone area.
2. Inability to chew hard foods, to talk for a long period of time, or to completely open the mouth.
3. Jaw joint noises (for example, clicking) when opening, closing, or chewing food.
4. Other seemingly unrelated symptoms such as dizziness, fatigue, or visual problems.

Signs. The findings of the clinician during the physical examination could be one of the following:

1. Facial asymmetry, such as different eye and ear levels, deviation of nose of chin to one side, or change in the height of the lower third of the face. The lower third of the face may appear shorter if the occlusion is disturbed.
2. Altered range of motion of the mouth opening, such as limited or hyperextended movement.
3. Abnormal pattern of mandibular movement, such as deviation or deflection of the mandible.
4. Malocclusion, such as missing, shifted, rotated, tipped, or deformed teeth.
5. Abnormal joint sounds, such as clicking or crepitation.
6. Muscle rigidity or change in consistency.

---

[13] L.A. Weinberg, *An Evaluation of Occlusal Factors in TMJ Dysfunction Pain Syndrome*, 41 J. Prosthetic Dentistry 636 (1979).

7. Radiographic findings, such as displaced, deformed, remodeled, hypoplastic, or hyperplastic condyle.
8. Soft tissue findings such as disc displacement, which can be confirmed through the use of magnetic resonance imaging (MRI) or an arthrogram.

Prevalence. The level of existence of TMJ-OSGS disorders within a specific population is difficult to determine due to the variety of sampling techniques used in studies. Rugh and Solberg[14] and Schiffman and Fricton[15] demonstrated that about 75 percent of the individuals they tested had at least one sign of TMJ disorder and about 33 percent had at least one symptom.

Signs and symptoms of TMJ-OSGS disorders usually increase in frequency and severity from the second through the fourth decade of life.[16] Different rates of occurrence between the sexes have been inconsistently reported: some studies catalog a 3:1 female to male ratio and others report a 9:1 ratio.

---

[14] J.D. Rugh & W.K. Solberg, *Oral Health Status in the United States: Temporomandibular Joint Disorders*, 49 J. Dental Education 398 (1985).

[15] E. Schiffman & J.R. Fricton, *Epidemiology of T.M.J. and Craniofacial Pain, in* Craniofacial Pain: Diagnosis and Management (J.R. Fricton, R.J. Kroenig, & K.M. Hathaway, eds. 1988).

[16] C. McNeil, *The Optimum Temporomandibular Condylar Position in Clinical Practice*, 5(6) Int'l. J. Periodontology and Restorative Dentistry 53 (1985); L. Centore, P. Bianchi, & C. McNeil, *The Relationship Between Non-Organic Multiple Physical Complaints and Narcissism*, 68 J. Dental Research 37 (1989).

CHAPTER 2

FUNCTIONAL ANATOMY

§ 2.1 Anatomical Planes

The study of the functional anatomy of TMJ-OSGS is essential for a thorough understanding of the diagnosis, prevention, and treatment of these disorders. It is also important for interviewing a client to develop and present a credible TMJ claim.

The anatomical relation of structures to each other is important in the study of anatomy. **Figure 2-1** illustrates terms used to describe anatomical relations.

Sagittal plane: running front to back, dividing the body into left and right portions

Coronal plane: running from side to side, dividing the body into front and back portions

Horizontal plane: parallel to the horizon

Occlusal plane: of the bite surface of the teeth parallel with the horizontal

Distal: away from the dental midline

Mesial: toward the dental midline

Medial: toward the body midline

Upper (superior): upward direction

Lower (inferior): downward direction
Lateral: to the side, right or left
Posterior: backward
Anterior: forward

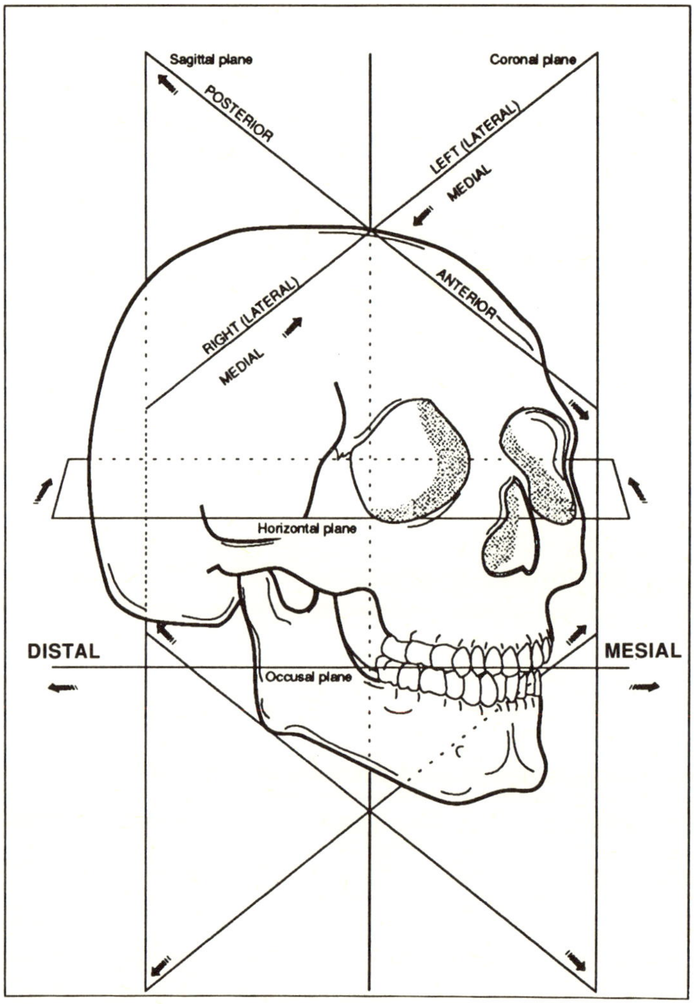

Figure 2-1. Anatomical planes.

Specific horizontal planes include the popular plane, otic plane, and occlusal plane, all shown in **Figure 2-2**. The occlusal plane is sometimes considered a curve rather than a plane because it follows the occlusal surface.

To illustrate how these terms are used, in certain types of TMJ disorders the condyle is displaced posteriorly and the disc is displaced anteriorly.

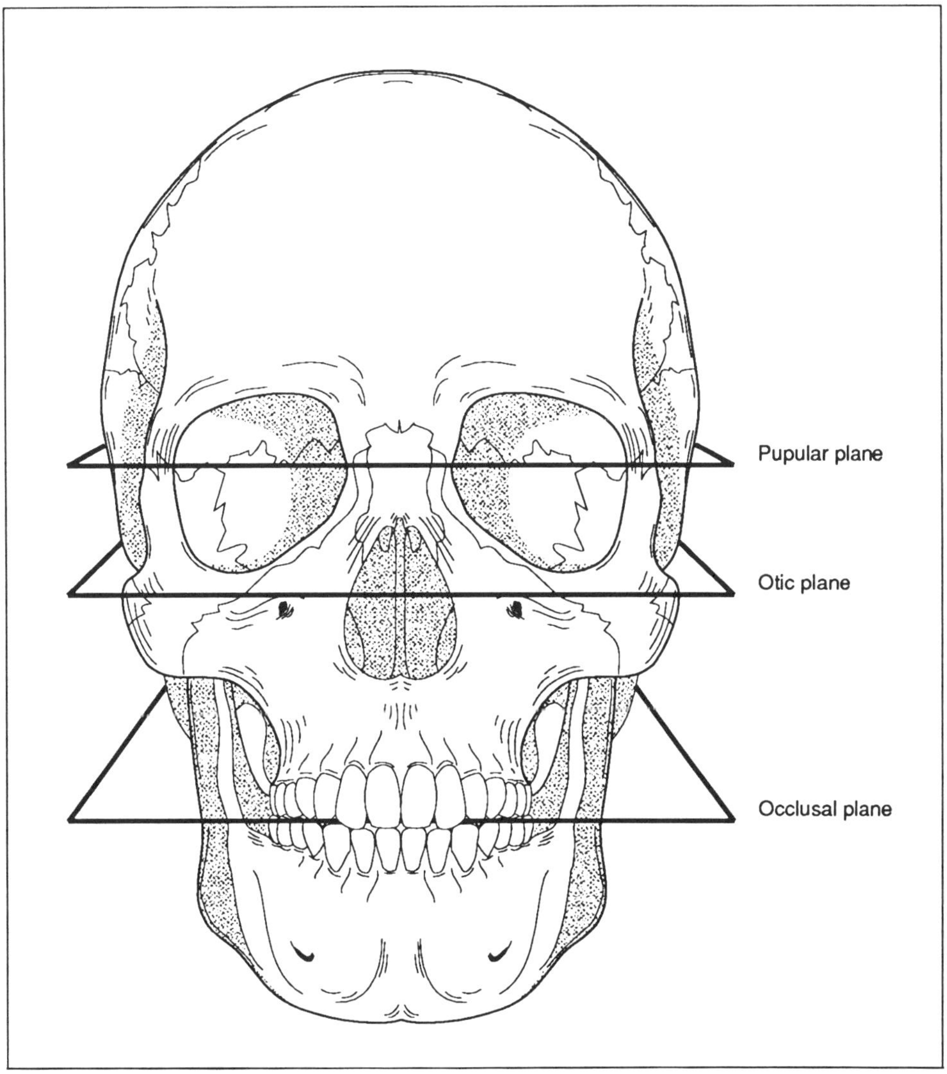

Figure 2-2. Horizontal planes.

§ 2.2 Osteology

TMJ-OSG disorders should be considered in the context of the entire head and neck, especially if the TMJ-OSG disorder is the result of massive trauma to that part of the body.

The following are descriptions of the skull views:

Figure 2-3 represents the anterior view of the skull which shows the most obvious landmarks of the orbits (eye sockets) separated medially and inferiorly by the pear-like opening, the anterior nasal aperature, through which

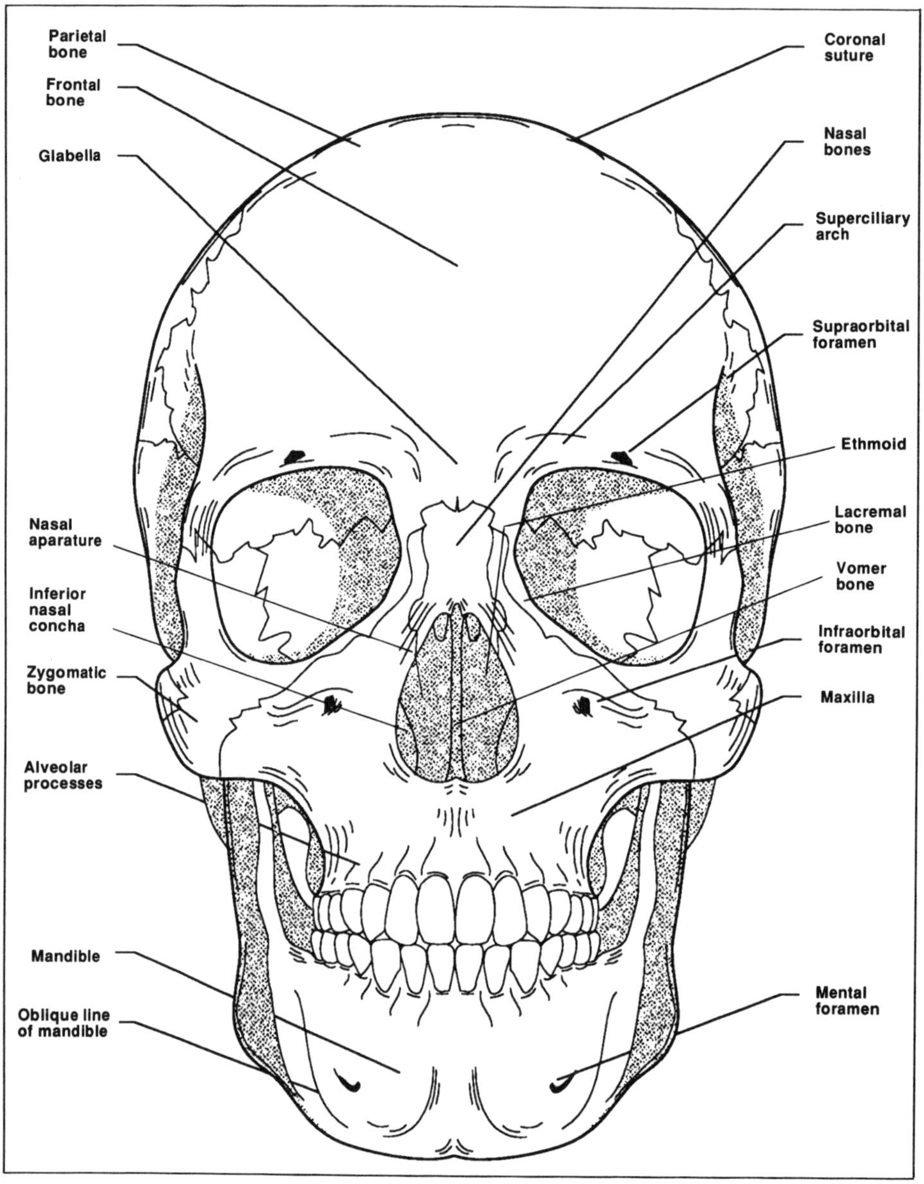

Figure 2-3. Anterior view of skull.

the nasal septum can be seen vertically in the midline. This nasal septum consists of vomer bone inferiorly and ethmoid bone superiorly. Laterally and through looking into the anterior nasal aperature curved thin bony plates extend laterally from the lateral wall of the nasal cavities. These are the inferior nasal conchae. The frontal bone, the bony prominence of the forehead, is superior to the orbits, while the zygomatic and maxillary bones are visible laterally and inferiorly.

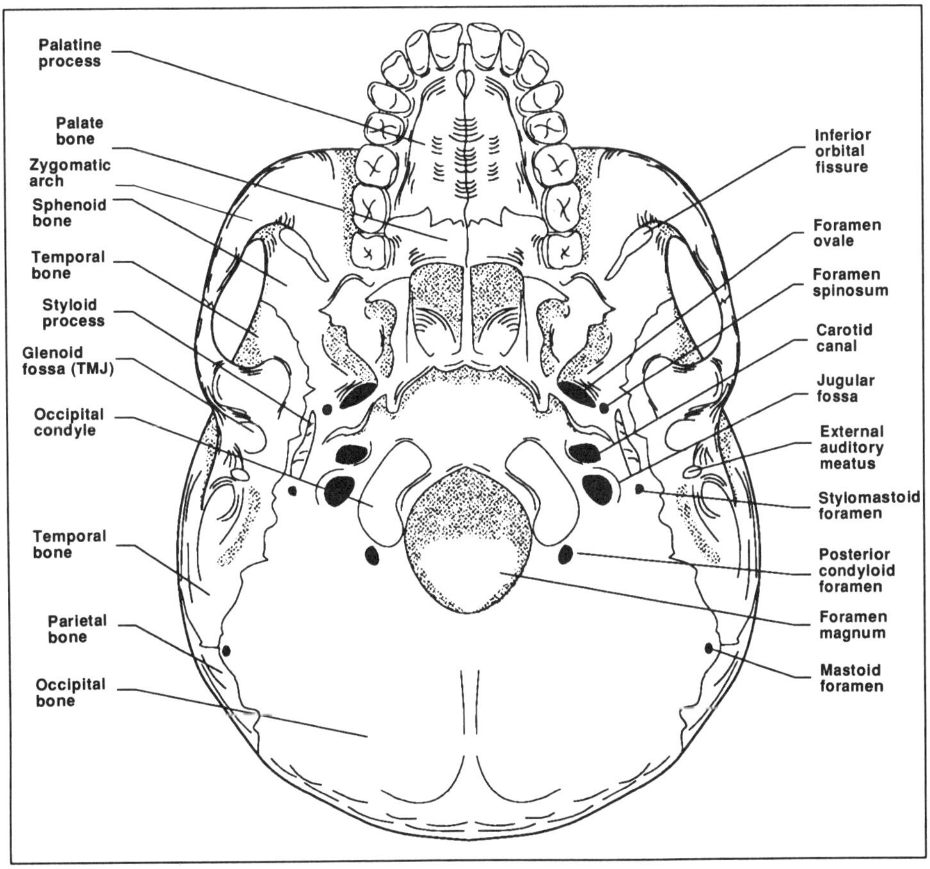

Figure 2-4. Basal view of skull.

The upper and lower dental arches (teeth) embedded in the upper and lower alvealar processes respectively are also obvious landmarks of the frontal view of the skull.

There are three foramena nearly located on a vertical line and named superior orbital, inferior orbital, and mental foramena for superior orbital, infraorbital, and mental nerves respectively.

Figure 2-4 shows the base of the skull with a major landmark in the middle of the skull, namely the foramen magnum through which the brain is connected to the spinal cord by the medulla oblongata. On each side of this foramen there are two processes called occipital condyles on which the skull rests on atlas (the first cervical vertebrae).

Lateral to the foramen magnum, there are numerous of foramina such as posterior condylar foramen for the hypoglassal nerve (XII cranial nerve), stylomastoid foramen for the facial nerve (VII cranial nerve), the jugular canal for the internal jugular vein, vagus nerve (X cranial nerve) and accessory nerve (XI cranial nerve), carotid artery, foramen spinosum for the

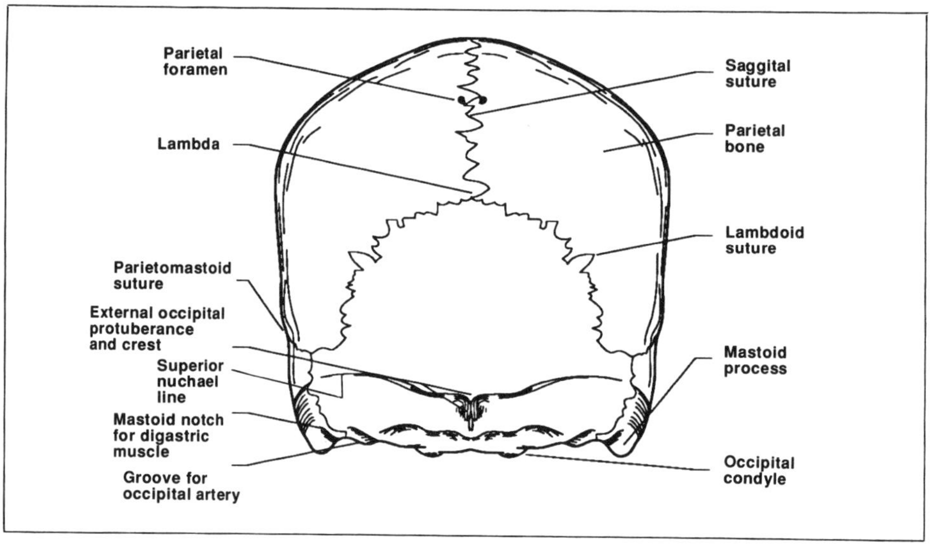

Figure 2-5. Posterior view of skull

middle meningeal artery, and foramen ovale for the mandibular nerve a branch of trigeminal nerve (V cranial nerve). Far laterally, the temporal bones are located on each side. Anteriorly, the maxillary dental arch surrounds the palatine processes and palatine bones. Lateral to the maxillary dental arch, the zygomatic bone, and arches are located.

The occipital bone is located posterior to the foramen magnum.

The posterior view of the skull indicated in **Figure 2-5** shows two parietal bones separated by the sagittal suture, occipital bone which is connected to the parietal bones through the lambdoid suture. The occipital bone has a horizontal thick ridge in the middle called the superior nuchael line. At its midpoint, it forms a raised point called the external occipital protuberance. Inferiorly, the occipital condyles where the skull rest on the atlas (first cervical vertebra) and the groove for the occipital artery are indicated. Laterally and inferiorly, the mastoid process which is a prominent projection containing the mastoid cells are present.

The cranial vault as indicated in **Figure 2-6** shows the two parietal bones connected at the midline by the sagittal suture, anteriorly to the frontal bone through the coronal suture and posteriorly to the occipital bone through the lambdoid suture. Nearly at the top of the skull, the parietal emmissary foramina are located on each side of the sagittal suture.

The lateral view of the skull shown in **Figure 2-7** shows the temporal bone in the middle connected to the parietal bone superiorly, frontal bone anteriorly superiorly, occipital bone posteriorly, and maxillary and malar bones anteriorly. The temporal bone is connected inferiorly to the mandible through the temporomandibular joint.

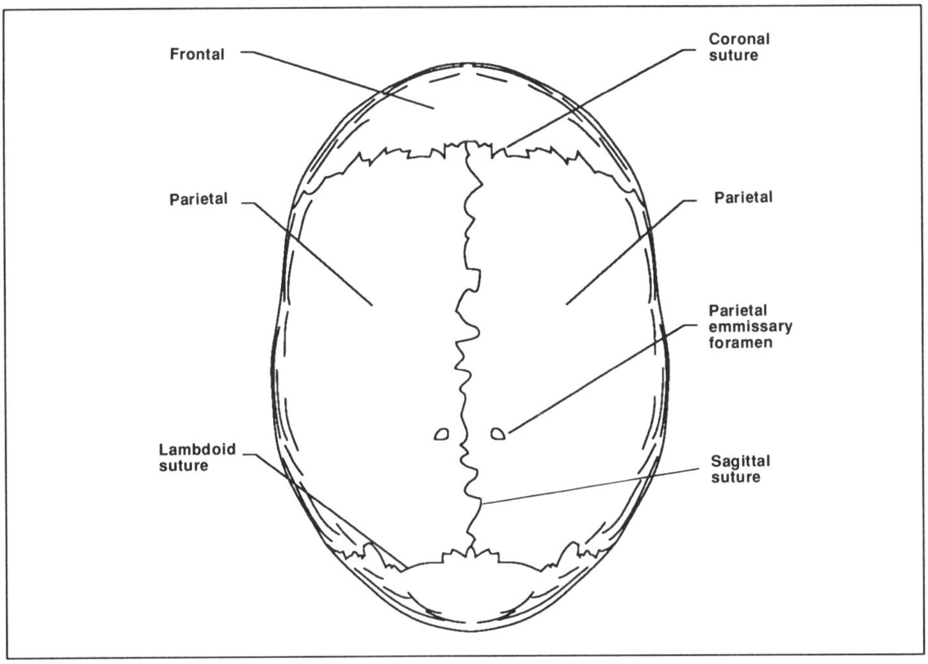

Figure 2-6. Top view of skull.

The skull is composed of cranial, facial, and miscellaneous bones.

The *cranial case*, or brain case, consists of eight bones. There are two parietal bones, which form the roof and sides of the skull connected together at the midline by the sagittal suture, as shown in **Figure 2-6** and **Figure 2-7**. The two parietal bones are connected inferior-laterally to two temporal bones. The two temporal bones are on both sides and the base of the skull. They include portions which enclose the hearing organs and the upper portion of the TMJ, namely glenoid fossae. See **Figure 2-7**. The occipital bone shown in **Figures 2-4** and **2-7** is the lower back part of the skull. It is connected superiorly to the parietal bones and laterally to the temporal bones and anteriorly to the sphenoid bone. Anteriorly from the side of the base of the skull is the sphenoid bone, see **Figure 2-4**. The ethmoid bone, located in the front of the skull, is a spongy bone containing cellular cavities which open into the nasal cavity. It is also connected to the vomer bone inferiorly and forms the upper portion of the nasal septum which can be viewed in **Figure 2-3**. The frontal bone shown in **Figure 2-3** and **Figure 2-7** is the forehead bone, it is connected to the partietal and temporal bones through the coronal suture. The sphenoid bone, a butterfly shaped bone is a large bone in the center and base of the skull. It is located between the occipital bone posteriorly and ethmoid bone anteriorly and connected to the parietal and temporal bones laterally. It is shown in **Figure 2-4**. The sphenoid bone contains vital structures such as optic nerves anteriorly, sellae turcica which

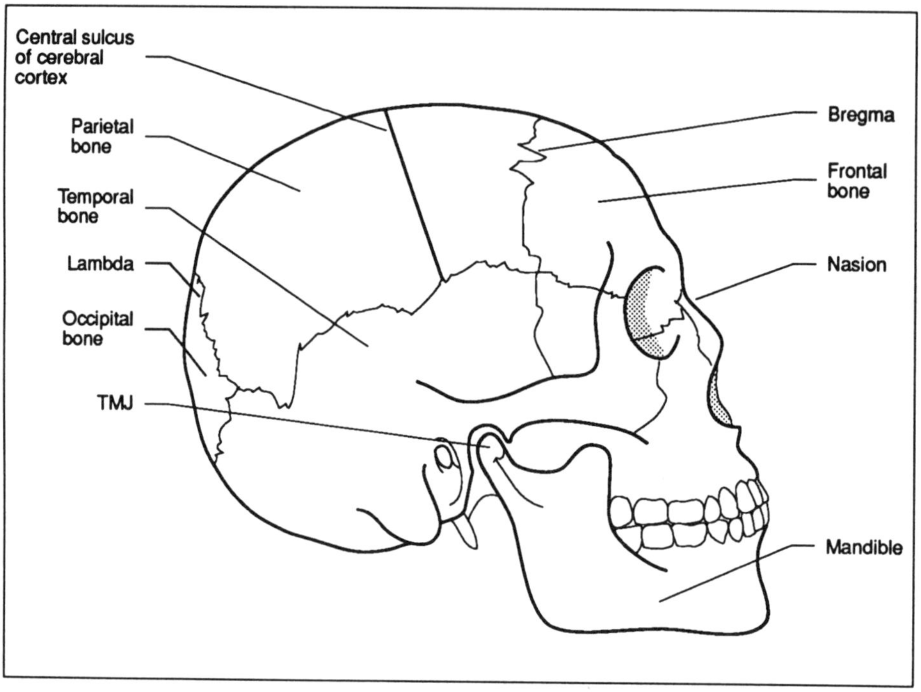

Figure 2-7. Lateral view of skull.

is the housing for the pituatary gland, cranial nerves III, IV, VI, and the trigeminal nerve divisions (maxillary nerve and mandibular nerve) jugular vein, and internal carotid artery. The cranial bones are articulated by sutures, these sutures are clinically considered immovable union of bones and contain thin layers of periostiums and tiny vascular supply. They are also considered to have micro movement. Several of these skull sutures are shown in **Figures 5**, **2-6**, and **2-7**.

There are fourteen *facial bones*. Six of them occur in pairs: the maxilla or the upper jaw bones, shown in **Figure 2-3**, the malar bone or cheek bone, and the palatine or bones of the palate, shown in **Figure 2-4**. The lacrimal bones are at the inner edge of the orbital cavity which serves to house the tear duct to transmit the tears from the eyes to the nasal cavity, and nasal bones which form the nasal bridge in between the eyes are also in pairs. The other nose bone, the vomer is a vertical one and forms the lower portion of the nasal septum and articulates with the ethmoid bone superiorly, sphenoid bone posteriorly superiorly, palatine and maxillary bones inferiorly. The two inferior conchae are curved layers of bone lying horizontally in the lateral walls of the nasal cavities. They can be observed through looking to the nasal opening. These inferior nasal conchae are forming more surfaces when covered with nasal mucosa for warming and clearing the air passing through the nose to the pharnyx. The mandible is the lower movable part of the face

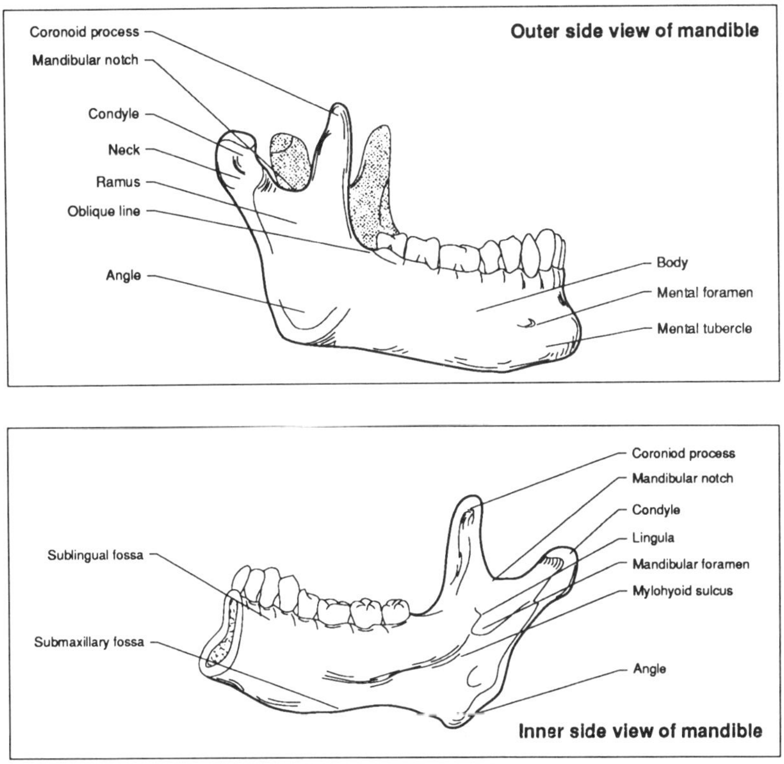

Figure 2-8. Outer and inner side views of mandible.

and forms a major part of the odontostomatognathic system and contains the condyles parts of the temporomandibular joints as shown in **Figure 2-7**. It is the focus of this book.

In **Figure 2-8** the mandible is shown. It consists of two halves, the right and left. Each half has two parts, a horizontal body and a vertical ramus attached posteriorly to the body.

The body contains the alvealar process superiorly in which the lower teeth are embedded. The mental foramen is located in the outerview of the mandibular body nearly below the apex of the second bicuspid root. The anterior portion of the mandibular body is thickened forming the mental protuberance (chin). The mylohyoid ridge is a bony ridge located in the inner surface of the mandibular body and allows the attachment of the mylohyoid muscles.

The ramus unites with the body to form the mandibular angle. The ramus has two processes named coronoid and condylar processes. The coronoid processes is the site for the temporalis muscle insertion and the condylar process contains the mandibular condyle which forms the movable part of the temporomandibular joint. The *neck bones* consist primarily of the cervical spine. In **Figure 2-9** the cervical spine is shown to consist of seven cervical vertebrae. They constitute the most superior extension of the

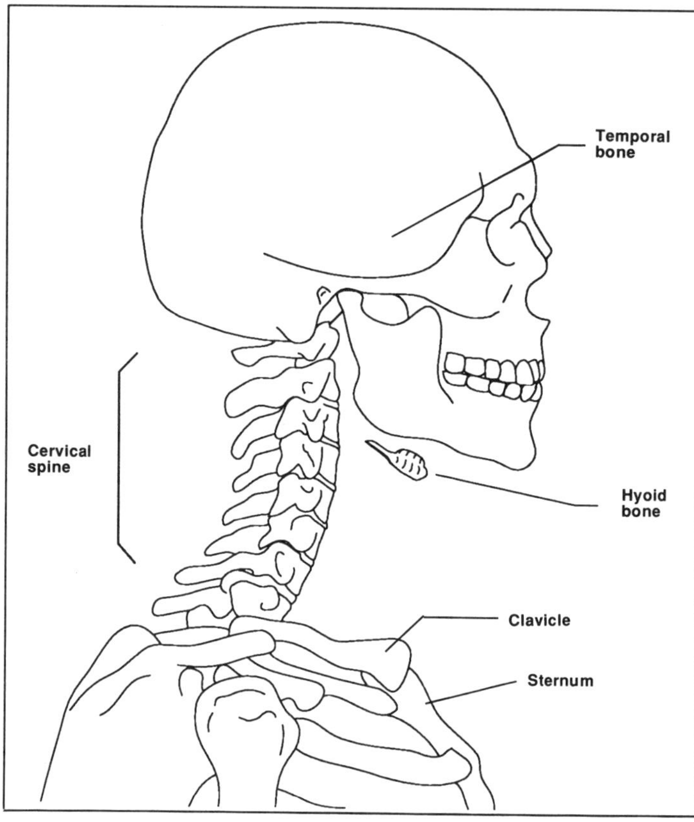

Figure 2-9. Anatomy of cervical spine (lateral view).

vertebral column. The superior two, the atlas and the axis are physiologically modified to support the head and allow its rotation and motion at the atlanto-axis joint. The most inferior cervical vertebra (C7) is also modified.

Any two vertebrae are interposed by an intervertebral disc as well as other cartilaginous structures to allow smooth movement and cushion and support the vertebral column.

The hyoid bone is a small, U-shaped bone suspended by ligaments and muscles between the temporal bones and sternum and located anterior to the cervical spine at the level of the third to fourth cervical vertebrae.

§ 2.3 Dental Occlusion (The Bite)

Dental occlusion refers to the manner in which the upper and lower teeth mesh when the jaw closes. The dentition of a human being comprises two sets of teeth over a lifetime. The first set, called primary or deciduous, is composed of twenty teeth: ten in the upper and ten in the lower arch. Each arch is composed of four incisors, two canines, and four molars. These deciduous teeth usually begin erupting at the age of six months, and the average child ends the ''teething'' stage by about twenty four months.

The second set is called permanent teeth and has thirty two teeth, sixteen in each arch. The individual arch consists of four incisors (two centrals and two laterals), two canines, two first bicuspids, two second bicuspids, and six molars. The incisors cut into the food, the canines tear it, the premolars or bicuspids grind food, and the molars more effectively mash or crush hard foods. The dental occlusion is illustrated in **Figures 2-10** and **2-11**.

Each tooth, as illustrated in **Figure 2-12** is constructed of two parts: the crown, which erupts from the gum or *gingiva*, and the root, which is embedded in the jawbone and covered with the *gingival tissue* (gums). Each tooth is composed of *enamel*, covering the crown, and the *cementum*, covering the root. Beneath the enamel and the cementum is a continuous layer of hard, cancellous tissue called the *dentin*. Within the dentin, there is a space filled by connective tissue that includes nerves, blood vessels, and the lymphatics as well as other tissues that serve to secure the nutrition and health of the tooth. This connective tissue is called dental pulp.

The teeth are surrounded by a soft tissue ligament called the periodontal membrane, and this cushions the attachment of the tooth to the jawbone.

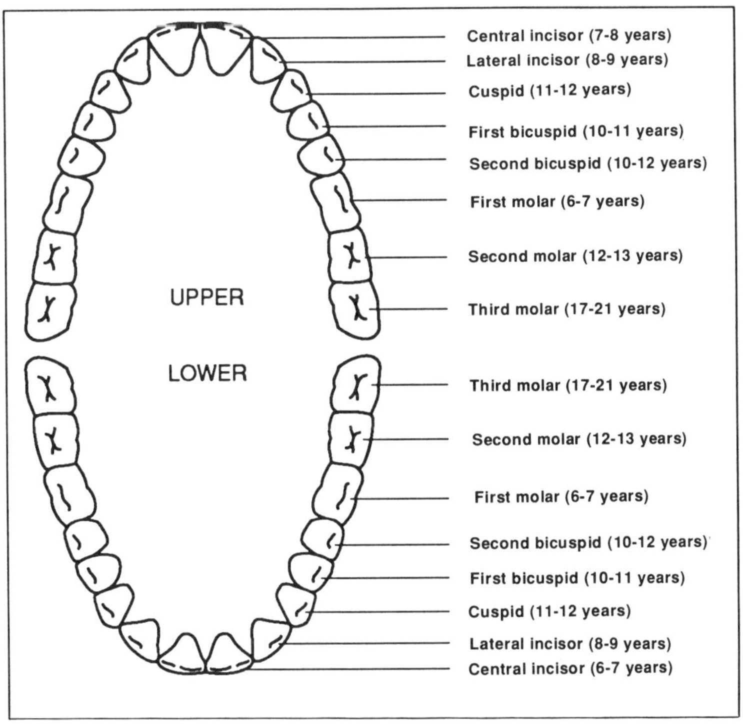

Figure 2-10. Dental occlusion (occlusal view). The date of tooth eruption is indicated by each tooth.

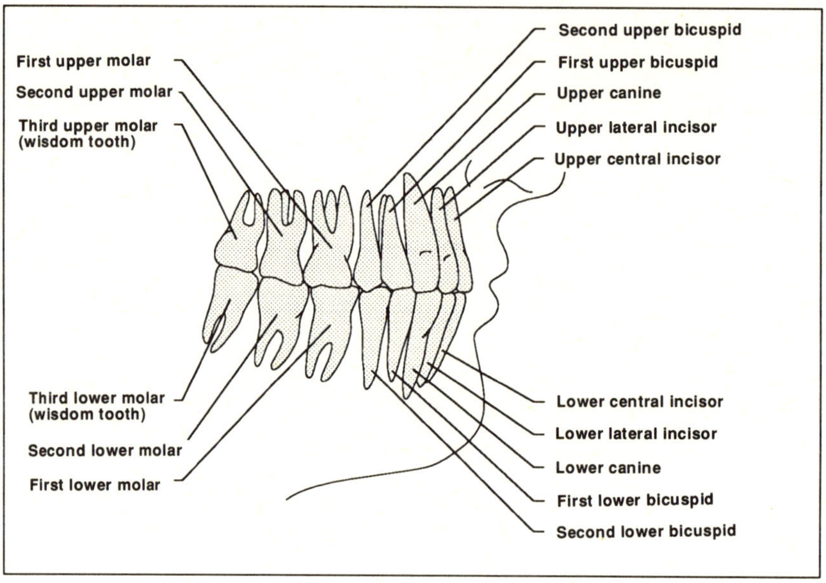

Figure 2-11. Dental occlusion (side view).

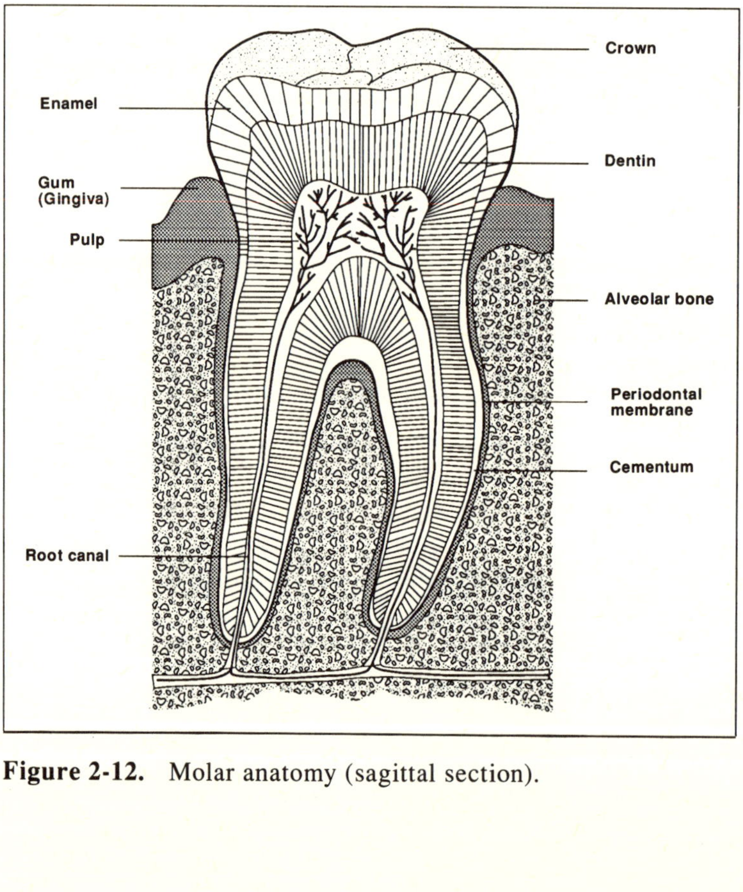

Figure 2-12. Molar anatomy (sagittal section).

§ 2.4 Myology

The TMJ-OSGS involves a large number of paired muscles, divided into four groups. The odontostomatognathic muscles control movement of the mouth and jaw together. There are also facial muscles, tongue muscles, and the cervical muscles.

Odontostomatognathic muscles. This group of muscles are subdivided by the type of movement they control: elevators, depressors, lateral movers, protruders, retruders, and two miscellaneous muscles. Some of the muscles are involved in more than one direction of movement and are in more than one of these groups.

The *elevators*, muscles which elevate the mandible, are illustrated in **Figure 2-13**. They include the *posterior temporalis*, which is located in the temporal fossa (a shallow depression in the temporal bone above and in front of the ear); *masseters*, which close the mouth and are the principle muscles in mastication; and the *medial pterygoids*, inside the mouth medial to the ramus of the mandible.

The temporalis muscle is a fan shaped muscle originating from the temporal fossa on each side of the skull. It is formed of three types of fibers: anterior, middle, and posterior. Temporalis muscle inserts in the middle surface, apex, anterior and posterior borders of the coronoid process, and the anterior border of the ramus of the mandible nearly as far as the last molar tooth. It is supplied by the posterior deep temporal branch of the maxillary artery and innervated by anterior and posterior deep temporal nerves of the mandibular division of the trigeminal nerve. Its function is to protrude and to move the mandible laterally by the anterior fibers; to move the mandible laterally by the middle fibers; and to elevate and protrude the mandible by the posterior fibers. When this muscle is in a spasm or dysfunction it will be tender and painful to chew and may refer pain to the upper posterior teeth. The masseter muscle is a thick muscle located on the side of the mandible formed of two deep and superficial groups of fibers originating from the zygomatic process and arch and inserted into the lateral aspect of the mandible ramus. It is supplied by the masseteric branch of the maxillary artery and innervated by the masseteric branch of the mandibular division of the trigeminal nerve. Its function is to elevate and protrude the mandible. It shows difficulty in chewing food and may refer pain to the lower posterior teeth when in spastic or dysfunctional condition. The middle pterygoid muscle originates from the middle surface of the lateral pterygoid plate and inserts in the middle surface of the mandibular ramus. It is supplied by a branch from the maxillary artery and innervated by the middle pterygoid nerve from the trunk of the mandibular division of the trigeminal nerve. Its function is to elevate, depress, protrude, and laterally move the mandible. When it is in a spasm

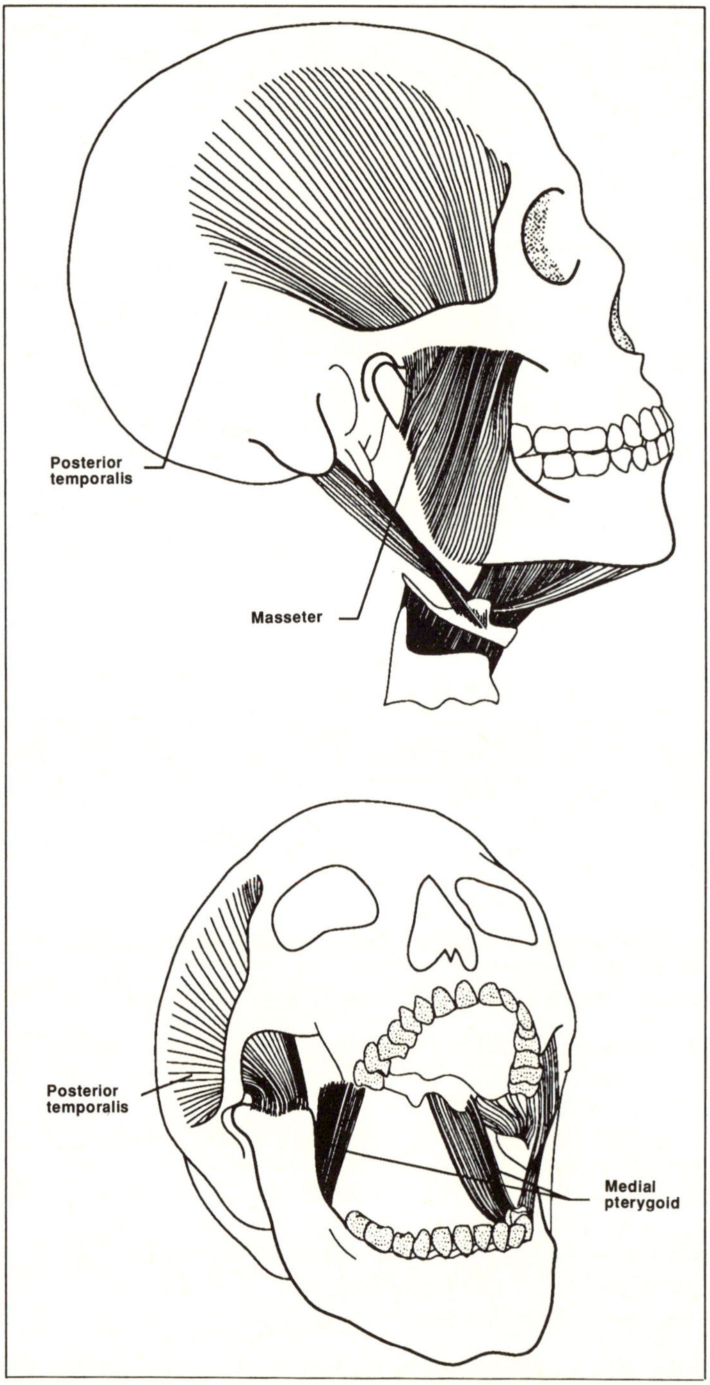

Figure 2-13. Mandibular elevator muscles.

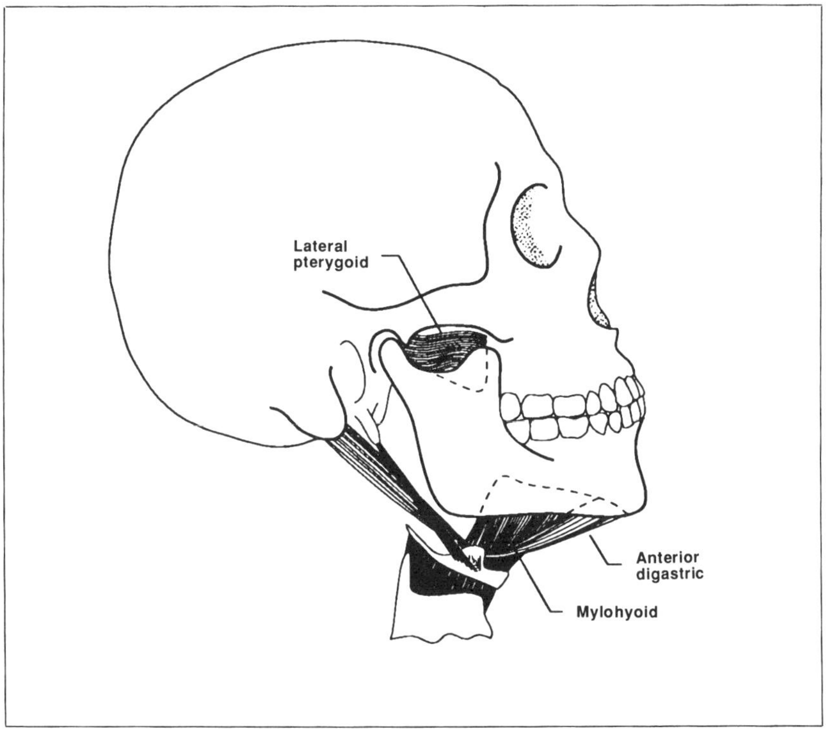

Figure 2-14. Mandibular depressor muscles.

or dysfunction it becomes tender causing difficulty in chewing food and may refer pain to the lower posterior teeth.

The *depressors*, muscles which depress the mandible, are illustrated in **Figure 2-14**. They include the *anterior digastrics*, which are located below the mandible; *lateral pterygoids*, connecting the TMJ to the lateral side of the skull; and *mylohyoid*, a pair of muscles that combine to form the floor of the mouth.

The diagastric muscle is an elongated spindle muscle which has two parts, anterior and posterior bellies. The anterior belly originates from the diagastric fossa on the lower border of the mandible near the symphasis and inserts in the middle tendon to the hyoid bone. The posterior belly originates from the mastoid notch and inserts in the middle tendon to the hyoid bone. The anterior belly of the diagastric is supplied by the submental branch of the facial artery. The posterior belly of the diagastric muscle is supplied by the posterior auricular artery with contributions from the supra-hyoid branch of the lingual artery and the muscle branch of the occipital artery. It is innervated by the mylohyoid nerve branch to the anterior belly and facial nerve to the posterior belly. Its function is to depress the mandible by anterior belly and retruded by the posterior one.

The lateral pterygoid muscle has two heads or bellies. The superior belly of the lateral pterygoid originates from the greater wing of the sphenoid bone and inferior temporal fossa and inserts through the articular capsule of the TMJ inserted into the disc and the neck of the condyle. The inferior belly of the lateral pterygoid muscle originates from the lateral surface of the lateral pterygoid plate and inserts in the anterior surface of the condylar process. The lateral pterygoid muscle is supplied by branches of the maxillary artery and innervated from the mandibular division of the trigeminal nerve. Its function to depress, protrude, and move the mandible laterally. When this muscle is in dysfunction or spasm condition it is painful to move the mandible. If the superior belly of the lateral pterygoid muscle is in severe spasm it may in some cases displace the disc anteriorly. Painful spasm of this muscle may refer pain to the upper posterior teeth and around the ears.

The mylohyoid muscle is the diaphragm muscle present under the mandible. It controls the mouth floor. It originates from the mylohyoid ridge, a thickening of bone in the inner surface of the mandible, and inserts medially into the medial raphe and at the body of the hyoid bone. The blood supply for the mylohyoid muscle is from a vascular amastomoses from the submental branch of the facial artery and the sublingual branch of the lingual artery. It is innervated by the mylohyoid branch inferior alvealar nerve a branch from the mandibular branch of the trigeminal nerve. Its function is to depress the mandible and elevate the hyoid bone during swallowing. When it is in a spasm or dysfunction it may cause dysphagia or difficulty swallowing.

The *lateral movers* move the mandible to both sides. As shown in **Figure 2-15**, they include the *lateral* and *medial pterygoids* already mentioned and also the *anterior* and *medial temporalis*.

The *protruders*, shown in **Figure 2-16**, move the mandible forward. They include the *lateral* and *medial pterygoids* plus the *masseters* and *anterior temporalis*.

The *retruders* are shown in **Figure 2-17**. In addition to the *posterior temporalis* and *digastric*, they also include the *suprahyoid*, above the hyoid bone.

The suprahyoid muscles are groups of muscles located between the hyoid bone and the lower border of the mandible and include the diagastric, mylohyoid, stylohyoid and the thyrohyoid. The diagrastric and the mylohyoid were explained previously. The stylohyoid and the thyrohyoid muscle will be explained in the discussion of the cervical muscles. This group of muscles acts together to assist in swallowing by lifting the hyoid bone, the floor of the mouth, and the tongue. As the food passes down the esophagus, the stylohyoid and the posterior diagastric muscle retrude the hyoid bone to prevent regurgitation. This muscle group may also assist in fixing the hyoid bone and in retruding the mandible when the hyoid bone is fixed by the infrahyoid muscle.

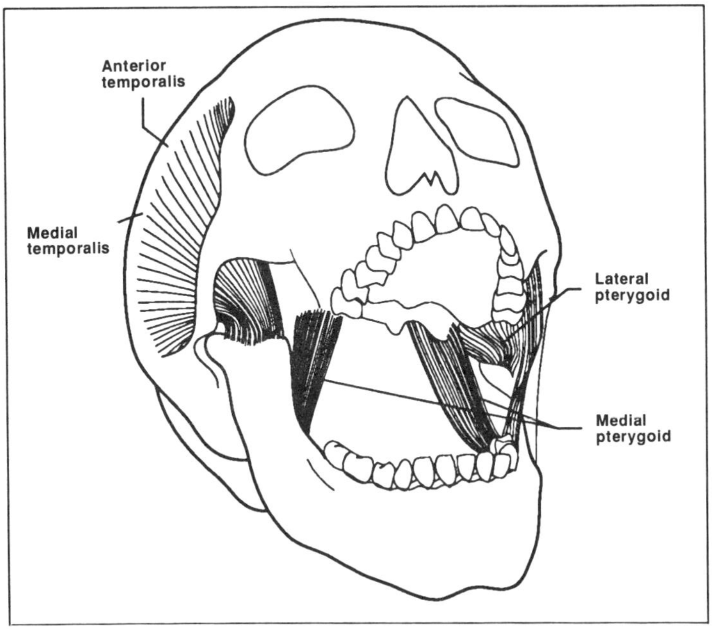

Figure 2-15. Mandibular lateral mover muscles.

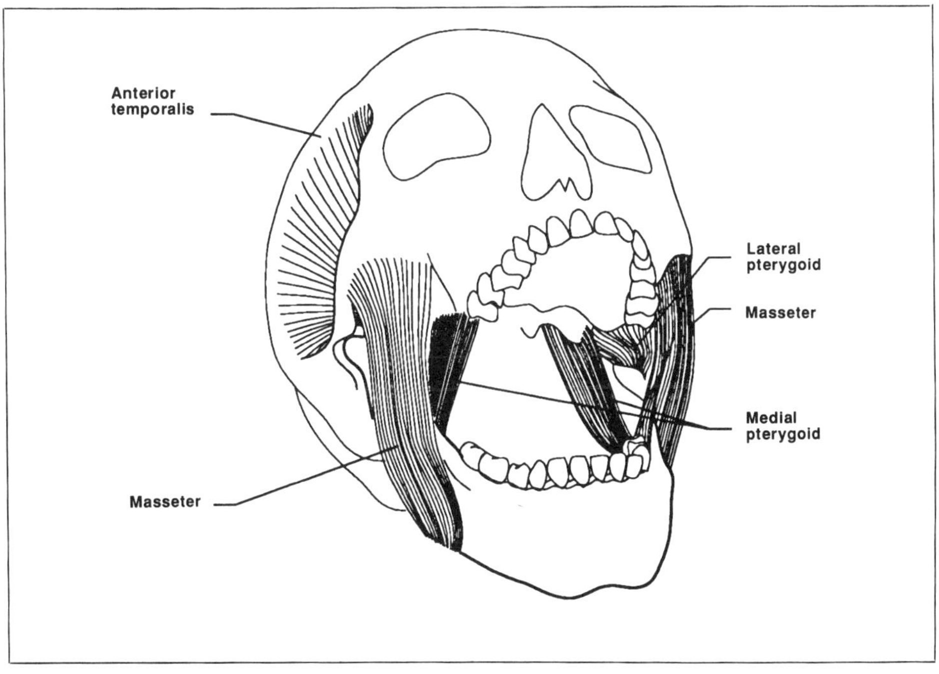

Figure 2-16. Mandibular protruder muscles.

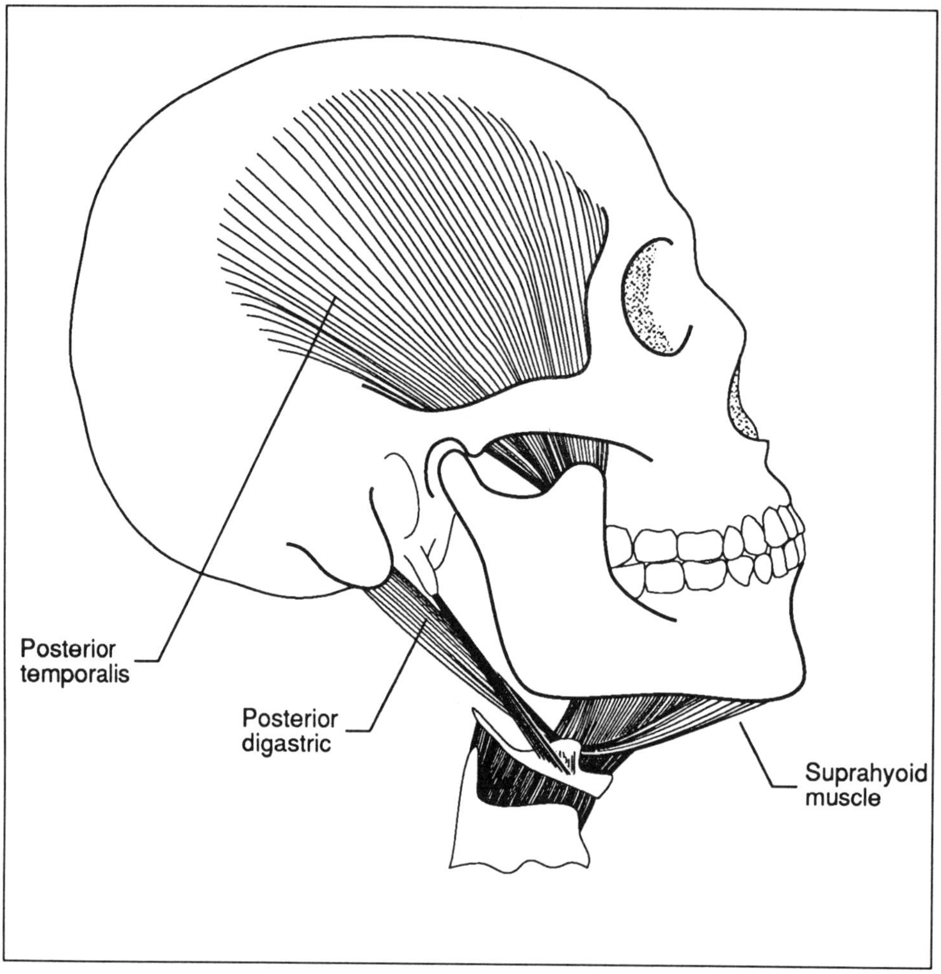

Figure 2-17. Mandibular retruder muscles.

The remaining muscles are the tensor tympani muscle, of the same origin as the medial pterygoids, which is responsible for keeping the proper tension of the eardrum. It exhibits ear symptoms when the medial pterygoid muscles are in spasm or dysfunctional stage because both the medial pterygoid and the tensor tempani originated from the same emberiologic source. The tensor veli palatini keeps the proper tension for the soft palate. It also originated emberiologically as the medial pterygoid muscle and may dysfunction when it does.

Facial muscles. Facial muscles are divided into large and small muscles which are illustrated in **Figures 2-18** and **2-19**. The large muscles are the orbicularis oris, buccinator, and the orbicularis oculi. The *orbicularis oris* is

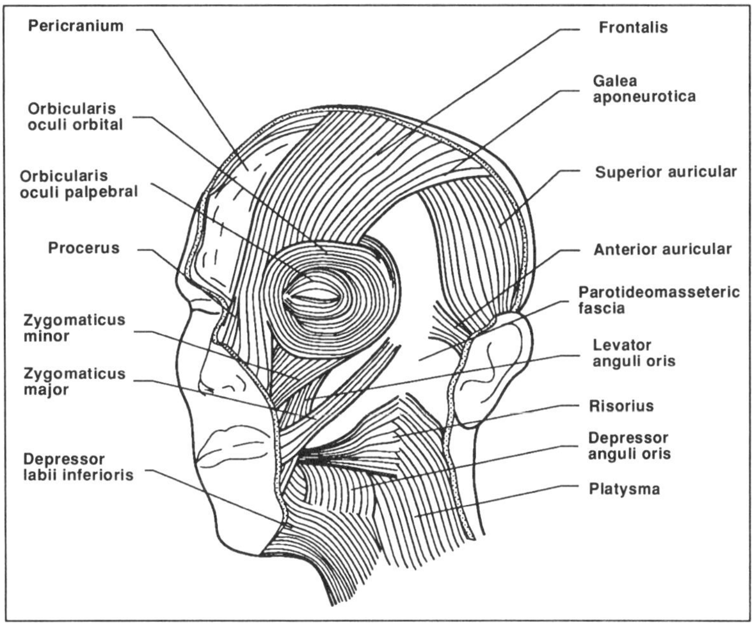

Figure 2-18. Muscles on the face (side view).

a sphincter muscle comprising two labial parts consisting of the fibers of the lips and marginal parts consisting of fibers blending with other adjacent muscles. It is innervated by the facial nerve and receives blood supply from the anastomoses of the facial artery. Its function is to close the lips as in speech, controlling the food during chewing, and kissing.

The *orbicularis oculi* are circular muscles surrounding the eyes and originate from the frontal process of the maxilla medially and incircling the orbit to insert in the zygomatic bone laterally. They are supplied by the facial nerve and receive blood supply from the anastomoses of the facial artery. Their function is to close the eyelids, wrinkles forehead, and compresses or dilates lacrimal sack.

The *buccinator* is the fleshy part of the cheek and originates from the maxilla, mandible and pterygo mandibular raphe and inserts in the orbicularis oris and the lips. It receives blood supply from the facial artery and is innervated by the buccal branch of the facial nerve. Its function is to compress the cheek.

The small muscles are more numerous by far. The *procerus* arises over the nose and connects with the forehead. Its function is to lower the eyebrows. The *compressor* and *dilator naris* compress and dilate the nostril. The *elevator labii superioris* elevates the upper lip; *levator labii superioris alaeque nasi* means to sneer by elevating the alaeque of the nose. The *zygomaticus major* and *minor* draw the upper lip upward and outward. The

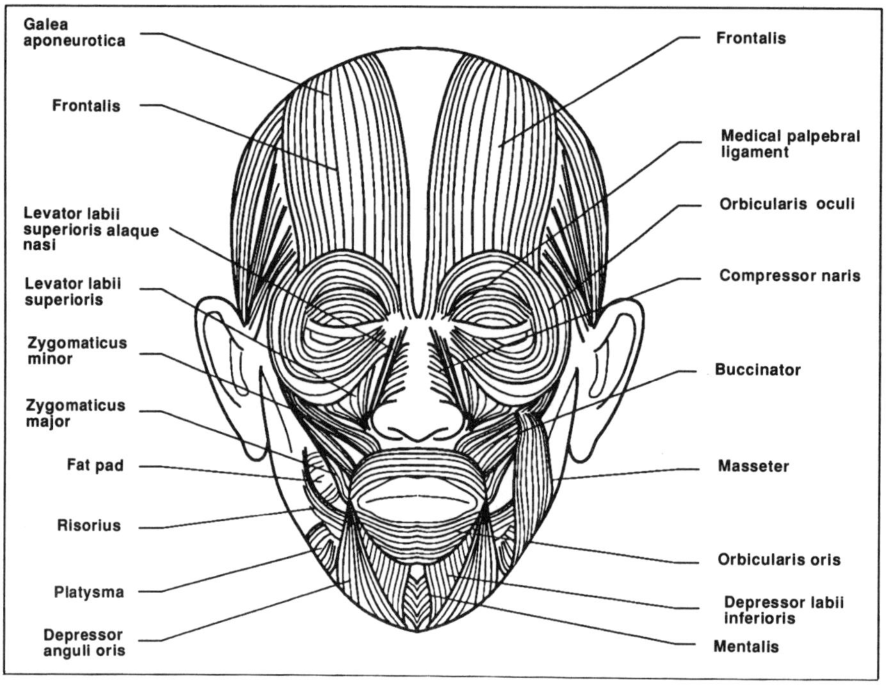

Figure 2-19. Muscles on the face (frontal view).

elevator and *depressor anguli oris* elevate and depress the corners of the mouth. The *depressor labii inferioris* depresses the lower lip.

The *mentalis* is the chin muscle. The *risorius* muscles, which arise over the masseters, connect with the corners of the mouth and are largely involved in smiling. The *platysma* is a muscle sheath covering the lateral aspect of the neck and face. The *frontalis* is the forehead muscle, and the *occipitalis* is the muscle in the back of the head. The *galea aponeurotica* is the scalp muscle. The *auricularis anterior* and *posterior* are the external ear muscles.

Tongue muscles. The tongue, illustrated in **Figure 2-20**, is comprised of a mass of muscle covered by the mucous membrane, which lies on the floor of the mouth. When the mouth is closed, the tongue nearly fills the oral cavity. The parts of the tongue are a tip, margins, a lower surface, and a dorsal or upper surface. The tongue has two groups of muscles, the external, which help in moving the tongue and can alter its shape, and the internal, which alter the shape of the tongue.

The external muscles are the *styloglossus*, which connects the tongue and styloid process and raises and retracts the tongue; the *palatoglossus*, which are at the sides and underside of the tongue to help elevate it; the *hyoglossus*, which arises from the hyoid bone to the tongue and draws down the sides and retracts the tongue; and the *genioglossus*, which connects the tongue to

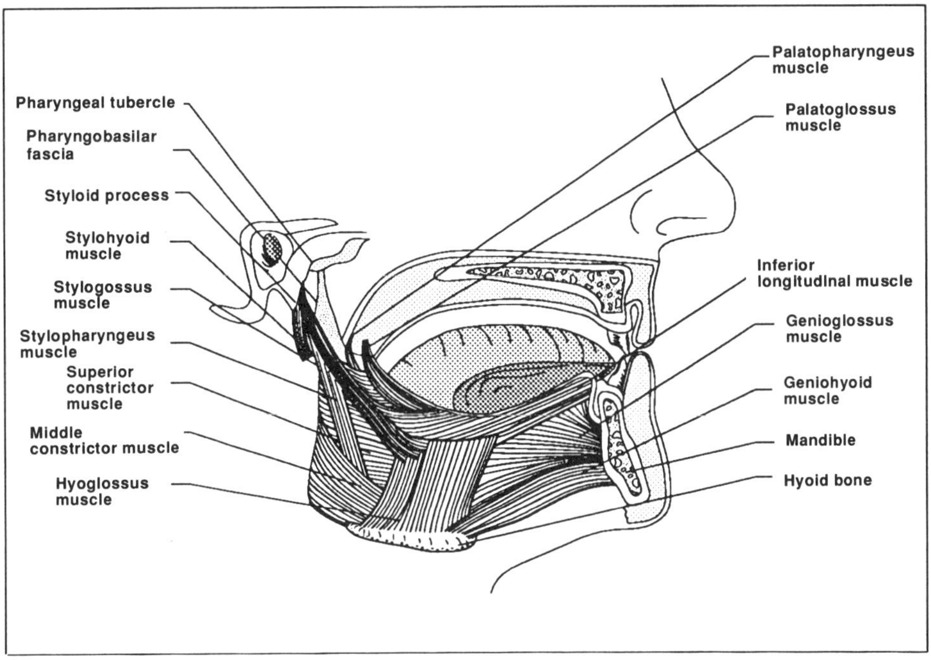

Figure 2-20. Muscles of the tongue, sagittal section.

the inner surface of the mandible at the symphasis. It draws the hyoid bone forward.

The internal muscles are confined within the structure of the tongue and are longitudinal, vertical, and transverse bundles of interfacing fibers separated by connective tissue. These muscles are responsible for altering the tongue shape during speaking and swallowing.

Cervical muscles. The cervical external skeletal muscles can be grouped by their location: anterior, posterior and lateral. The anterior muscles are further divided by whether they are above or below the hyoid bone.

Anterior cervical muscles are shown in **Figure 2-21** and **Figure 2-22**. The suprahyoid muscles shown in **Figure 2-21** are the diagastric, mylohyoid (both were explained previously), and stylohyoid muscle. The *stylohyoid* muscle originates from the styloid process or the temporal bone at the base of the skull and inserts in the hyoid bone. It is supplied by branches from the external carotid artery and innervated by the facial nerve. Its function is to draw the hyoid bone and pound upward and backward.

The infrahyoid muscles in **Figure 2-22** are the sternothyroid, thyrohyoid, sternohyoid, and omohyoid. The *sternothyroid* originates from the manubrium, a part of the sternum, and inserts at the thyroid cartilage. It is innervated by ansacervicals nerve and works to depress the thyroid cartilage. The *thyrohyoid* muscle originates from thyroid cartilage and inserts

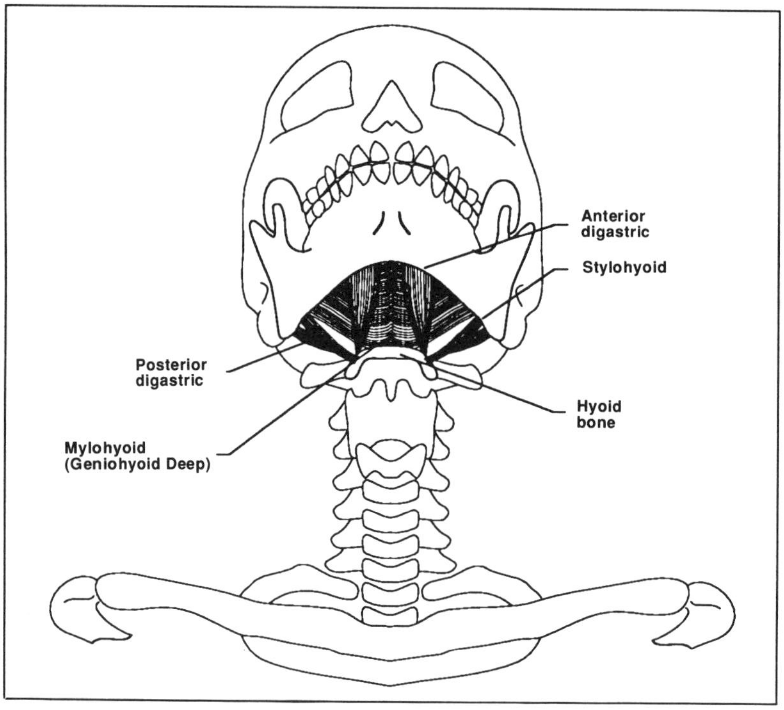

Figure 2-21. Suprahyoid muscles.

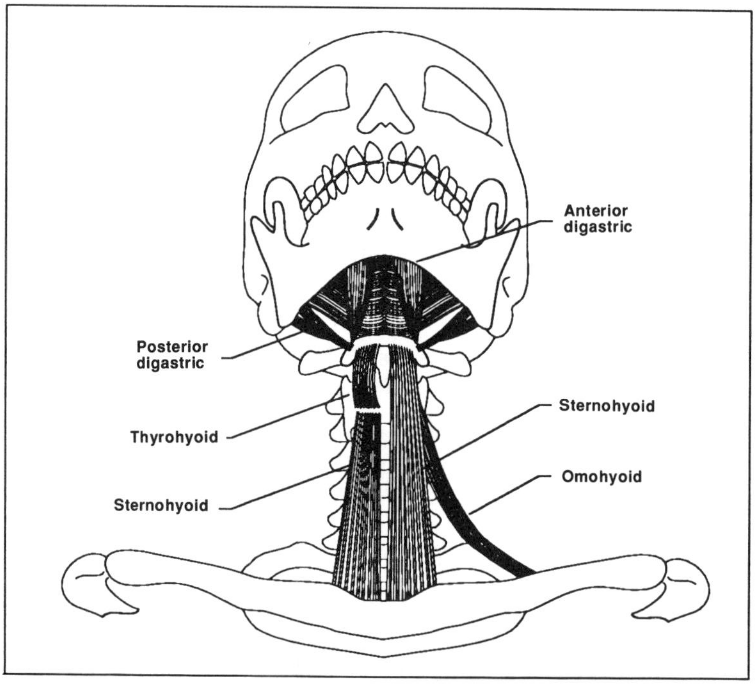

Figure 2-22. Infrahyoid muscles.

in the hyoid bone. It is innervated by the recurrent laryngeal nerve and its function is to raise the larynx. The *sternohyoid* muscle originates from the sterno clavicular joint area and inserts in the inferior border of the hyoid bone. It is innervated by the ansacervicals. Its function is to depress and fix the hyoid bone. *Omohyoid* muscles originates from the superior border of the scapula and inserts in the inferior border of the hyoid bone. It is innervated by the ansacervicals and acts to depress and fixes hyoid bone.

Posterior cervicals muscles are shown in **Figure 2-23**. They include the *suboccipital* muscles, consisting of the *rectus capitus posterior minor*, which originates from the second vertebrae and runs nearly vertically to insert in the occipital bone; the *rectus capitus posterior major*, which runs obliquely under the rectus capitus posterior minor; the *obliqueous capitus superior*, which runs from the transverse process of first cervical vertebrae (atlas) and inserts in the occipital bone and the nuchadl line; and the *obiqueous capitus inferior*, which runs from the posterior spine of the second vertebrae axis and runs obliquely laterally to be inserted in the transverse process of atlas.

This group of muscles is innervated by the greater occipital nerve, third occipital nerve, and lesser occipital nerve. Its common use is in backward tilt of the head. It should be mentioned that the vertebral artery runs in the foramina in the transverse processes of the cervical spine and curves around the first vertebrae. Postural problems, as in forward head position, may constrict this vertebral artery and cause vertebral artery syndrome which is characterized by headaches, nausea, high blood pressure, and other symptoms.

The lateral cervical muscles, as shown in **Figure 2-24** and **Figure 2-25** are the sternocleidomastoids, trapezius muscle, and intrensic neck muscle, or scalenes.

The *sternocleidomastoid* muscle, shown in **Figure 2-24** is a spindle three-headed muscle located obliquely on the side of the neck. It originates from the sternum and clavicle bone inferiorly and runs posteriorly and upwardly to insert in the mastoid process. It is supplied by sternocleidomastoid branch of the occipital artery, a branch of the external carotid artery. It is innervated by the accessory nerve branch from the second, third, and fourth cervical spinal nerves.

Its function is to flex the vertebral column and rotate the head. Sternocleidomastoid muscle dysfunction or spasm cause head tilt as seen in Torticollis when the sternocleidomastoid becomes shorter and the head tilts to the affected side and the individual seems to have a raised shoulder.

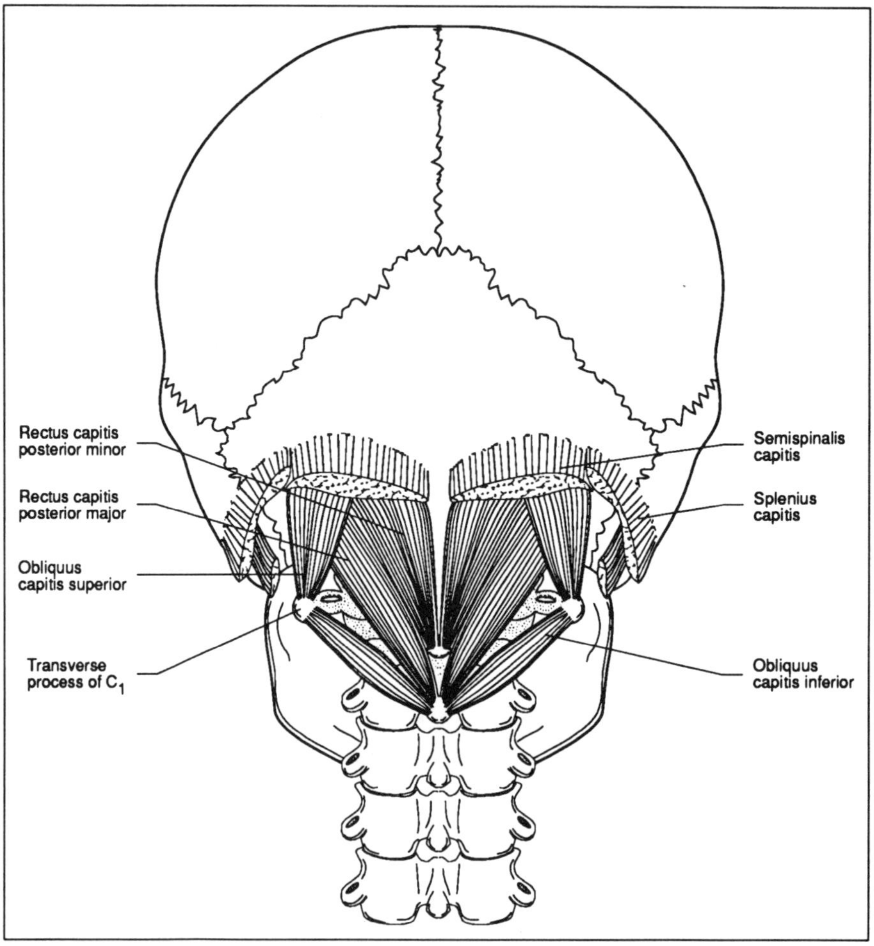

Figure 2-23. Suboccipital muscles.

The trapezius, shown in **Figure 2-25**, is a large flat triangular muscle at the back of the neck and thoracic spine. It originates from the occipital bone at the ligamentum nuchae, spinous processes of seventh cervical, and all twelve thoracic vertebrae and inserts in the clavicle, acromion, and the spine of the scapula. It is innervated by the accessory cranial nerve (XI) and the third and fourth cervical spinal nerves. Its function is to raise the scapula, shoulder, and arms. It also maintains posture, holding the head posteriorly. Its spasm may affect posture.

The scalenes muscles are groups of four muscles: anterior, minimus, medius, and posterior. They originate from the transverse processes of the cervical vertebrae and insert in the first and second ribs. They are innervated by branches from the cervical spinal nerves and supplied by branches from the subclavian artery. Their function is to raise the first and second ribs and laterally flex the cervical spine.

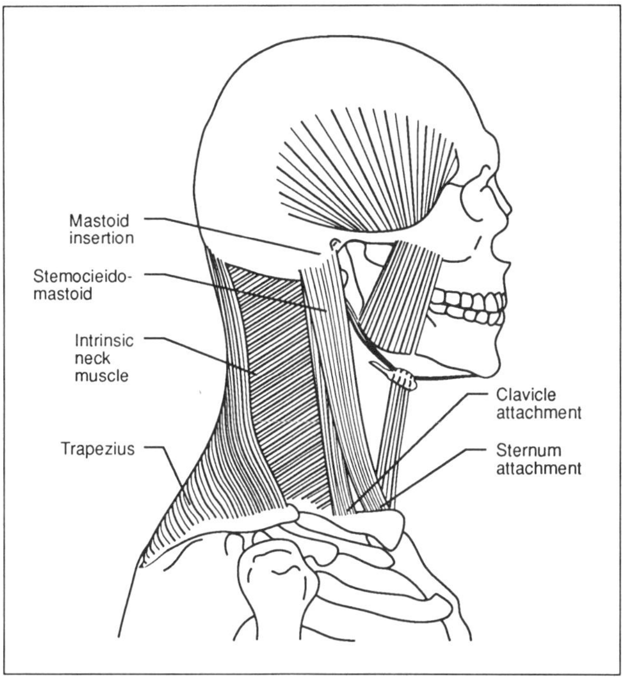

Figure 2-24. Cervical muscles (Lateral view).

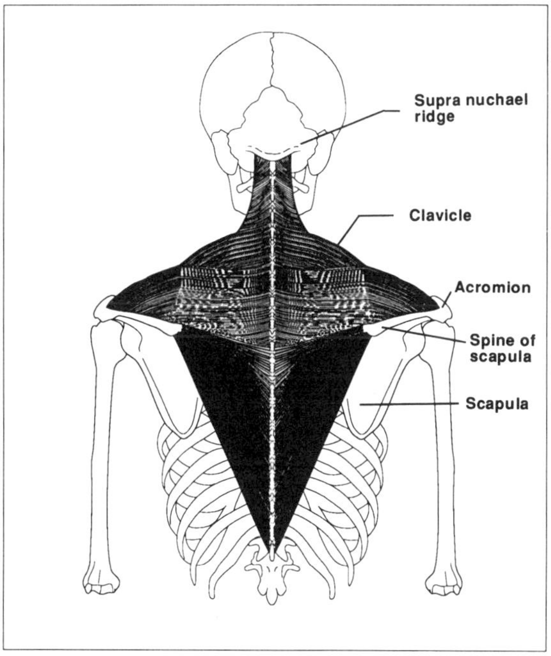

Figure 2-25. Trapezius muscles.

Ligaments. Ligaments are defined as tough bands of collagenous, slightly elastic fibers connecting bones or supporting viscera. They also prevent excessive movement of the joints and may sprain if bones are hyperextended. The ligamentous structures, shown in **Figures 2-27, 2-28**, and **2-29**, in and around the OSGS include:

1. The articular capsule, a dense, fibrous tissue sheet enclosing the joint in a 360° fashion, with insertion at the neck of the condyle below and the glenoid fossa above.
2. The lateral temporomandibular ligament, a thickening of the lateral portion of the TMJ capsule. This ligament, which attaches to the temporal bone above and to the lateral neck of the condyle below, works like a pendulum during condylar translation and resists excessive lateral condylar displacement. It can be loose in an injured or stressed TMJ.
3. The sphenomandibular ligament, a thin, flat, fibrous band of about 2 to 3 cm in length, attaches to the sphenoid bone spine in the base of the skull anterior to the TMJ capsule and to the mandibular lingual side of the ramus below the lingula. In many cases, some of its fibers go through the petrotympanic fissure to the malleus bone of the middle ear; therefore, problems associated with trauma to the ligament may cause hearing impairment or tinnitus (ringing in the ears).
4. The stylomandibular ligament, a thin, fibrous band, attached above to the styloid process of the temporal bone and below to the medial aspect of the mandibular angle. The styloid process runs parallel to the posterior belly of the digastric muscles. In hyperextension—hyperflexion cervical trauma, this ligament may be sprained and may cause referred pain to its site and surrounding areas. This is called Ernest syndrome.
5. The mandibular malleolar ligament (Pinto's ligament), a fibroblastic tissue with an elastic, dense nature, connecting the neck and anterior process of the malleus to the medioposterosuperior part of the TMJ capsule, the articular disc, and the sphenomandibular ligament. This anatomical connection may explain the correlation between symptoms which occur in the ear and TMJ disorders.

§ 2.5 Blood Supplies to the TMJ-OSGS and Face

Arterial blood supplies. The arterial supply to the OSGS and face, illustrated in **Figure 2-30**, emanate mainly from the external carotid artery. Arteries are blood vessels that carry oxygenated blood from the heart to all parts of the body. The external carotid artery supplies the following branches:

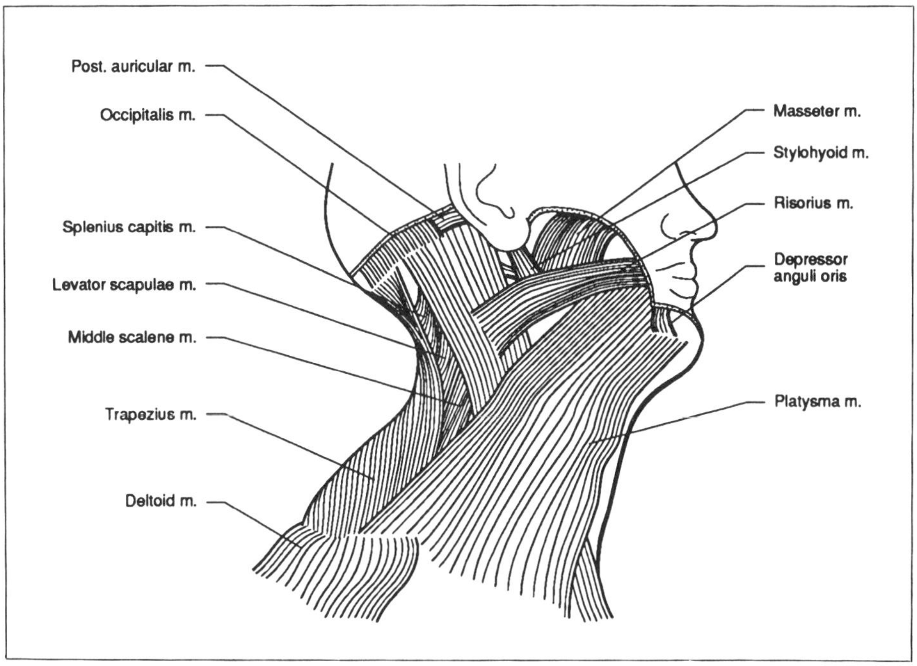

Figure 2-26. Cervical muscles (anteriolateral view).

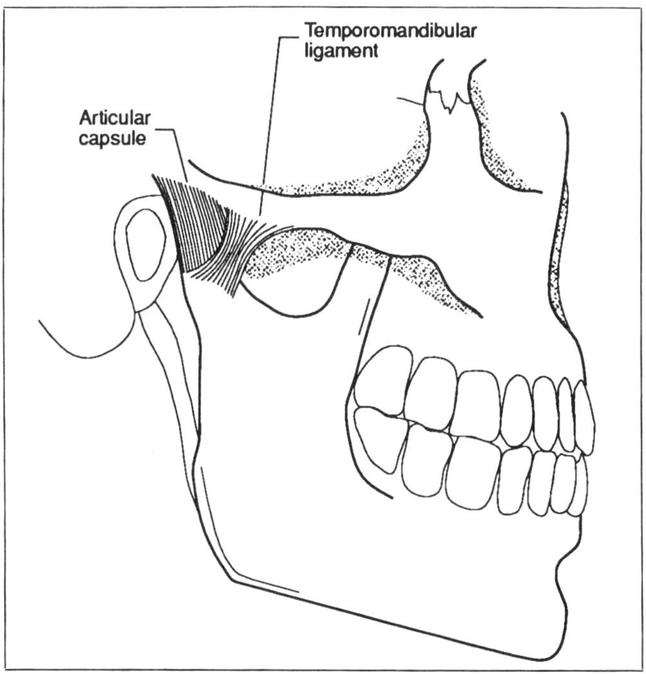

Figure 2-27. Ligaments of TMJ (lateral view).

1. Ascending pharyngeal artery, to the wall of the pharynx.
2. Superior thyroid artery, to the upper pole of the lobe of the thyroid gland.
3. Lingual artery, to the tongue.

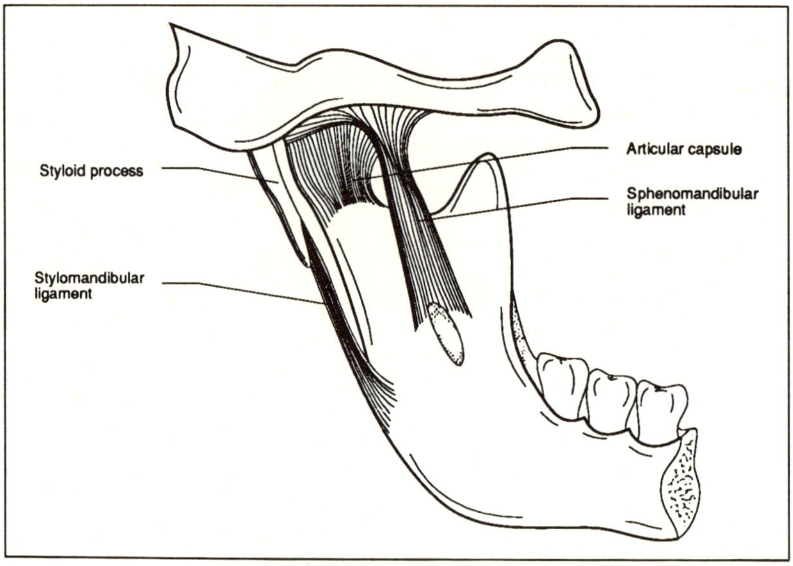

Figure 2-28. Ligaments of TMJ (medial view).

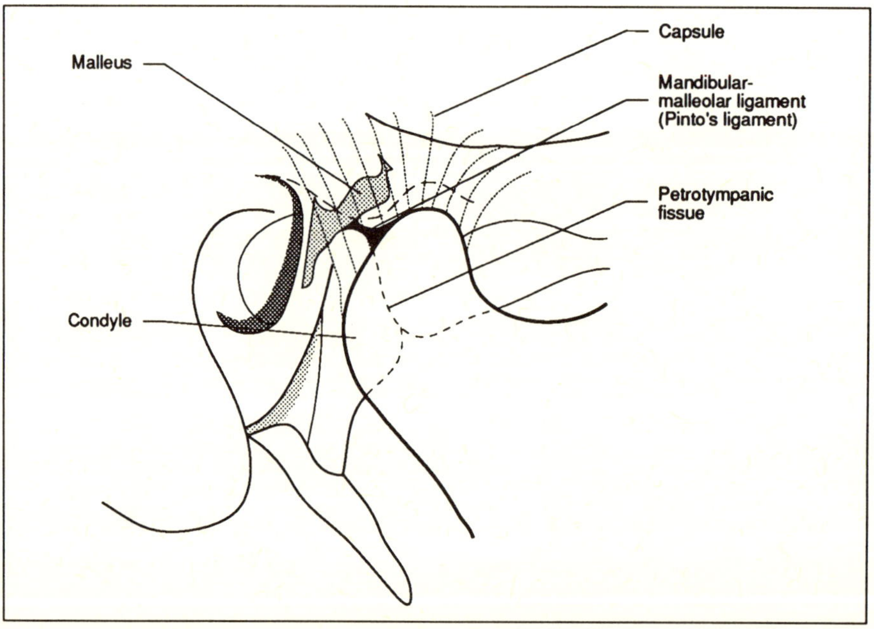

Figure 2-29. Mandibular malleolar ligament (Pinto's ligament).

4. Facial artery, to the neck and face.
5. Occipital artery, to the posterior part of the scalp.
6. Posterior auricular artery, to the scalp.

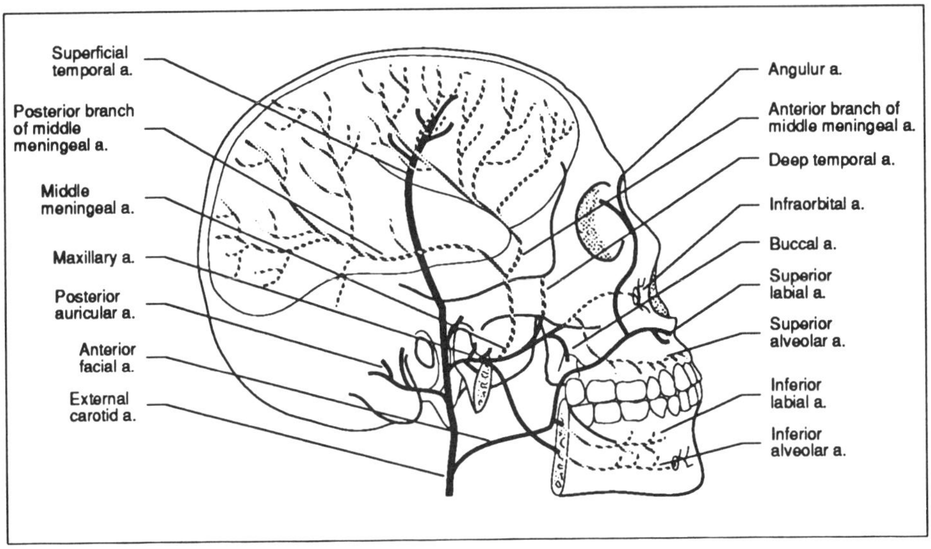

Figure 2-30. Arterial blood supplies (lateral view).

The external carotid artery then splits into two terminal branches: the maxillary artery, supplies to the infratemporal fossa (and the TMJ area), and the superfacial temporal artery, supplies to the temporal region.

The arterial blood supply to the TMJ emanates from the superfacial temporal artery (posterior to the joint), posterior auricular artery, deep auricular artery, lateral pterygoid pedicle (a significant blood supply) and masseteric artery. The latter three arteries are branches of the maxillary artery.

Venous drainage. Veins are vessels that return nonoxygenated blood toward the heart. The venous return from the face and OSGS, shown in **Figure 2-31**, consists of:

1. Anterior facial vein, formed by the union of the supraorbital vein and the supratrochlear vein.
2. The tributaries of the anterior facial vein: the superior ophthalmic vein and the deep facial vein, which connects it with the pterygoid venous plexus.

The posterior facial vein is formed by the union of the superficial temporal and the maxillary veins. Both anterior and posterior facial veins form the common facial vein, and this in turn unites with the maxillary vein to form the external jugular vein.

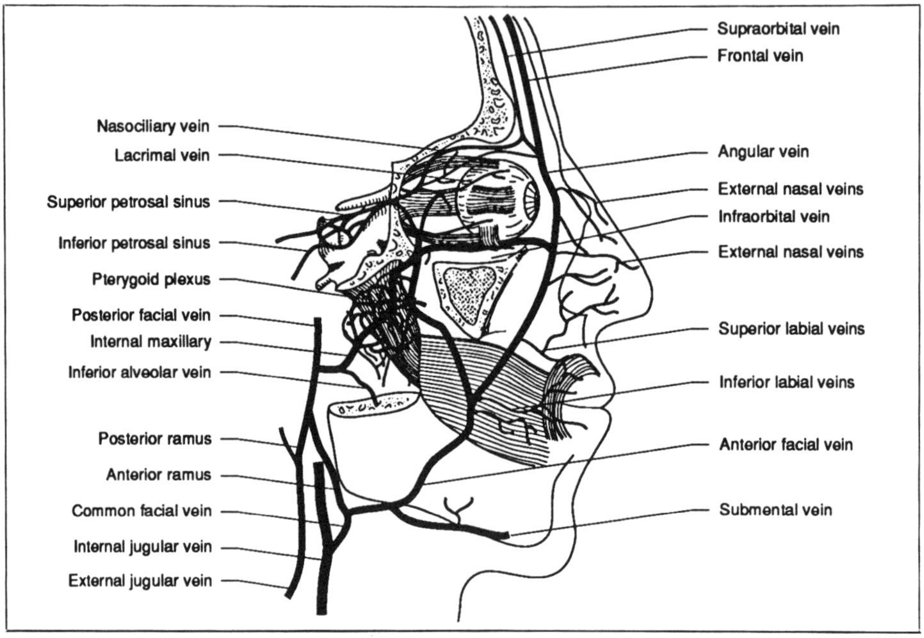

Figure 2-31. Venous drainage (lateral view).

Lymphatics. Lymphatics are defined as vessels that drain lymph from the body to the blood stream. Lymph is a milky body fluid that contains white cells produced by bone marrow, the thymus, and the spleen, providing defense against infection. Lymph nodes are small, round organs lying along the lymphatics, containing fibrous lymphoid tissue. They work as barriers to prevent the spread of infection. Lymph drainage of the face and OSGS, illustrated in **Figure 2-32**, occurs in the following ways:

1. The anterior part of the scalp drains with the face into the submandibular lymph nodes.
2. The temporal region drains into the superfacial parotid lymph nodes.
3. The lateral and medial parts of the eyelids drain into the parotid and submandibular lymph nodes, respectively.
4. The nose, cheek, upper lip, and lateral part of the lower lip drain into the buccal, parotid, and submandibular lymph nodes.
5. The central part of the lower lip drains into the submental lymph nodes.
6. The mouth drains into the submental, submandibular, and deep cervical lymph nodes.
7. The tongue drains into the submental and submandibular lymph nodes.
8. The tissue in the teeth drain into the submental, submandibular, and deep cervical lymph nodes.

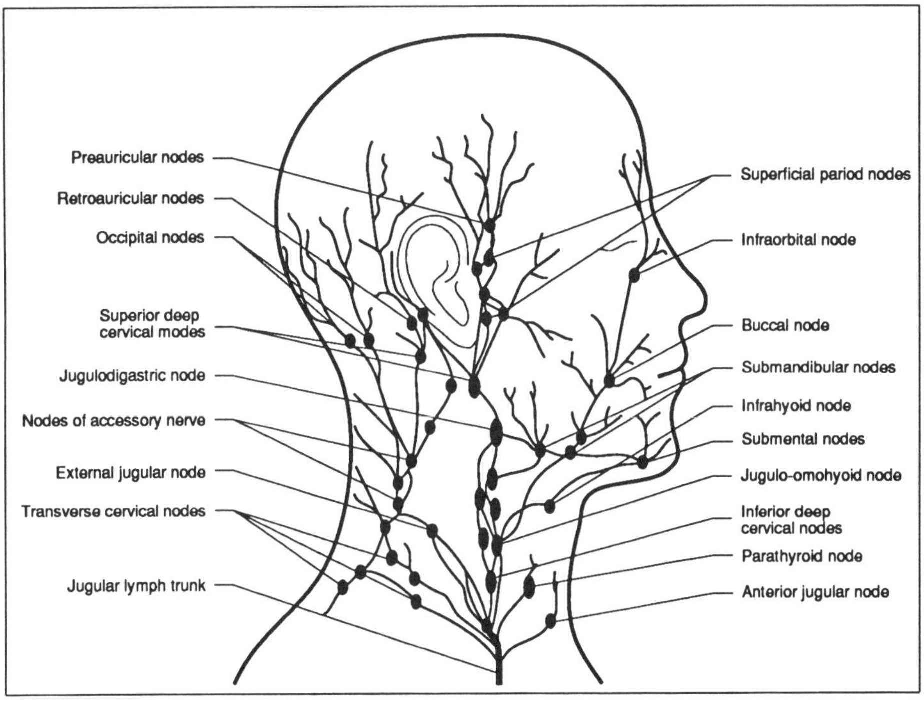

Figure 2-32. Lymphatics.

§ 2.6 Arthrology of TMJ

TMJ is the articulation of the mandibular condylar process (condyle) and the temporal bone (articulating fossa and eminence). The fossa is the concavity hosting the mandibular condyle and the eminence is the bony convexity anterior to the fossa. Each condyle has a elliptical shape and its long axis is oriented mediolaterally and at a right angle to the surface of the mandibular ramus plane. The mandibular ramus plane runs parallel to the posterior surface of the ramus of the mandible, which is the vertical posterior position of the mandible. The condyle measures about 20 mm mediolaterally (side to side) and about 10 mm anteroposteriorly (front to back). Considerable variations in condylar shape and angulation have been reported.

The articulating surface of the temporal bone is anterior to the tympanic bone and consists of a concave thin bony surface, or fossa, and a convex thick bony surface, or eminence. See **Figure 2-33**. Because of the absence of the cartilaginous covering found on articulating surfaces and the thinning of its bony surface, the fossa is not considered to be a functional component of articulation and is incapable of carrying heavy loads. The medial and lateral borders of the articular eminence are accentuated bony ridges. The anterior boundary is continuous with the infratemporal surface of the temporal bone.

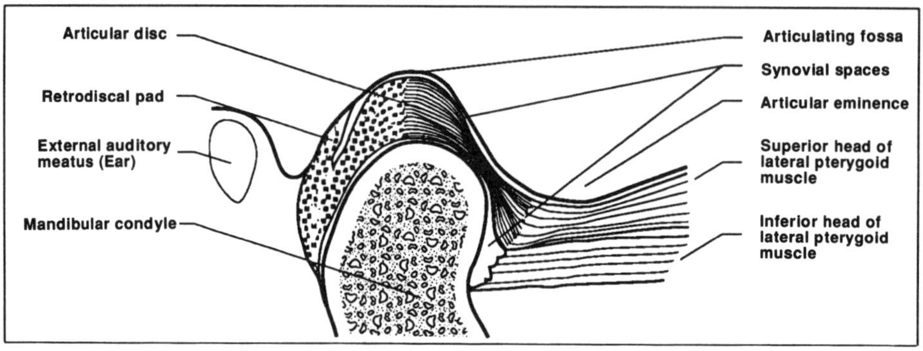

Figure 2-33. Sagittal section TMJ anatomy.

In addition, the TMJ includes the articulating disc, retrodiscal tissue, joint capsule, and synovium, which are all soft tissue structures. The articulating disc is an oval plate of flexible fibrous tissue that divides the joint into an upper and lower compartment. The central part of the disc is firm, avascular, without innervation. The disc continues posteriorly into a thick layer of loose connective tissue called the retrodiscal pad. The collateral ligament of the disc medially and laterally inserts into the medial and lateral poles of the condyle. Anteriorly, the disc is continuous with the superior portion of the lateral pterygoid muscle. The temporomandibular capsule is a dense, fibrous tissue sheet completely enclosing the joint in a 360° fashion with its insertion lines at the neck of the condyle below and at the temporal bone above. A thickening of the lateral portion of the capsule forms the temporomandibular ligament. See **Figure 2-34**.

The final soft tissue structure is the synovial lining, a very thin, delicate structure that lines the upper and lower compartments of the TMJ. This lining usually consists of three different types of cells contained in a monolayer.

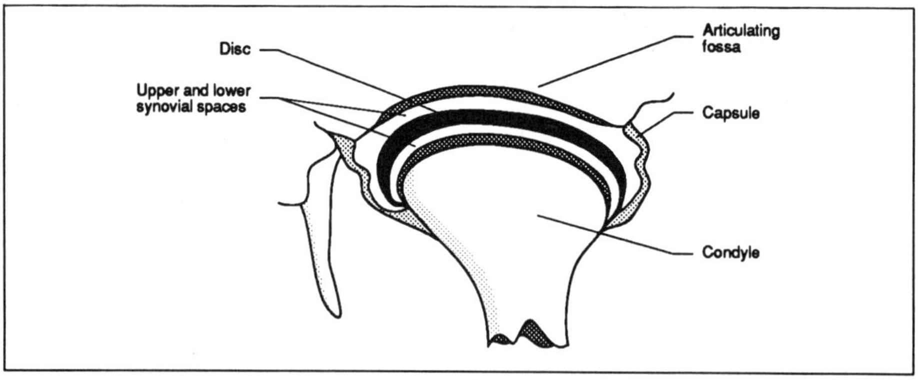

Figure 2-34. Coronal section TMJ anatomy.

One type secretes collagenase to dissolve collagen formation in minor bleedings or trauma, the second has a phagocytic ability to clean the area by engulfing foreign bodies or dead cells, and the third has a highly active immunologic ability to produce antibodies such as the rhematoid factor, as well as other products to insure the health of the joint.

§ 2.7 Innervation to the TMJ and OSGS

The TMJ is innervated by the auriculotemporal nerve posteriolaterally, the masseteric nerve anteriomedially, and the deep temporal nerve anteriolaterally. **Figures 2-35, 2-36,** and **2-37** give an overview of the innervation. Two principle nerves, the trigeminal and the facial, innervate the TMJ and OSGS. Although they are mixed in function (sensory and motor), the trigeminal nerve is mainlysensory and the facial nerve is mainly motor.

Sensory nerve supply. Branches of the trigeminal nerve, shown in **Figure 2-38**, supply sensation to the skin of the face, except in the area over the angle of the mandible, which is supplied by the great auricular nerve (from C2 and C3 branches). The trigeminal nerve (5th cranial nerve) is a ''mixed'' nerve; in other words, it contains both sensory and motor fibers. It has three cutaneous branches: the ophthalmic, maxillary, and mandibular.

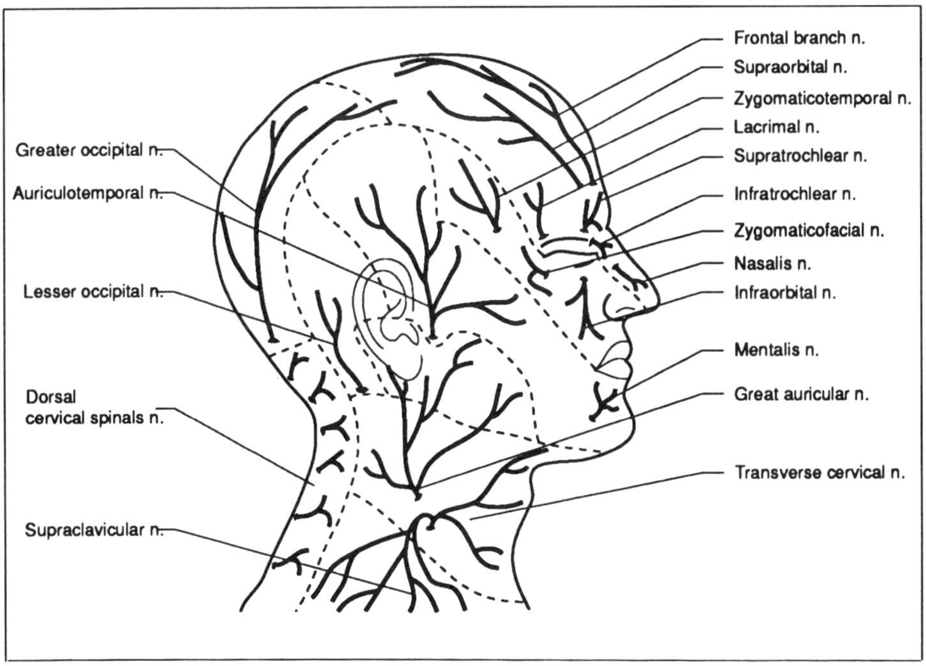

Figure 2-35. Innervation of the face (lateral view).

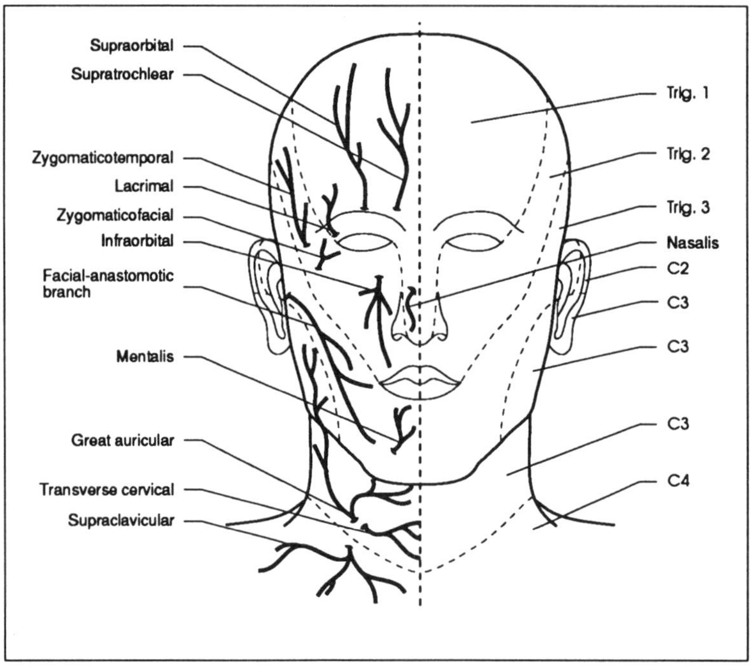

Figure 2-36. Innervation of the face (anterior view).

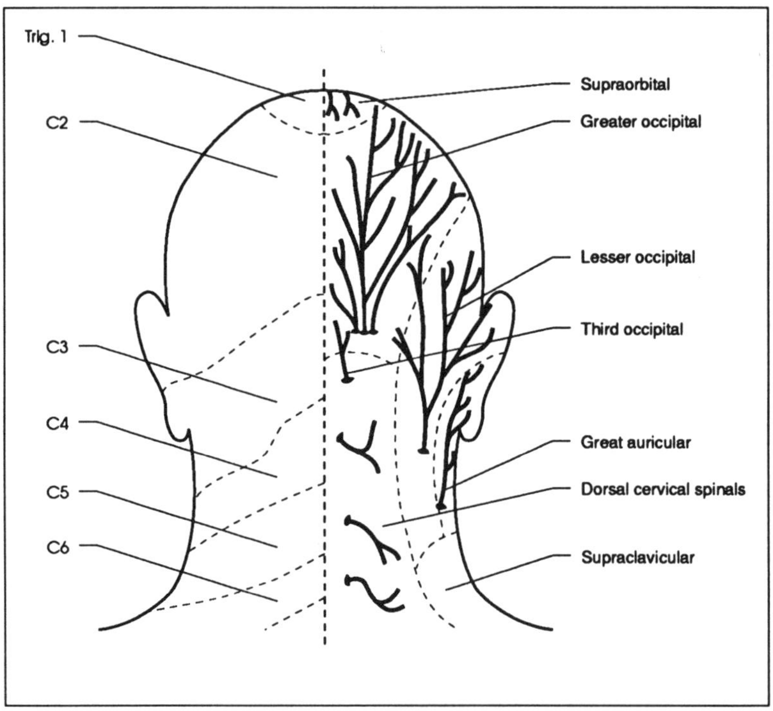

Figure 2-37. Innervation of the head (posterior view).

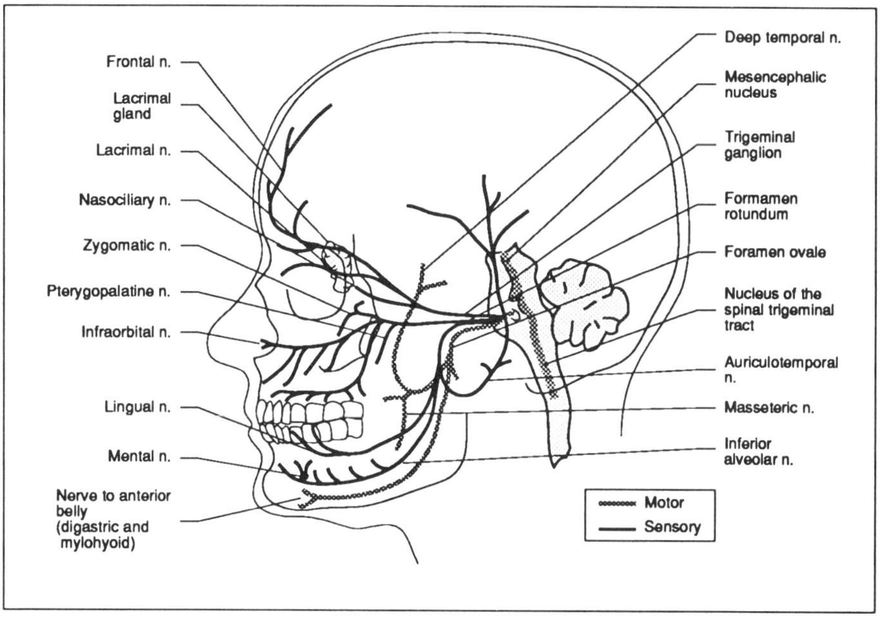

Figure 2-38. Trigeminal nerve.

The ophthalmic branch is subdivided into three nerve branches: the frontal, which supplies the supratrochlear and supraorbital nerves; the lacrimal, which supplies the palpebral nerve; and the nasociliary, which supplies the infratrochlear and external nasal nerves.

The maxillary branch leaves the cranium through the foramen rotundum. After a special course in the floor of the orbit, it sends nerve branches to supply the upper arch of the teeth, and eventually becomes the infraorbital nerve, which supplies the midface. The sphenopalatine ganglion is suspended from the maxillary nerve in the pterygopalatine fossa and sends the pharyngeal branch to supply the nasopharynx, the greater and lesser palatine nerves to supply the mucosa of the hard and soft palate, respectively, and the long and short sphenopalatine nerves to supply the lateral wall of the nose and the anterior part of the hard palate, respectively.

The mandibular branch has two sensory branches (buccal, which supplies the cheek, and the mental, which supplies the skin over the chin and over the anterior part of the mandible). The mandibular nerve has other branches:

Nerve to medial pterygoid muscle (motor).

Deep temporal nerves (sensory).

Masseteric nerve (motor).

Nerve to the lateral pterygoid muscles (motor).

Auriculotemporal nerve (supplies the TMJ and passes behind it to emerge distal to the temporomandibular condyle and then moves to the temporal area—sensory). See **Figure 2-39**.

Lingual nerve to the tongue (sensory).

Inferior dental nerve supplies the lower teeth and finally emerges out of mental foramen as a mental nerve (sensory).

Motor innervation. In addition to the motor branches of the mandibular nerve (a branch of the trigeminal nerve) and the muscles of mastication, the OSGS and the face are supplied by the facial nerve, shown in **Figure 2-40**. This is a "mixed" nerve, although primarily motor. It has seven motor terminal branches:

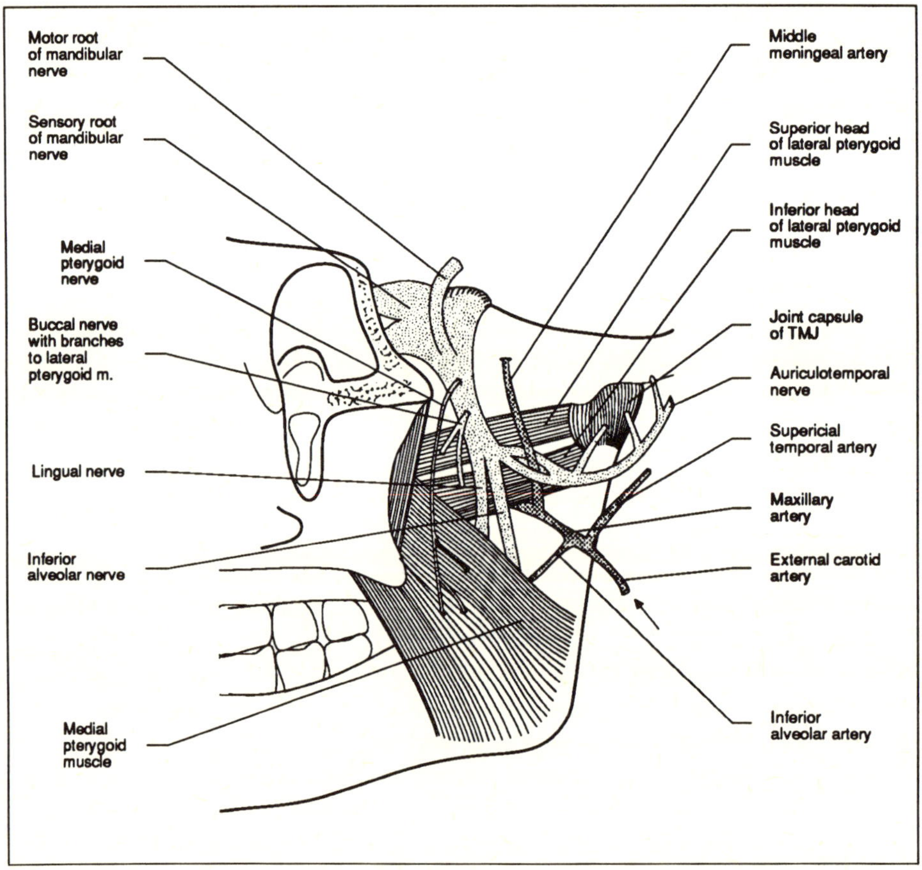

Figure 2-39. Auriculotemporal nerve (medial view).

1. Posterior auricular nerve which supplies the occipitalis muscle.
2. The nerve to the posterior belly of the digastric muscle.
3. Temporal branch to the frontalis and orbicularis oculi muscles.
4. Zygomatic branch to orbicularis oculi muscle and the muscles between the mouth and the nose.
5. Buccal branch to the buccinator and orbicularis oris muscles.
6. Mandibular branch to the muscle of the lower lip.
7. Cervical branch to the platysma muscle.

The sensory fibers in the facial nerve are the chorda tympani nerve which leaves the facial nerve to join the lingual branch of the mandibular nerve. It conveys the sense of taste in the anterior two thirds of the tongue. The taste sensation of the posterior one-third of the tongue is through the glasopharyngeal nerve. The hypoglossal nerve is the motor nerve to both extrensic and interensic muscles of the tongue, except the palatoglossus, which is supplied by the pharyngeal plenx.

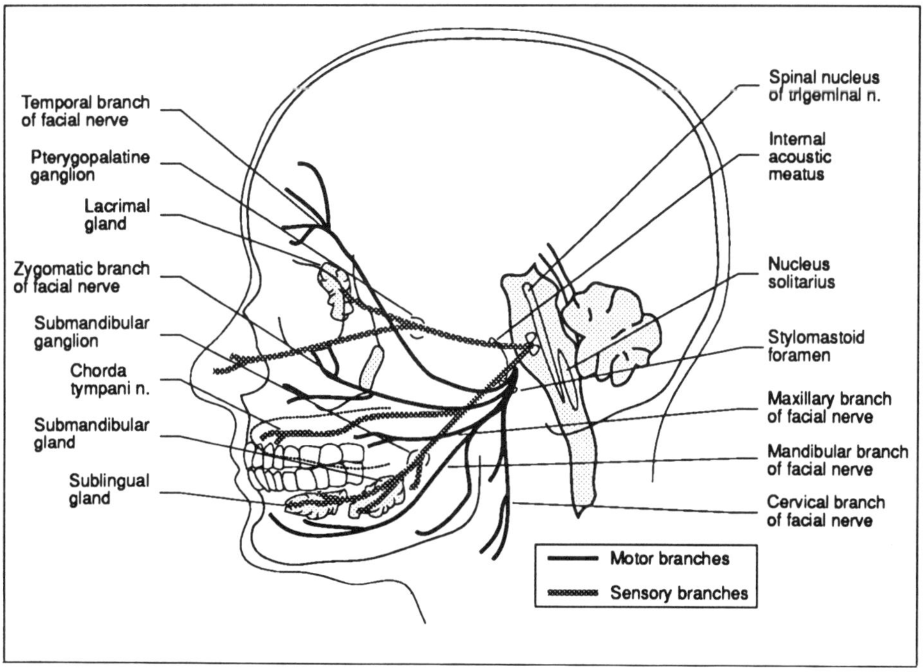

Figure 2-40. Facial nerves (lateral view).

§ 2.8 Distinguishing Characteristics of TMJ

The TMJ is distinguished from other synovial joints of the body as follows:

1. TMJ articulating surfaces are covered by fibrocartilage rather than hyaline for more protection.
2. TMJ is divided by a fibrous disc into upper and lower compartments. This disc facilitates the unique movements of rotation and translation.
3. Right and left TMJs work in coordinated movements as they are coordinated by one piece of bone, the mandible, which necessitates diagnosing and treating both even if only one is symptomatic.
4. The maximum closure of the TMJ is determined by the teeth. Therefore, any adverse change in the occlusion can cause a TMJ disorder.
5. The unique movement of the condyle in the fossa and its relation to the disc forms a complex dual rotational and translational movement. The rotation allows opening the mandible up to 20-27 mm. Translation is the movement of the mandible with the disc on the condyle forward to avoid impingement of the mandibular body on vital structures in the neck, such as the pharynx, trachea, caratid and jugular vessels.

In addition the anatomical relations of the TMJ are unique. Medially, the TMJ is close to the internal carotid artery, the internal jugular vein, the sphenomandibular ligament, the eustachian tube, the tensor palatine muscle, and the middle meningeal artery. Superiorly, the TMJ is close to the middle cranial fossa. Laterally, the TMJ is close to the parotid gland and the facial nerve, a motor nerve to the face. Posteriorly, the TMJ is also close to the tympanic cartilage, the auditory canal, and the mastoid process. Many of these relationships are shown in **Figure 2-41**. The proximity of all these features make the TMJ a particularly challenging area for diagnosis and treatment.

§ 2.9 References

For further details, the author strongly recommends the use of an anatomical text; several are listed:

1. P.L. Williams & R. Warwick, Gray's Anatomy (36th British ed. W.B. Saunders 1980).

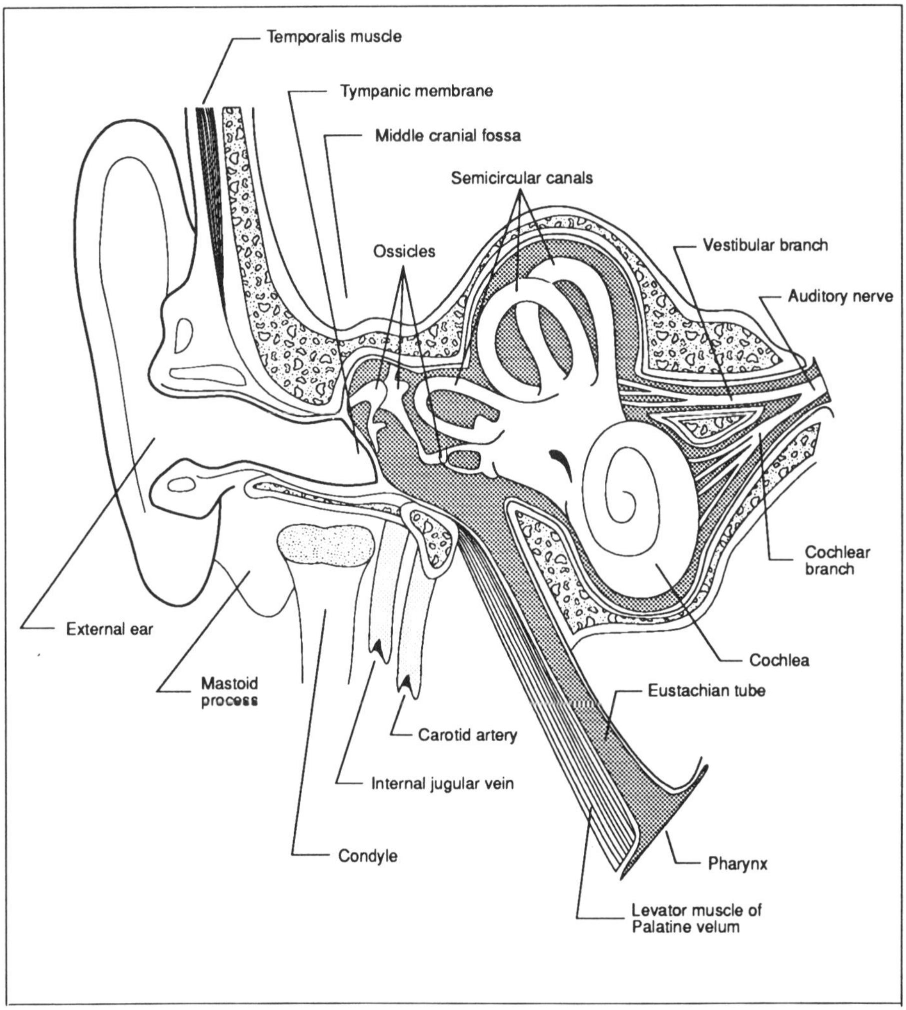

Figure 2-41. Coronal section through the TMJ and ear.

2. E.L. DuBrul, Sicher's Oral Anatomy, (7th ed. C.V. Mosby 1980).

3. J.L. Hiatt & L.P. Gartner, Textbook of Head and Neck Anatomy (Appleton-Century-Crofts 1982).

4. W.H. Hollinshead, Anatomy for Surgeons, Vol. 1, The Head and Neck (2d ed., Harper & Row 1968).

5. R.M.H. McMinn, R.T. Hutchings, & B.M. Logan, Color Atlas of Head and Neck Anatomy (Year Book Medical Publishers 1981).

CHAPTER 3

PHYSIOLOGY AND BIOMECHANICS

PHYSIOLOGY

§ 3.1 Functional Matrix Concept

The functional matrix is a convenient term encompassing the soft tissues within which the functional skeletal components are embedded. It is composed of all the muscles of the mastication process (masseter, temporalis, medial pterygoid, lateral pterygoid, anterior belly of digastric, platysma, mylohyoid, geniohyoid, genioglossus, and the facial expression muscles), ligaments (TMJ capsule and ligament, stylomandibular, sphenomandibular), and an articulating disc. The size, shape, and structure of the skeletal unit of the TMJ-OSGS are controlled by the actions of the functional matrix. Therefore, functional matrix problems, such as muscle spasms, lack or diminished blood supply and loose or torn ligaments, can affect the morphology (size, shape, and symmetry) of the mandible, maxillae, and the condyles. Subsequently, a disturbed morphology causes unbalanced skeletal structure leading to further disorders. It is possible to conclude that the primary function of the condylar cartilage is to provide enough growth to enable the condyle to remain in contact with the fossa (interposed by the disc). At the same time, the soft tissues surrounding the mandible exert an adequate amount of force to direct the mandibular growth forward and downward. This is the functional matrix concept.[1]

§ 3.2 Condylar Growth

Except for the condyle, mandibular growth is a membranous type of growth. It forms through the precipitation of calcium salts in membranous tissue. This is also called membranous ossification (bone formation). The mandibular condyle is a major growth site, acting as a regional filed of mandibular growth that adapts to its own growth environment. See **Figure 3-1**.

The mandibular condyle growth is a cartilaginous type of growth. It forms through precipitation of calcium slats in cartilaginous matrix. The articulating surface growth occurs through an endochondral process in which a pressure exerted on the condylar surface causes localized *ischemia*, anemia caused by mechanical obstruction of the blood supply, and *anoxia*, absence of oxygen. The ischemia and anoxia cause formation of a cartilage surface rather than cortical bone.The medullary portion of the condyle is formed in association with this contact cartilage. The cortical bony surfaces, at which the tension is created by muscle and connective tissue attachments, are formed by cells from *periosteum*, membrane covering bone, and *endosteum*, lining membrane of hollow bone.

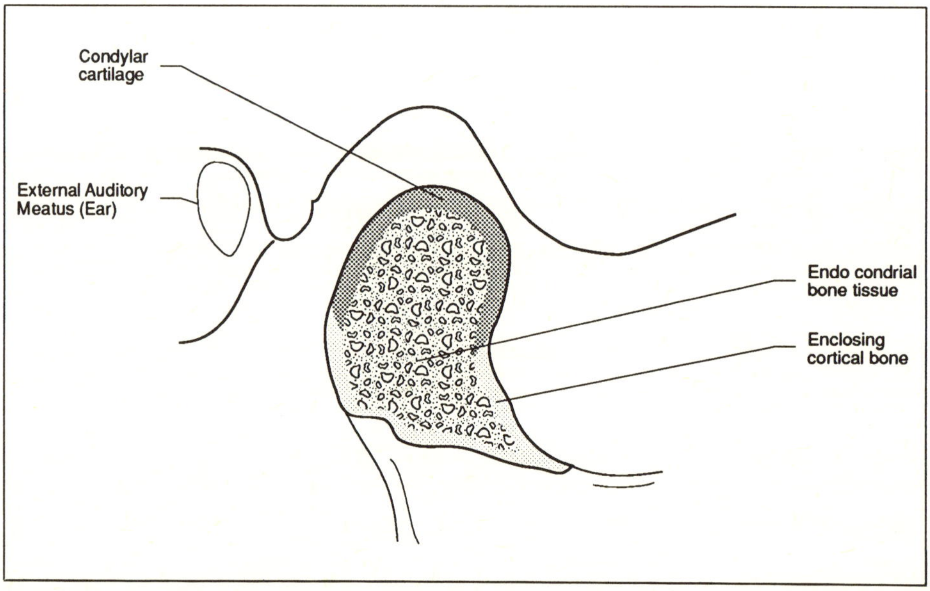

Figure 3-1. Condylar growth.

[1] M.L. Moss, *The Functional Matrix Concept and its Relationship to TMJ Dysfunction and Treatment in* 27 Temporomandibular Joint Dysfunctional and Treatment 445 (H. Gelb, ed., W.B. Saunders 1983).

The condylar cartilage is a secondary type of cartilage, that is, it is not a direct aid in mandibular growth. Rather, it provides regional, adaptive growth and maintains the proper condylar relationship to the temporal articulating surface. In addition, it has a multidirectional capacity of growth and remodeling as a selective response to different mandibular displacement movement and rotation.

Understanding the condylar growth is essential to prevent TMJ-OSGS disorders through eliminating factors which can disturb growth, such as trauma, missing teeth, bad habits and other factors. In addition, understanding the condylar growth helps clinicians predict recovery from a disorder or recognize a pre-existing condition.

As **Figure 3-2** illustrates, there is continuing development of the TMJ throughout life. The articulating fossa is usually flatter in childhood. The surface becomes deeper during adolescence and deepest in adulthood. This increase in depth is caused by increased function.

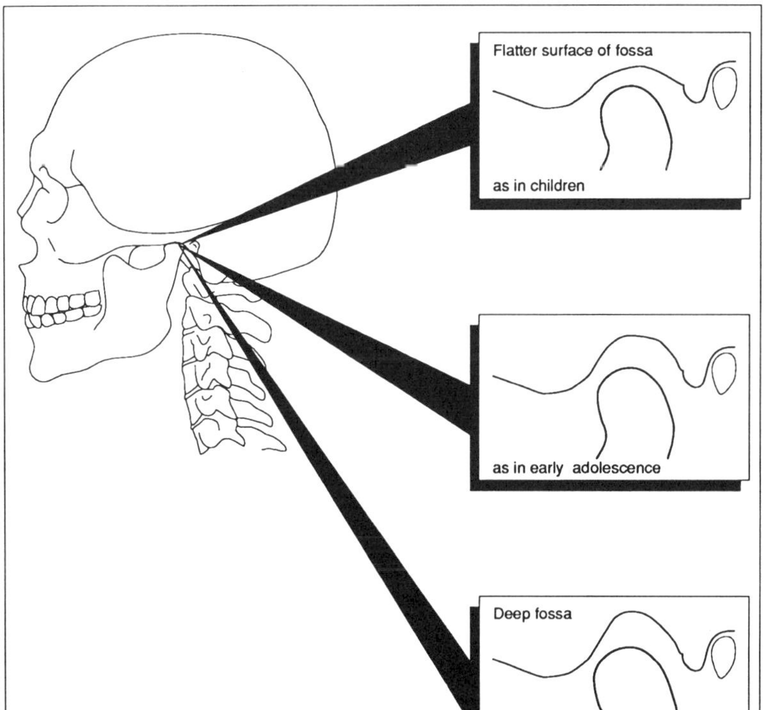

Figure 3-2. TMJ development

§ 3.3 Articular Remodeling

The TMJ is congenitally established by the twelfth week of intrauterine life and is frequently altered by function and usage postnatally and throughout the life span. Articular remodeling is the percipitation of new bone in one direction and resorption of bone in the opposite direction. It causes a change of form and possible deformity. It takes three forms (see **Figure 3-3**).

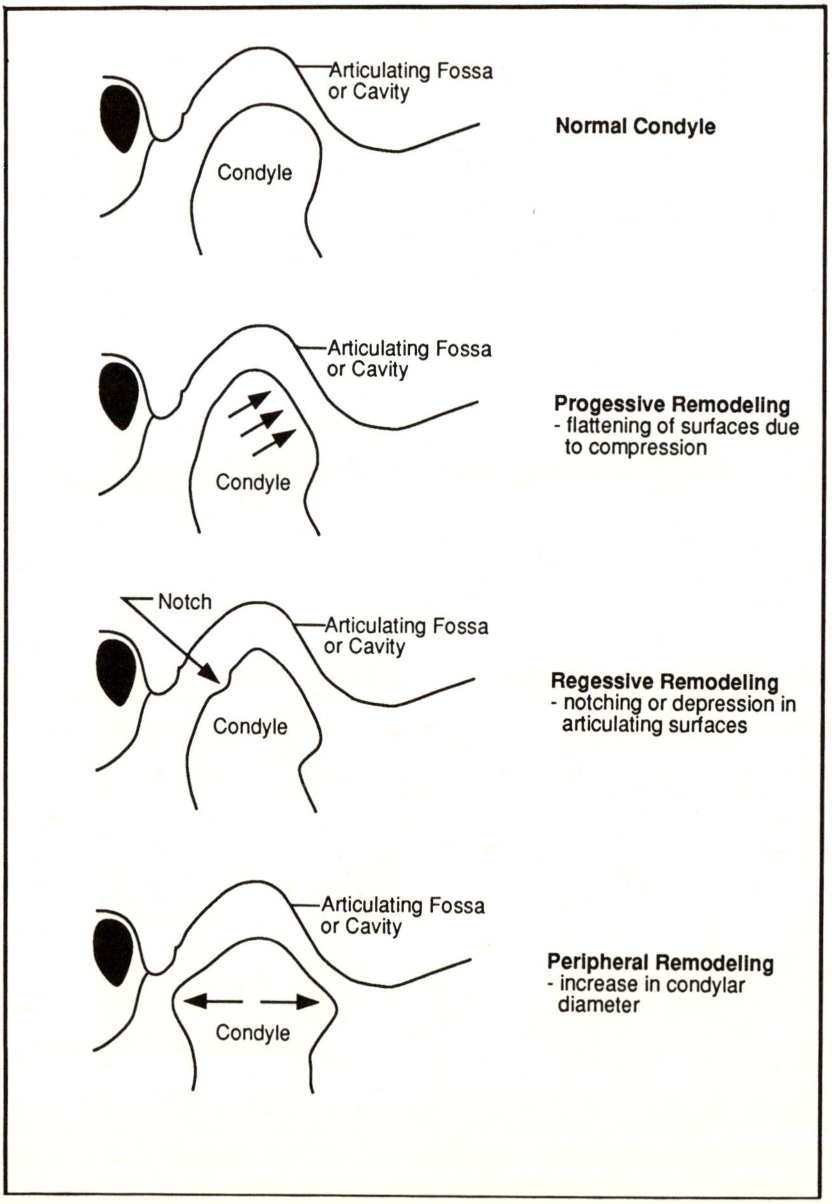

Figure 3-3. Articular remodeling.

1. Progressive, in which the joint surface advances toward the articular cavity as in articular surface flattening due to condylar compression.
2. Regressive, in which the joint surface moving away from the articular cavity as in articular surface notching or denting.
3. Circumferential or peripheral, in which the articular surface increases in diameter as in condylar enlargement due to stimulating stress (commonly seen in degenerative arthritis).

Clearly, the TMJ can be viewed as a dynamic structure with a capacity for morphologic adaption to temporally influenced functional stresses.[2]

In addition, mechanical stimuli can initiate condylar remodeling.[3] Mechanical stimuli, such as repeated, excessive use of the OSGS and occlusal changes, can exert pressure on the joint, sometimes causing arthritic changes. Furthermore, the amount of remodeling and arthrosis of the TMJ is probably higher in those individuals with depleted or compromised dental occlusion.[4]

§ 3.4 TMJ Condylar Position

The condylar position is described relative to the fossa. It is the product of many dynamic changes in the body, which are due to growth and remodeling,

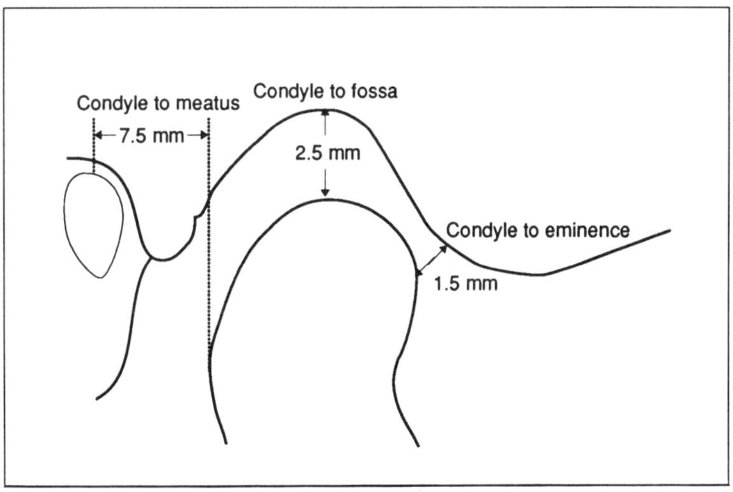

Figure 3-4. Rickett's condylar position.

[2] B. Moffett, *The Morphogenesis of the Temporomandibular Joint*, 52 Am. J. Orthodontics 401 (1966).

[3] H.J. Blackwood, *Cellular Remodeling in Articular Tissue*, 45 J. Dental Research 480 (1960).

[4] T. Oberg, G.E. Carlson, & C.M. Fajers, *The Temporomandibular Joint: A Morphologic Study on Human Anatory Material*, 29 Acta Odontology Scandinavia 349 (1971).

functional matrix activities, the occlusal condition, functional adaptation, and individual variation.[5] Several clinicians[6] have recommended optimal condylar positions and found them to be in a forward position in the fossa. As **Figures 3-4**, **3-5**, and **3-6** show, the recommended positions differ more in the methodology describing them than in the actual position.

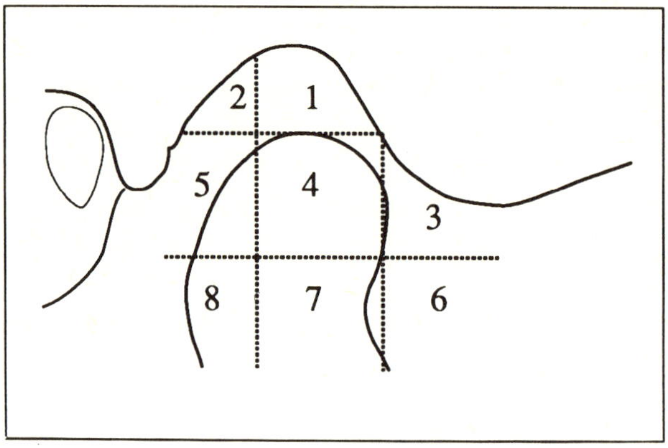

Figure 3-5. Gelb's condylar position.

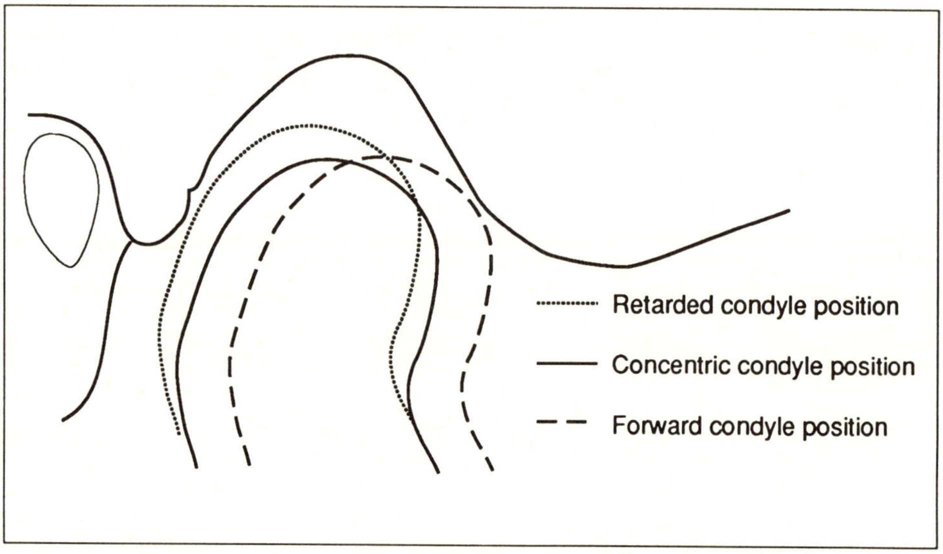

Figure 3-6. Weinberg's condylar positions.

---

[5] R.A. Abdel-Fattah, *Optimum TMJ Condylar Position*, Today's Scientific Florida Dental Assoc. J. (Nov. 1989).

[6] R.M. Ricketts, *Laminography in the Diagnosis of Temporomandibular Joint Disorders*, 46 J. Am. Dental Assoc. 620 (1953).

BIOMECHANICS

§ 3.5 Movement of the Condyle

The mandibular condyle is freely movable in the glenoid fossa. Movement occurs in the orthogonal spatial planes, namely the horizontal, facial, sagittal, or a combination of planes. In the sagittal plane, the condyle moves to open the interincisal distance to a range of twenty to twenty seven millimeters by the rotation of the condylar body around its center. During rotation, the articulating disc remains stationary between the condyle and the posterior slope of the articular eminence. When the interincisal distance becomes greater than twenty seven millimeters, the condyle travels, or translates, downward and forward along the posterior slope of the articular eminence and beyond its most convex portion, with the articulating disc located interstitially to the condyle and the eminence. Rotation and translation are normally smooth motions, and with minimal noise or interference, a combination of the two types of motion can occur. See **Figure 3-7**.

In addition, condylar movement is controlled by the neuromuscular and ligamentous attachments to the lower mandible, cranium, and spine. The incisal point moves within the borders of the envelope of Posselt.

The envelope of Posselt describes the sagittal movement of the mandible. If one can imagine a point between the lower central incisors as a midpoint, it describes the movement of the mandible during function. Trace the pathway of this midpoint as the mandible is moved backward, forward, and downward in a sagittal direction. See **Figure 3-8**. This tracing forms the sagittal boundaries or limits of mandibular motion known as the envelope of Posselt.

When the same point is traced in a frontal direction, adding movement to the right and left as well as downward, it will form the frontal boundaries or limits of mandibular motion. See **Figure 3-9**. Together the sagittal and frontal boundaries form the envelope of mandibular motion in three dimensions.

As in the sagittal plane, in the frontal and horizontal planes, the condyle slides along the posterior slope of the eminence or medial wall of the glenoid fossa, with the articulating disc interposed between the condyle and the eminence. Again, the lower incisal point follows the envelope of motion. See **Figure 3-10**. When the mandible is compressed or displaced posteriorly due to trauma, a pathogenic condition, or any other factor, the TMJ overloads, loosening the collagen fibers and overstretching the temporomandibular ligaments and capsule. These actions result in a disturbed condyle-disc-fossa assembly which leads to a clicking noise in the joint, spasms of the lateral pterygoid muscles, and subsequent pain and dysfunction.

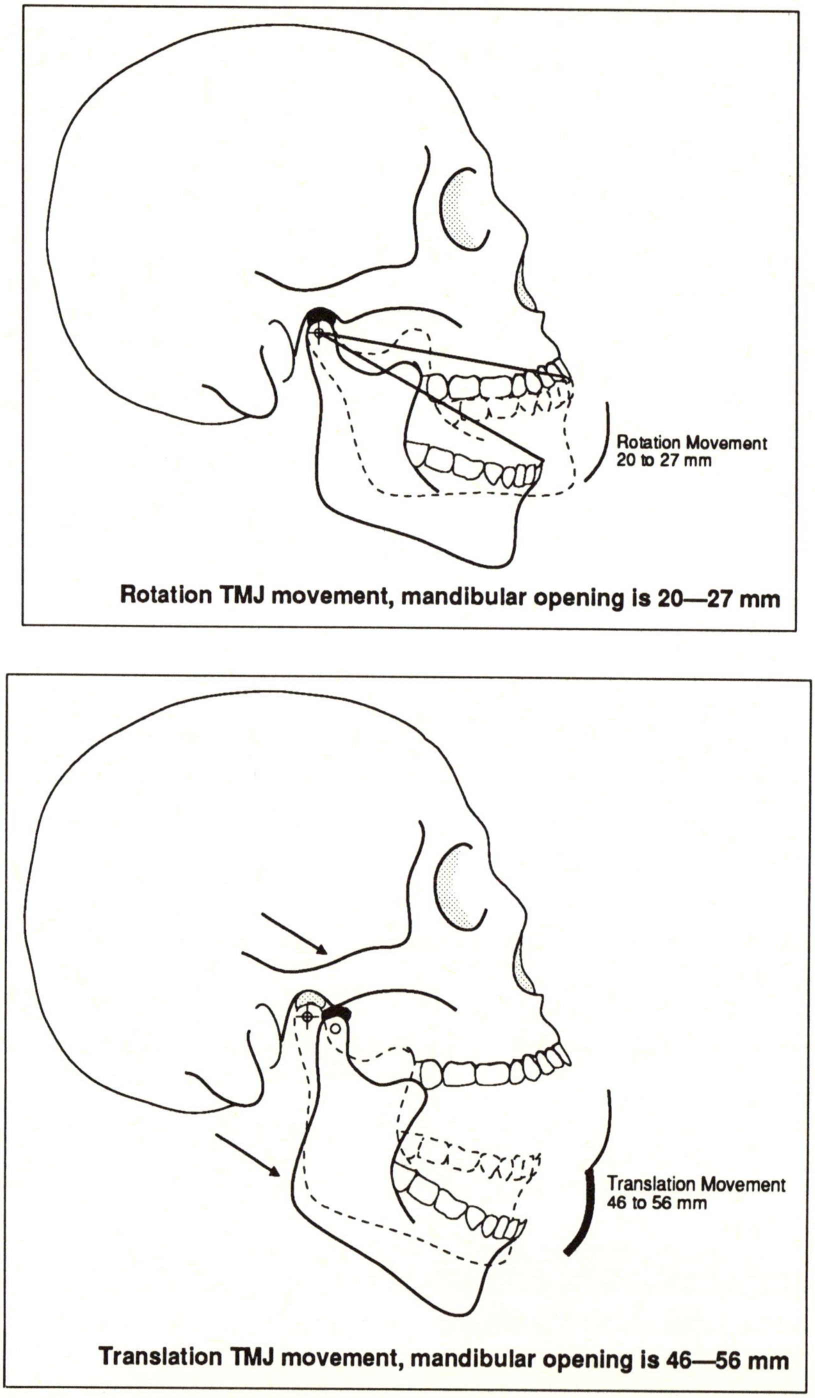

Figure 3-7. Movement in the TMJ.

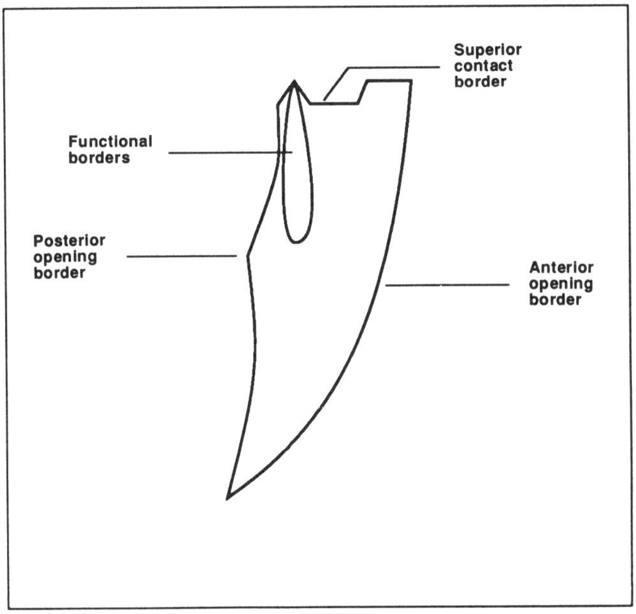

Figure 3-8. Sagittal boundaries of mandibular motion (envelope of Posselt).

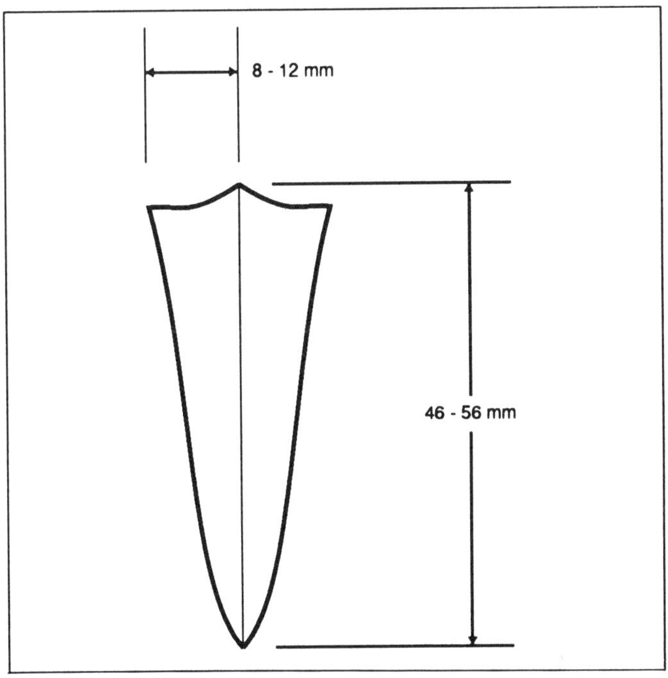

Figure 3-9. Frontal boundary of mandibular motion (envelope of motion).

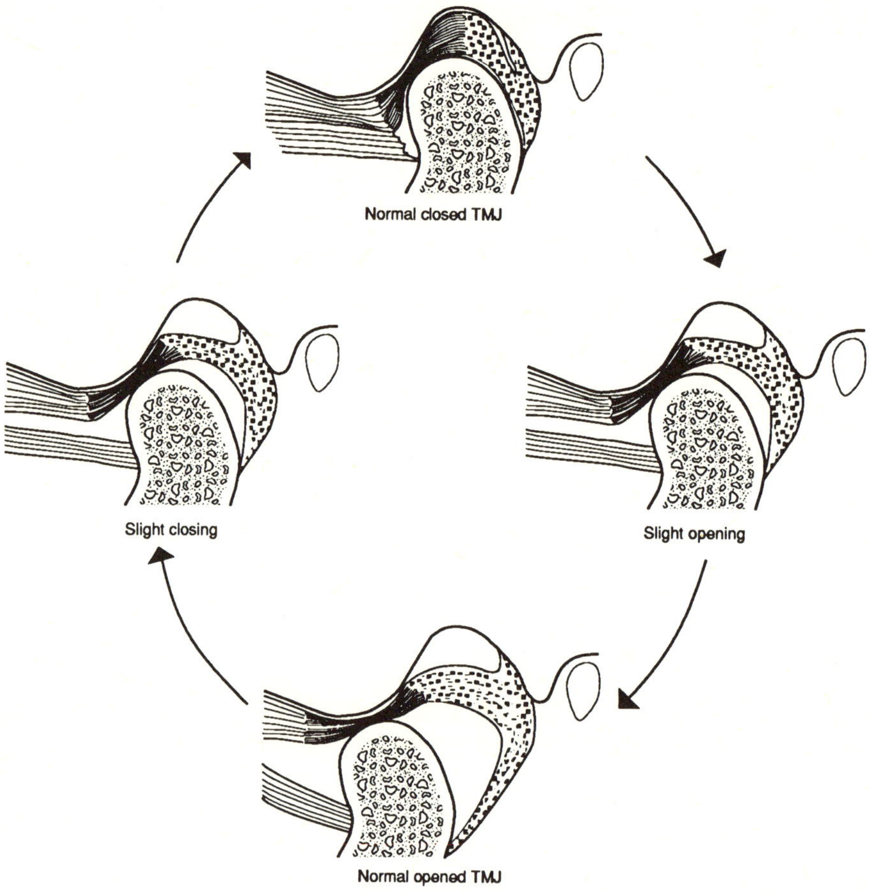

Figure 3-10. Normal condylar movement while opening and closing the mouth.

There is a complementary influence between the inclination of the teeth and the TMJ. If the inclinations of the dental occlusion and the TMJs are symmetrical as regards centric occlusion and during eccentric movement, the joints and the teeth can remain healthy. On the other hand, when no harmonious inclination exists, due to loss, shift, damage, restoration, or an erosion of the teeth, a pathologic joint condition may result. The teeth may become the dominant factor; therefore, the joint will bear the brunt of the malocclusion. Alternatively, if the TMJ is predominant, the teeth and their supporting structure will be traumatized and demonstrate attrition, cracks, fractures, migration, or traumatic periodontal disease.

Investigators have reported a relation between head posture and occlusal (bite) contact, as illustrated in **Figure 3-11**. The arrows in **Figure 3-11** show

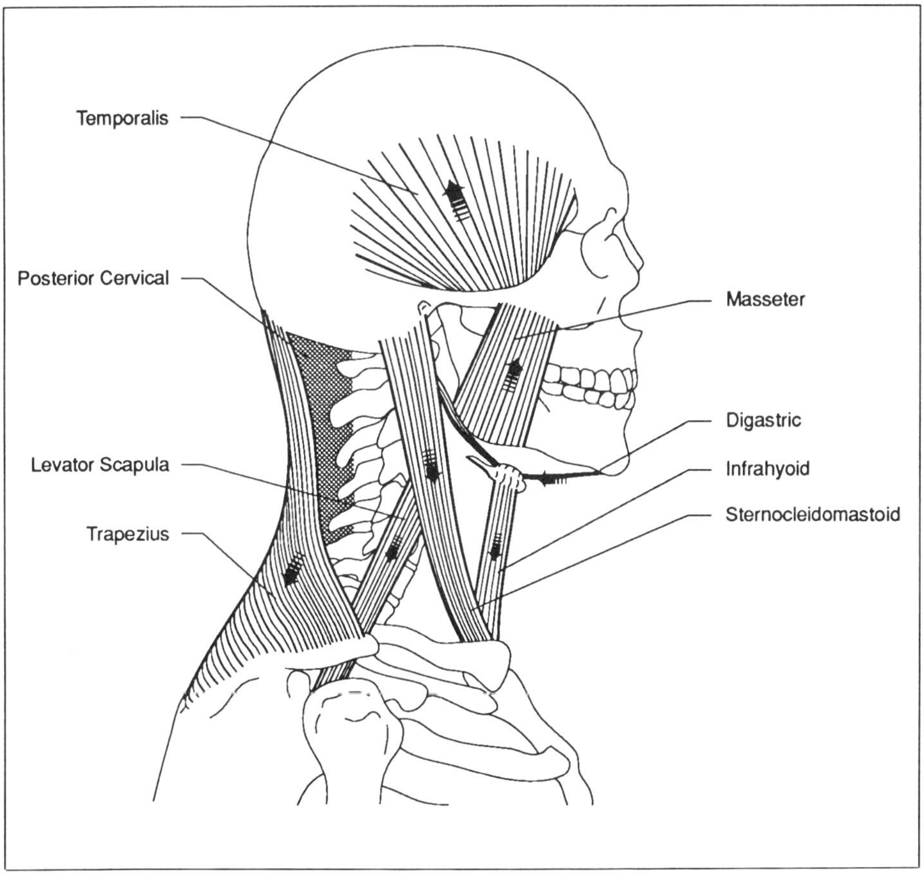

Figure 3-11. Postural balance through cervical and cranial muscle balance.

the direction of muscle action to balance posture and keep the head erect. A misalignment of the head posture forward increases the contact and pressure on the posterior teeth, See **Figure 3-12**. An erect, normal posture allows maximum, even contact of the upper and lower dental arches. This has been proven clinically through the work of Mariano Racabado.[7]

[7] M. Racabado, *Diagnosis and Treatment of Abnormal Craniocervical and Craniomandibular Mechanics in* Abnormal Jaw Mechanics: Diagnosis and Treatment (W.K. Solberg & G.T. Clark, eds. 1984).

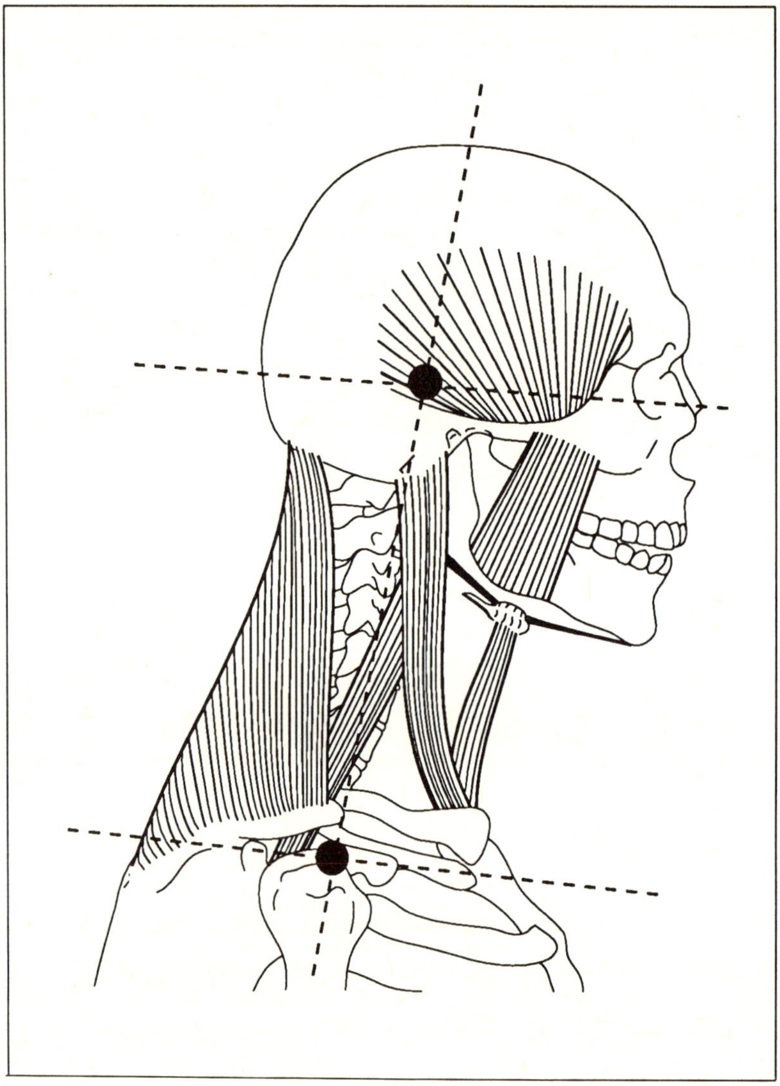

Figure 3-12. Forward head posture.

CHAPTER 4

CAUSATION OF TMJ-OSG DISORDERS

§ 4.1 Proximate Cause

Causation is the relation of a certain injury to a certain effect within a reasonable degree of medical and dental probability. In determining the proximate cause of a TMJ-OSGS disorder, the expert witness selected for the purpose of presenting a legal case often faces a difficult task, depending on the severity of injury.

TMJ-OSGS disorders are often causally related to a certain trauma. Trauma, or injury, can be classified into these groups:

1. Direct physical or mechanical.
2. Indirect, to the neck and to the side of the head.
3. Psychological and/or emotional, such as a death in the family, loss of job, or divorce.
4. Chemical, such as medications that increase muscle tension and subsequently cause TMJ-OSGS disorders.
5. Thermal, such as overexposure to cold, can affect muscle condition and cause contracture or blood vessel dilatation.

It is also possible for nontraumatic factors, such as nutritional or behavioral factors, infections, neoplasms, and growth disturbances, to be the cause of TMJ-OSGS disorders.

Proximate causation is very important and all pertinent factors should be carefully analyzed. Acute mechanical trauma is not always the first or the only causative factor. Other factors should be considered, such as condition of the individual, amount and direction of trauma, and follow-up treatment.

Causation analysis includes consideration of preexisting conditions, predisposition and susceptibility, initiation and perpetuation of symptoms.

Preexisting factors. Preexisting factors are those that existed prior to the incident being litigated. They may be readily apparent or detectable only by examination. The more common preexisting factors include:

1. Facial asymmetry as an indication of mandibular displacement and growth disturbances, e.g., higher level of one eye, nose deviated to one side, higher level of one ear, chin deviated to one side, shorter lower third of the face.
2. Dental malocclusion as an indication of mandibular displacement, e.g., crossbite, increased overjet, midline shift, irregular occlusal plane.
3. Pathological conditions of bones or muscles, e.g., condylar bone osteoarthritis, flattening or excessive remodeling, asymmetrical mandibular rami or condyles, muscle disease, neurological disorders.

Predisposing factors. Predisposing factors are pathological, physiological, or structural processes that alter (usually weaken) the TMJ-OSGS, thereby increasing the probability that a disorder will develop. Examples include rheumatological disease, hormonal changes, nutritional deficiencies, metabolic disorders, and debilitating diseases.[1]

Eggshell theory. Predisposed or preexisting conditions may exist; however, the final precipitating or aggravating factor is responsible for the damage sustained in an injury. A clichéd manner of expressing this theory is a fragile individual who is an accident waiting to happen or the injury is the straw that broke the camel's back.

Initiating factors. Initiating factors lead to the onset of the symptoms and are primarily related to the overload of the TMJ-OSGS. Trauma, either direct or indirect, is the most common factor in litigated cases. Emotional stress can be an important initiating factor in nonlitigious cases.

Perpetuating factors. These factors, including psychological, nutritional, mechanical, and biological factors, perpetuate the disorder and thus aggravate or complicate its management. Psychological factors are usually depression, tension, anxiety, hypochondria, and desire for financial gain. Vitamin

---

[1] H.L. Goldberg, *Trauma and the Improbable Anterior Displacement*, 4 J. Craniomandibular Disorders, Facial, Oral Pain 131 (1990); O.J. Rogel, Mandibular Whiplash (Owen J. Rogel 1988).

deficiencies and metabolic inadequacies may perpetuate the disorder. Skeletal assymetry and chronic infection may also perpetuate the disorder.

General adaptation syndrome. Compensatory or adaptive mechanisms enable an individual to function without symptoms. Once the tolerance level is exceeded the body will no longer endure the injury and symptoms surface.

Some factors can be perpetuating, predisposing, mitigating, or aggravating depending on strength of the factor and the onset of the disorder. For example, trauma can initiate TMJ-OSGS disorder in a normal individual or the trauma may aggravate a pre-existing condition. Mechanical internal trauma from malocclusion is a perpetuating factor and leads to TMJ-OSGS disorders by itself. That can also be a predisposing factor in a specific individual who subsequently suffers an aggravating factor which reveals the disorder.

§ 4.2 Mechanism of Injury

Analysis of the mechanism of injury to the TMJ-OSGS can assist in the understanding of its effects. These effects, or the extent, of an injury may depend on many factors, such as the amount of trauma, direction of trauma, the individual's position during receipt of trauma and the individual's general condition. The occurrence of trauma can be direct or indirect; macro- or micro-; mechanical, chemical, or psychological; acute or chronic; and closed or open.

Direct mechanical trauma to head and neck. **Figure 4-1** shows several possible directions for direct trauma to the head and neck.

Horizontal injury to the mandible, driving it backward, may be caused by a direct blow during a fight or a boxing match, hitting the steering wheel in an automobile accident, or falling from a bicycle or motorcycle. Any of these could displace the mandible posteriorly, causing posterior condylar displacement, bruised retrodiscal tissue, anterior displacement of the articulating disc or even disc perforation in severe or rare cases, spasm of the retruding (backward moving) and protruding muscles, or mandibular ligament sprain.

Horizontal injury to the mandible, pushing it from right to left and vice versa, as may result from a direct blow during a fight, hitting the steering wheel or door in an automobile accident, or by a blow from a ball during sports activity, such as racquetball or golf. Any of these injuries could displace the mandible laterally, causing lateral condylar displacement, lateral articular disc displacement, spasm in the laterally moving muscles, or mandibular ligament sprain.

Injury to the temporal bone, forcing it inside the skull, which, similar to horizontal actuations of the head and neck, is often caused by impact with

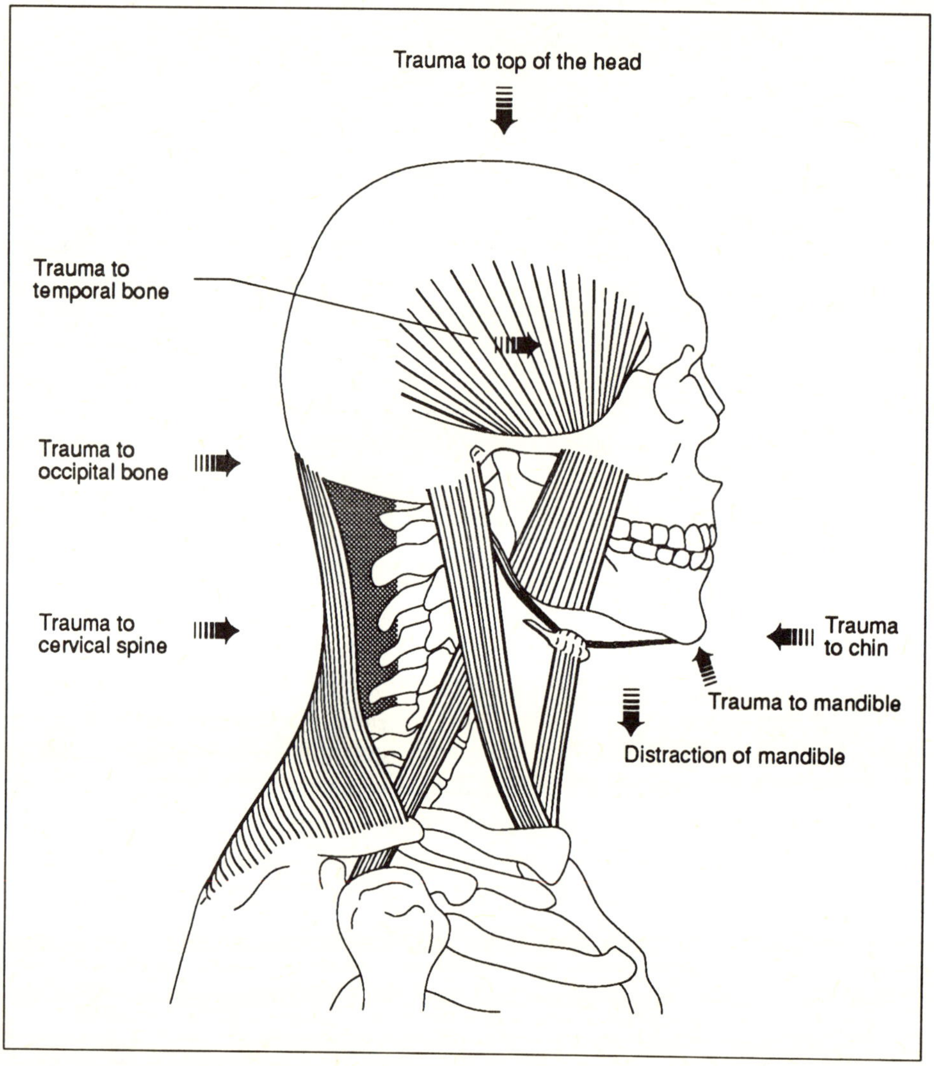

Figure 4-1. Direct traumas to head and neck.

car door in an automobile accident, accidental contact with sports equipment, a club or bat, a free weight, or a ball, or fist fighting and boxing.

The result may be muscle spasm and/or temporal bone displacement, and these may lead to spasm of the temporalis muscle, temporal bone rotation, inward or outward, disturbing the condyle-disc-fossa assembly, pressure on the contents of the temporal bone that presents in symptoms such as hearing impairment, headache, or blurred vision, or sprain of the temporalis tendon.

Injury to the occipital bone, propelling the occipital bone forward; as with the head and neck injuries previously described, the origin may be head trauma during a vehicular collision, a blow from a ball or other sporting equipment, fisticuffs, or a blow to the back of the head, such as a slip, trip, or fall. Any of these or a combination of injuries may cause the occipital bone to move forward, resulting in disturbed TMJ condyle-disc assembly or muscle spasm.

Injury to the top of the head may be caused by a falling object or hitting the roof of an automobile in the course of an accident. This may cause downward compression of the parietal bones into the temporal bones and may result or lead to disturbed TMJ condyle-disc-fossa assembly or muscle spasm in the OSGS.

Vertical compression of the mandible, as in forcible cervical traction, may cause muscle spasms and a disturbance of the TMJ condyle-disc-fossa assembly.

Injury to or distraction of the mandible, as in forcible oral intubation or mandibular manipulation, could cause spasms of the odontostomatognathic muscles and ligament sprain and disc displacement of TMJ.

Indirect trauma causing cervical or mandibular hyperextension-hyperflexion injuries. Indirect trauma, such as caused by a rear end auto collision, is illustrated in **Figure 4-2**. The actual injury sustained may depend on the individual's position at the time of injury. The normal position is shown in **Figure 4-2A**.

1. The teeth are clenched in an adequate occlusion (stable bite) upon injury. This is a controlled position of the TMJ and OSGS in which there is minimal or no mandibular displacement and may manifest in slight mandibular stiffness as a result of minor muscle spasm and *capsulitis*: inflammation of the TMJ capsule.
2. The teeth are clenched in an inadequate occlusion (unstable bite) upon injury. This is an uncontrolled position of the TMJ and OSGS and an overcontracture of the muscles of mastication as well as compression of TMJ may occur. Among the consequences are muscle spasms and capsulitis. Anterior disc displacement may be a result of a severe trauma in a person with a disturbed occlusion.
3. Upon injury, if the jaw is relaxed and the teeth are apart so that the condyles move freely in the fossa, trauma radiates from the cervical spine to the mandible. This is an uncontrolled displacement or distraction of the joint and will cause soft tissue and cervical muscle problems and pain. Hyperextension is noted particularly in motor vehicle rear end collisions.

The sudden impact may cause the head to move faster than the mandible, which is "fastened" to the head via muscles and ligaments and held to the neck by the anterior cervical muscles. See **Figure 4-2B**. This action may force the mouth open excessively wide, and causes the joint to overload. See **Figure 4-2C** and **D**. This is the common "snapping" of the head backward that usually results in whiplash and can be seen in slow-motion demonstration films of vehicular accidents. During hyperflexion, the head is pushed

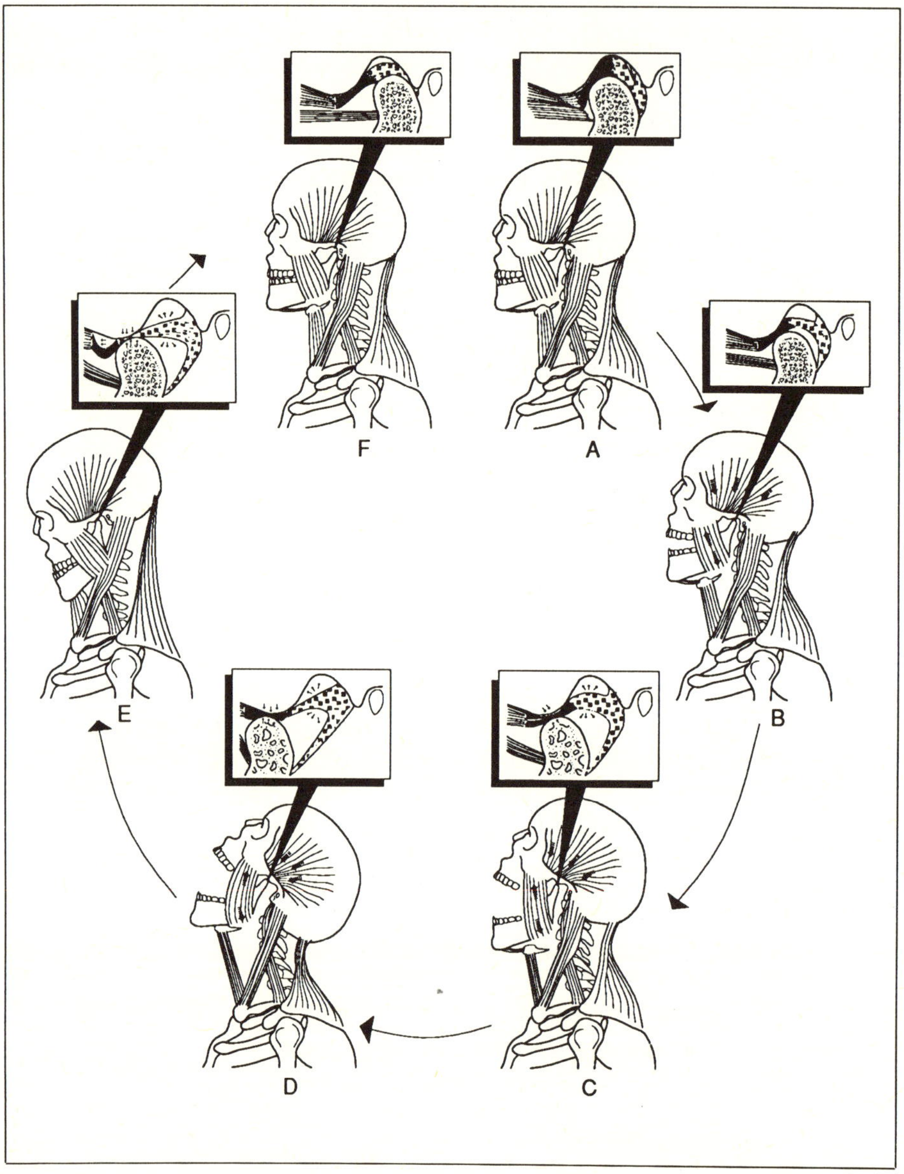

Figure 4-2. Cervical hyperextension-hyperflexion as a result of a rear-end collision. (A) Normal craniomandibular relation. (B) The head moves backward; mandible follows the head, albeit at a slower speed; condyle moves forward. (C) Head moves further in a posterior direction; mandible moves upward at a slower rate of speed; condyle is forced forward. (D) Further movement of the head; further distraction of craniomandibular articulation; further force on TMJ; the OSGS muscles are overstretched. (E) When head is forced forward in hyperflexion, the mandible is thrust forward, overloading the TMJ. (F) Appearance of the OSGS post-injury with anterior disc displacement, posterior condylar displacement, and retrodiscal tissue edema.

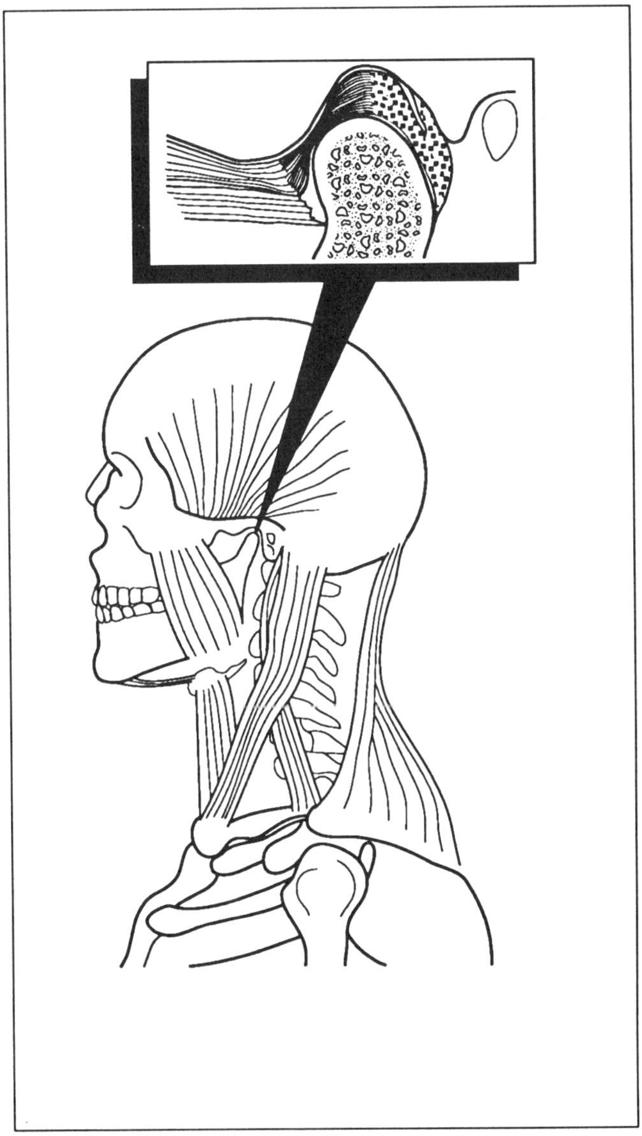

Figure 4-2A. Detailed magnification of normal craniomandibular relation.

forward quite suddenly, **Figure 4-2E**, with the mandible smashing against the maxilla, causing overload of the TMJ. Sometimes the head moves downward and forward forcing the mandible between the maxilla and the chest; this forward movement of the mandible leads to TMJ trauma and possible disc displacement. See **Figure 4-2F**. The actual mechanism of whiplash involves a very complex series of stretching, compressing, and twisting forces radiating throughout the skeletal structure and living tissue

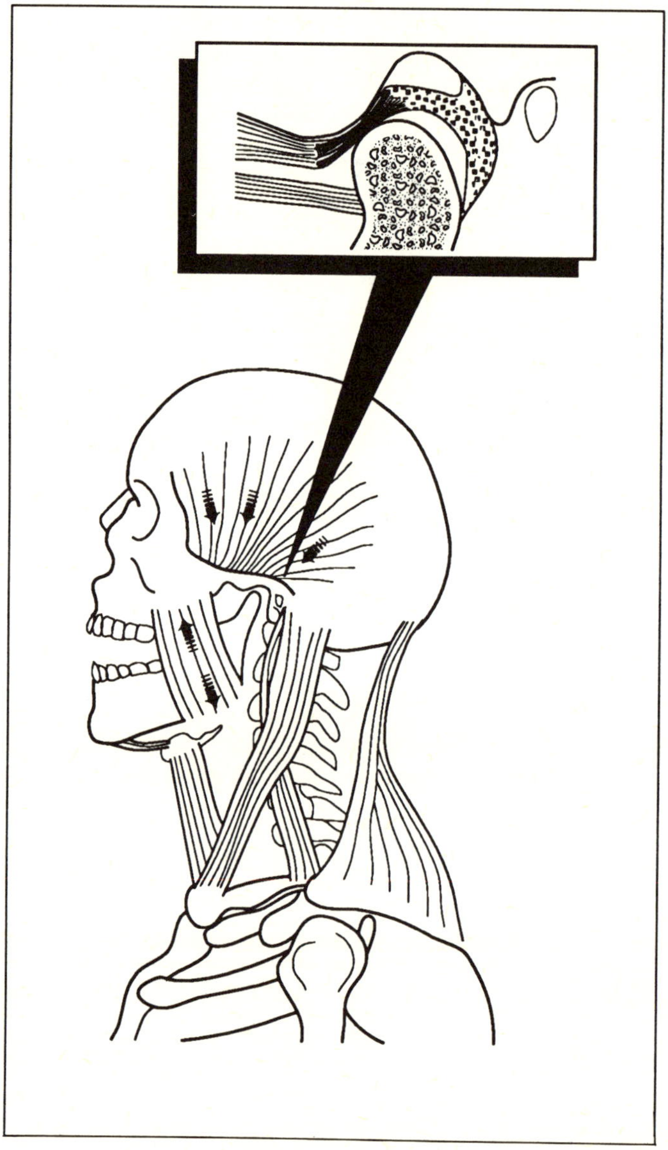

Figure 4-2B. Detailed magnification of cervical hyperextension-hyperflexion: the head moves backward; mandible follows the head, although more slowly; condyle moves forward.

in various directions. There is no doubt that some victims of motor vehicle accidents have experienced a type of shock, whether blunt trauma or cervical spinal whiplash, and the severity of it is unique to each individual.

The facility or difficulty of explaining how anterior disc displacement occurs varies among patients. It is certainly true that not all cases of disc displacement are caused by accident-related trauma. A preexisting condition

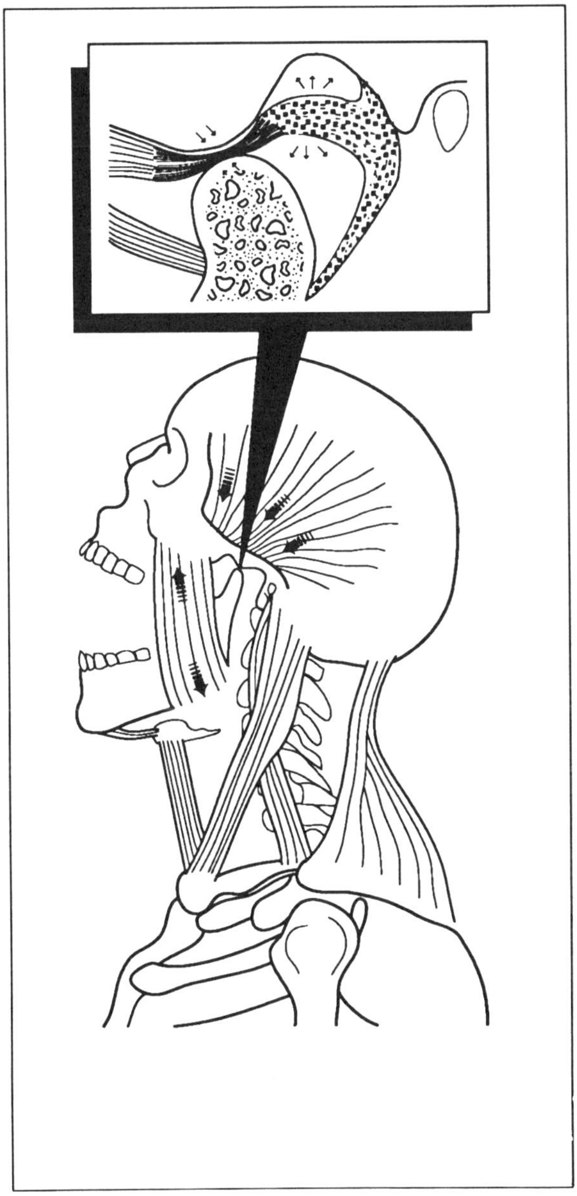

Figure 4-2C. Detailed magnification of cervical hyperextension-hyperflexion: head moves further posteriorly; mandible moves upward, slower than the head; condyle is forced forward.

not previously diagnosed by the accident victim's regular physician may be the actual cause, or the first therapist or diagnostician visited by the victim may never have previously examined the patient.

If blunt trauma occurs to the mandible when the teeth are apart, disc displacement may result from condylar displacement. If forty eight hours pass after onset of the trauma, the mandible may not return to its original position because of the soft tissue injury with the attendant possible edema and hemorrhage, and patients may complain of pain and temporary malocclusion (noted for the duration of active inflammation). With accurate diagnosis and treatment of the inflammatory process (synovitis, capsulitis, retrodiscitis, and/or myocytis), the patient should enjoy a rapid recovery without complex therapy. A large percentage of these TMJ complaints are found to be asymptomatic after a short time; however, in the case of continuous contraction of the lateral pterygoid muscles and condyle displacement, morphological changes take place in the disc. Anatomically, the disc has a bow tie shape with an anterior and a posterior head (thickening) and an intermediate band. Ultimately, the condyle, with compression, can force the disc anteriorly or medially without retrodiscal retraction.

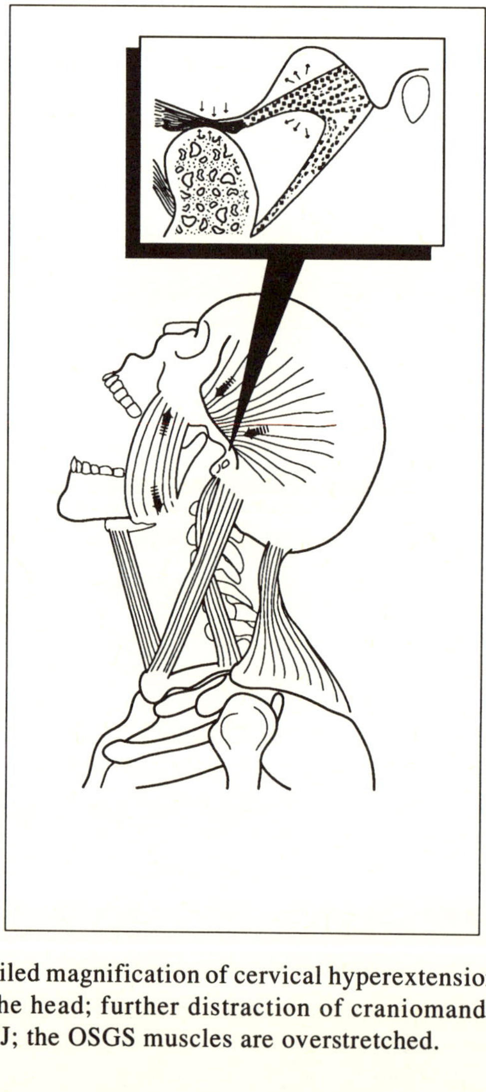

Figure 4-2D. Detailed magnification of cervical hyperextension-hyperflexion: further movement of the head; further distraction of craniomandibular articulation; further force on TMJ; the OSGS muscles are overstretched.

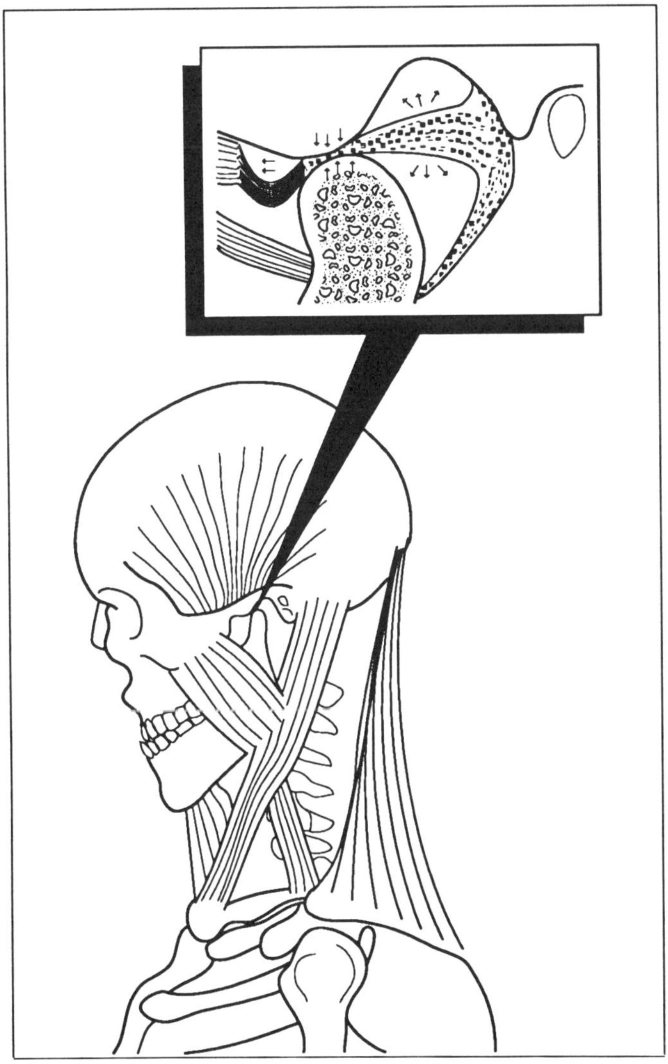

Figure 4-2E. Detailed magnification of cervical hyperextension-hyperflexion; head is forced forward, causing the mandible to be thrust forward, overloading the TMJ.

Blunt trauma to the mandible may also occur if the individual clenches his teeth at the time of the trauma. Upon opening the mouth after receiving a blow, the jaw locks and is accompanied by a clicking sound and some slight discomfort. Displacement of the condyle usually is not possible since the mandible is fixed by the clenching of the teeth. Local soft tissue injury depends on the point of trauma. A blow to the masseter, temporalis, or directly to the TMJ with the teeth locked in the occlusion (bite) may result in myofibrotic contraction with inflammation; however, disc disreplacement is not seen in this case.[2]

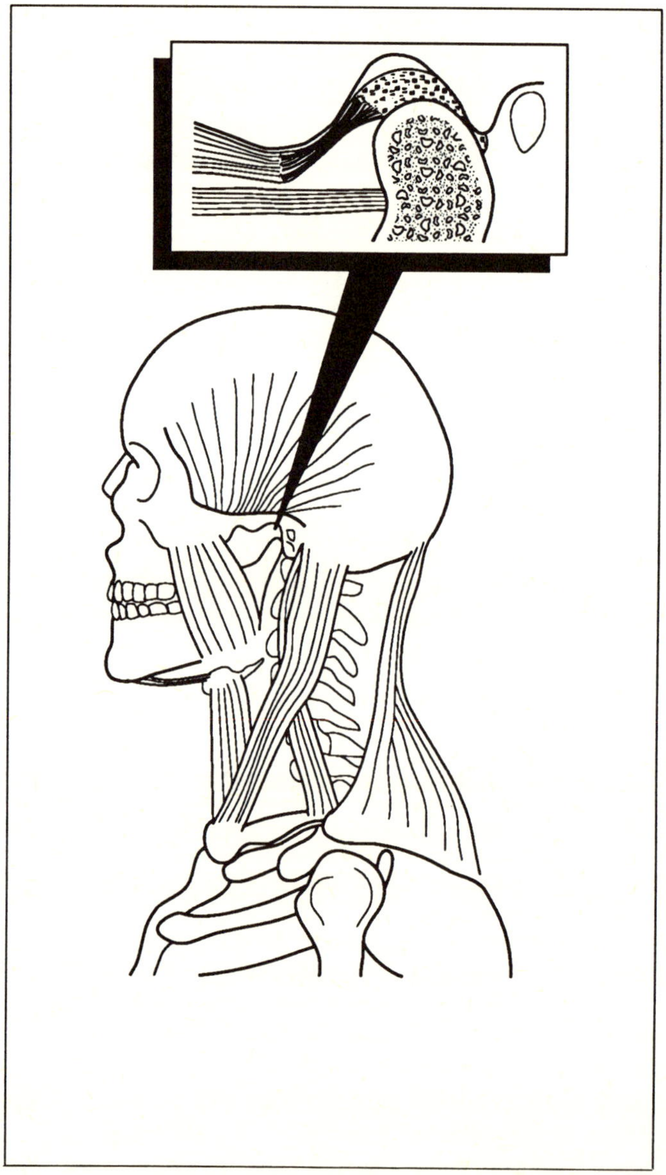

Figure 4-2F. Detailed magnification of cervical hyperextension-hyperflexion: disc is displaced forward and the condyle is displaced backward.

---

[2] H.L. Goldberg, *Trauma and the Improbable Anterior Displacement*, 4 J. Craniomandibular Disorders, Facial, Oral Pain 131 (1990); O.J. Rogel, Mandibular Whiplash (Owen J. Rogel 1988).

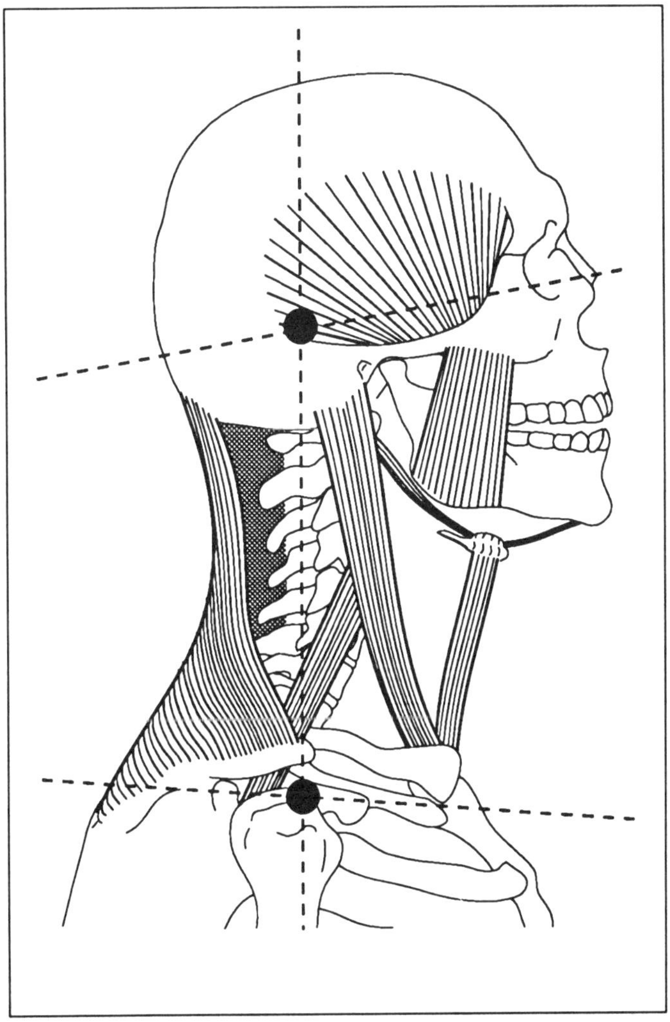

Figure 4-3. When a cervical injury occurs, posterior cervical muscles spasm, causing backward movement of the head.

Remote effect of cervical muscle spasm. In cases of persistent cervical muscle spasm, a TMJ-OSGS disorder may develop as a secondary effect, sometimes occurring six to twelve months after the trauma that triggered the spasm. The spasms that result from cervical injury follow this pattern: a posterior cervical muscle forces the head backward as shown in **Figure 4-3**. Then, due to a reflex input through the mechanoreceptors, the head assumes a forward posture shown in **Figure 4-4**. In addition, the increased tension on hyoid muscles displaces the mandible posteriorly and exerts pressure on the posterior teeth. This causes bruxism (grinding) as well as displacement of the condyle posteriorly, and leads to anterior disc displacement. Assuming the availability of other contributing factors, such disc displacement could lead to osteoarthritis.

Excessive parafunctional activities cause long-term, low-grade trauma. Moving the mandible vigorously and excessively places a compression strain on the TMJ and fatigues the muscles of mastication, causing spasm. Common types of activities that may cause problems include gum chewing, talking, biting on hard foods, playing a musical instrument, and "unusual" oral activities. These causes are further discussed in § **4.3**.

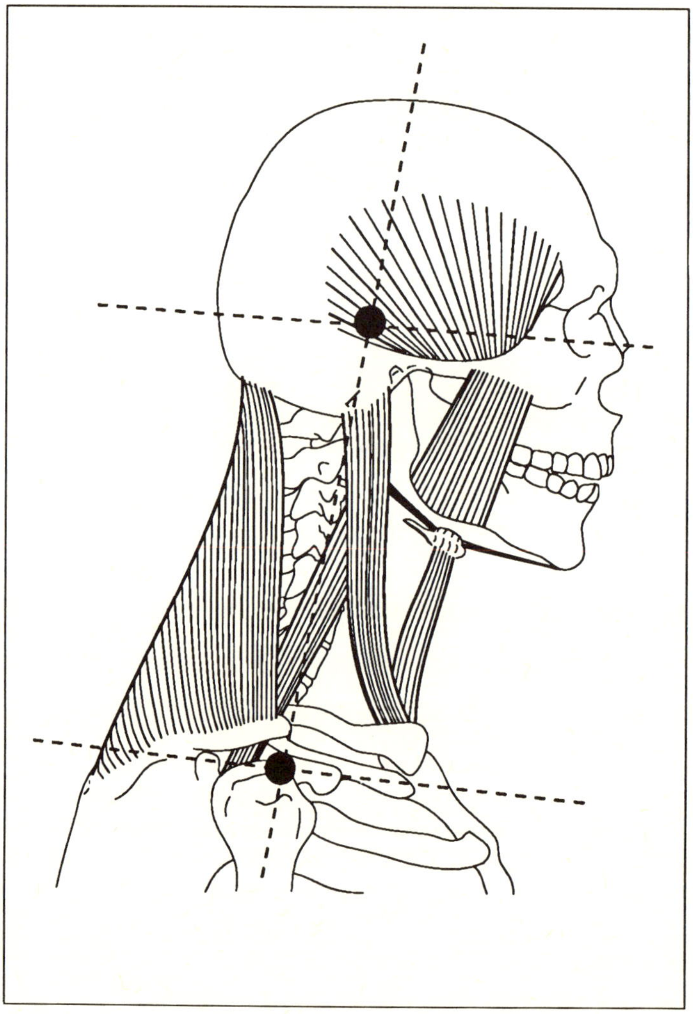

Figure 4-4. Due to a reflex input through the mechanoreceptors, the head will assume a forward position.

§ 4.3 Etiology

There are several etiologic factors in TMJ-OSGS disorders, most of which disturb the condyle-disc-fossa assembly relation, discussed in **Chapter 3**, and/or cause an imbalance in the maxillofacial musculature, which lead to the signs and symptoms of the disorder.

Psychosomatic factors such as anxiety, anger, depression, sadness, worry, fear, frustration, or irritability can play an important part in causing muscle spasms and subsequent internal derangement of the TMJ.[3] Stressful situations such as marital difficulties, family problems, or an unpleasant work environment can influence the balance of TMJ-OSGS.

Bruxism (grinding teeth) and clenching (pressing the upper and lower arches of the teeth together, causing pressure) are examples of parafunctional, and often unconscious, activities that predispose some individuals to TMJ-OSGS disorders. Clenching and bruxism are protective reflexes against unwanted tooth interference (early tooth contact) and can cause the disintegration of various structures, leading to TMJ-OSGS disorders, pupal inflammation, and periodontal disease. Other parafunctional activities such as excessive gum chewing, yawning, thumb-sucking (**Figure 4-5.**), unilateral chewing of food, nail biting, rhythmic tooth tapping, or vigorous, "unusual" use of the mouth (such as fellatio) place stress on the joint and fatigue in the lateral pterygoid muscles and lead to TMJ-OSG disorders. **Figure 4-6** illustrates a TMJ disorder caused by parafunctional activity.

Several clinicians[4] have related malocclusion (abnormal bite) to TMJ disorders. Crossbite, increased overbite, increased overjet, midline shift, maxillary crowding, open bite, premature contacts, and other forms of malocclusion cause TMJ strain and subsequent dysfunction. See **Figure 4-7**.

---

[3] Craniomandibular Disorders: Guidelines for Evaluation, Diagnosis, and Management (C. McNeill, ed. 1990); R. Abdel-Fattah, *Diagnosis and Prevention of Temporomandibular (TMJ) and Odontostomatognathic System (OSG) Injuries in Dental Practice*, 2 Today's Scientific Florida Dental Assoc. J. 5C (1990); G.H. Smith, Headaches Aren't Forever (International Center for Nutritional Research 1986); W.K. Solberg & D.A. Seligman, *Temporomandibular Orthopedics in* New Vistas in Orthodontics (L.E. Johnson, ed., Lea & Febiger 1985); J.D. Rugh & W.K. Solberg, *Psychological Implications in Temporomandibular Pain and Dysfunction*, 7 Oral Science Rev. 30 (1976).

[4] C. McNeill, W.M. Dawing, W. Farrar, H. Gelb, M. Lerman, B. Moffett, R. Pertes, W. Solberg, & L. Weinberg, *Craniomandibular (TMJ) Disorders—The State of the Art*, 44 J. Prosthetic Dentistry 434 (1980); D.A. Keith, *Etiology and Diagnosis of Temporomandibular Pain and Dysfunction*, (Paper presented at the President's Conference on the Examination, Diagnosis and Management of Temporomandibular Disorders, American Dental Association, 1982).

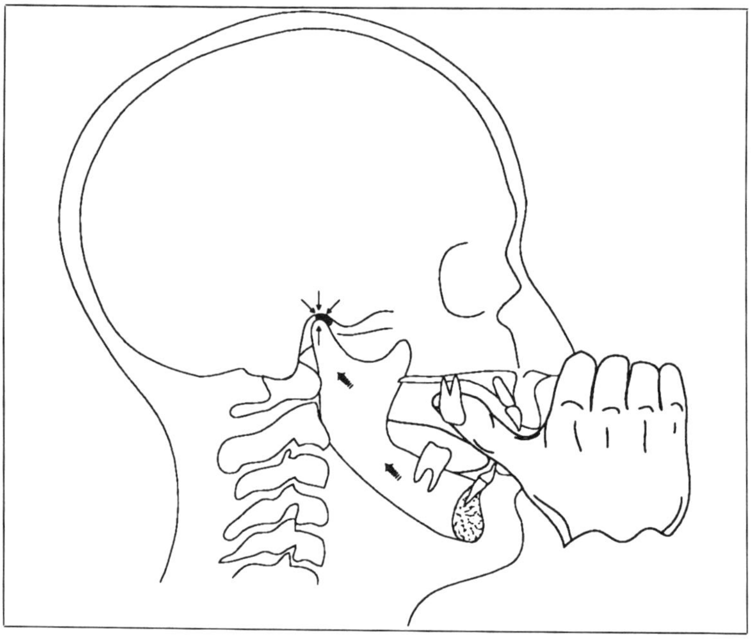

Figure 4-5. Parafunctional activity—thumb sucking.

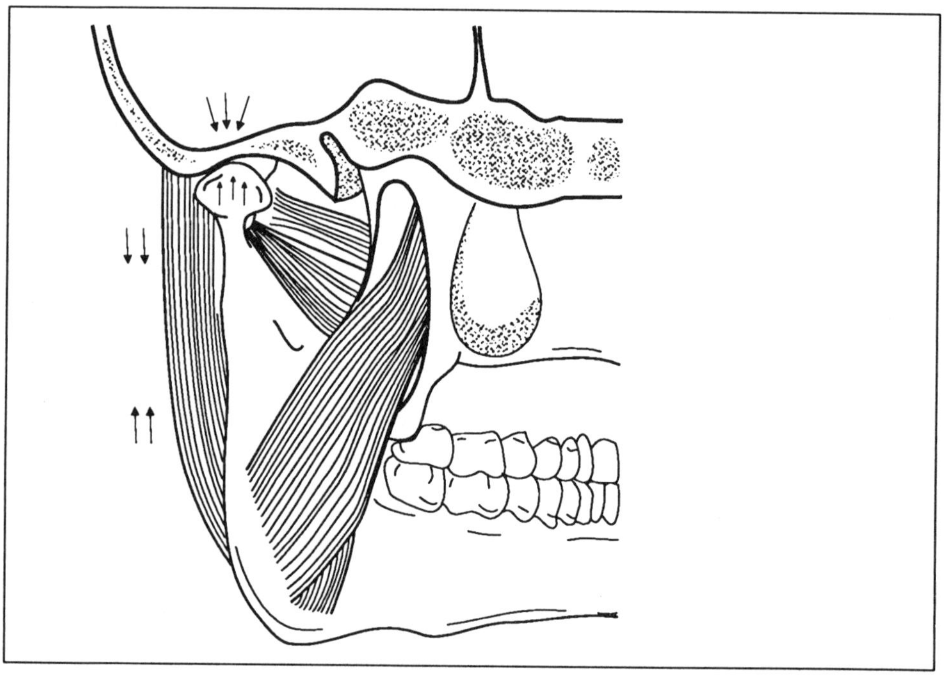

Figure 4-6. Muscle spasm overloading the TMJ as a result of parafunctional activity.

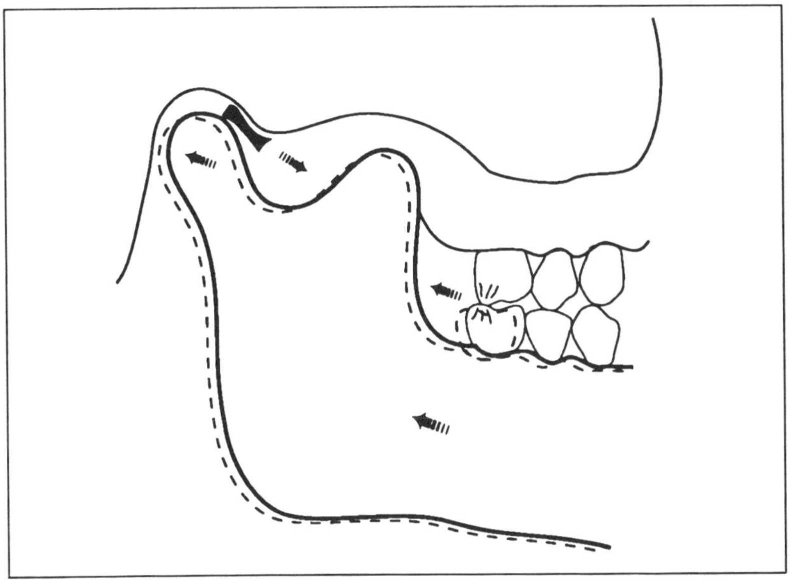

Figure 4-7. Malocclusion or cuspla interference can cause mandibular displacement leading to TMJ-OSGS disorder.

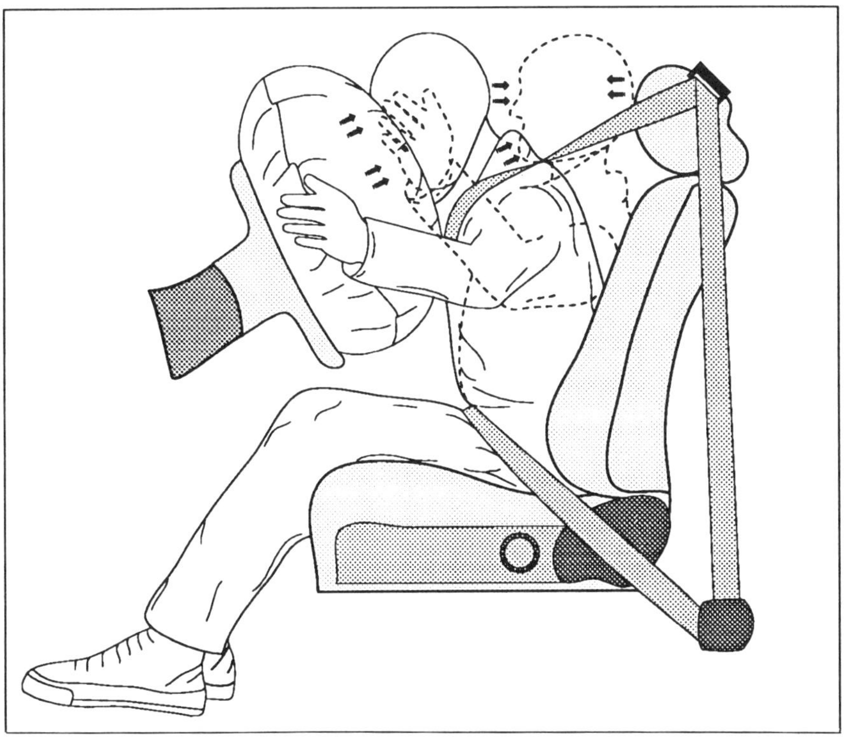

Figure 4-8. Air bag could cause macrotrauma.

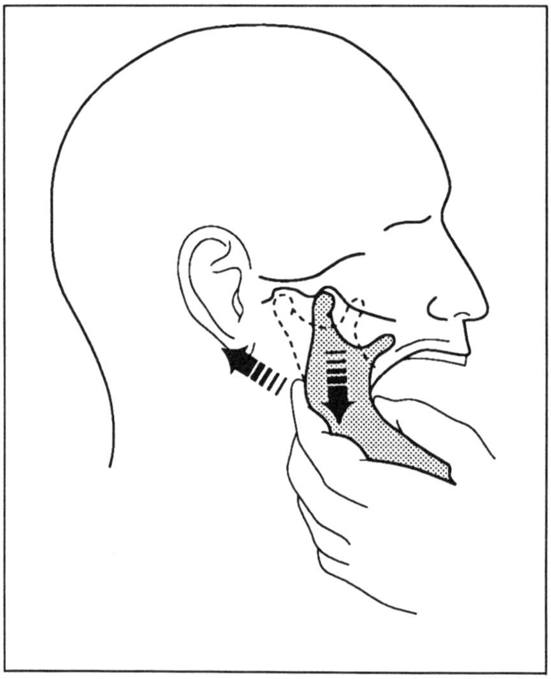

Figure 4-9. Overstretching the mouth during dental procedure.

Repetitive, chronic, low-grade trauma from parafunction or malocclusion may stimulate remodeling of the joint or may, if increased, initiate degenerative arthritis.

Macrotrauma, such as a blow to the chin or the lateral aspect of the face, an automobile accident, a sports injury, or that which may occur at a recreational area, such as a park or on a carnival ride,[5] inflation of an airbag against a forward-moving face could force the mandible to move posteriorly, causing condylar distalization and anterior disc displacement. See **Figure 4-8**. Overloading of the joint as a result of trauma causes hyperextension of the ligaments and disturbs the condyle-disc-fossa assembly.

Other causes of TMJ disorders include misdiagnosis of preexisting TMJ-OSGS disorders; creating a pathogenic situation that will result in a TMJ-OSGS disorder, such as inducing cervical muscle spasms or disturbing the dental occlusion; aggravating a latent TMJ disorder by changing the dental occlusion of a patient with facial muscle tenderness and joint noise; and precipitating a TMJ-OSGS disorder by the use of excessive, forcible dental procedures. Various procedures such as forcible extractions, overstretching the mouth opening, as shown in **Figure 4-9**, forcible pressure during impression taking, third molar extraction, endodontic therapy of the posterior teeth,

[5] D.A. Keith, *Etiology and Diagnosis of Temporomandibular Pain and Dysfunction* (Paper presented at the President's Conference on the Examination, Diagnosis and Management of Temporomandibular Disorders, American Dental Association, 1982).

forcible oral-endotracheal intubation during the delivery of general anesthesia, as shown in **Figure 4-10**, and improper cervical traction when pressure is applied to the mandible, improper cervical manipulation when the mandible is used as support, as shown in **Figure 4-11**.

Numerous conditions may predispose an individual to TMJ disorders. Nutritional problems like calcium deficiency; food additives, like the MSG in oriental foods and tyramine in wine; caffeine; and vitamin D deficiency, can cause muscle spasm. Metabolic, hormonal, vascular, psychological, or neurologic disorders and other systemic conditions such as the debilitating diseases of diabetes, liver cirrhosis, and alcoholism, may also predispose the patient to a TMJ-OSGS disorder.[6]

Development of the TMJ from infancy to adulthood is a complex series of events that may affect the possible variations in the condylar growth rate. These variations disturb facial and mandibular growth and can manifest as the elevation of one eye socket over the other in the skull, deviation of the chin or nose, or a flattened zygomatic bone.[7] TMJ neoplasms (abnormal growth) such as osteoma, chondroma, osteochondroma, giant cell lesions, myxoma, fibromyxoma, fibroosteoma, pigmented villinodular synovitis, synovial chondromatosis, hemangioma, and glomus tumor are not common. Neoplasms cause condylar enlargement and subsequent joint dysfunction. They may also disturb the mandibular balance when they occur in the mandible or maxillae.[8]

Medicaments such as antipsychotic tranquilizers, oral contraceptives, diuretics, and digitalis can cause muscle and TMJ pain. The scientific literature contains much information regarding the deleterious effects, such as muscular rigidity, dystonia, akathisia, tardive dyskinesia, and convulsions, of antipsychotic tranquilizers such as Promethazine (Phenergan), Haloperidal (Haldol), Thioridazine (Mellaril), and Chloropromazine (Thorazine). These side effects adversely impact the oral-facial-cranialcervical musculatures and cause dysfunction.[9]

§ 4.4 Pathogenesis

If the mandibular condyle is displaced posteriorly due to any etiological factor as discussed in § **4.3**, this may *overload* the TMJ. Such overload, or

---

[6] C. McNeill, W.M. Dawing, W. Farrar, H. Gelb, M. Lerman, B. Moffett, R. Pertes, W. Solberg, & L. Weinberg, *Craniomandibular (TMJ) Disorders—The State of the Art*, 44 J. Prosthetic Dentistry 434 (1980).

[7] D.A. Keith, *Etiology and Diagnosis of Temporomandibular Pain and Dysfunction*, (Paper presented at the President's Conference on the Examination, Diagnosis and Management of Temporomandibular Disorders, American Dental Association, 1982).

[8] *Id.*

[9] F.H. Meyers, E. Jawetz, & A. Goldfien, Review of Medical Pharmacology (Lange Medical Publications 1980).

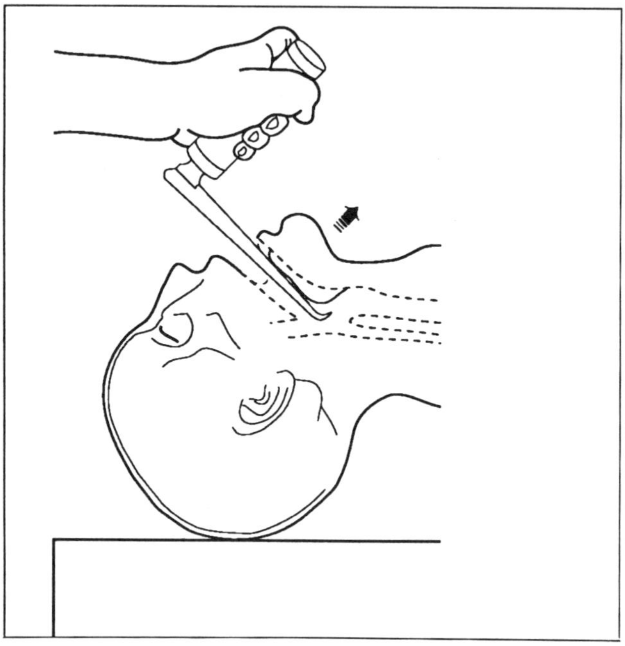

Figure 4-10. Forcible oral-endotrac intubation during delivery of general anesthesia.

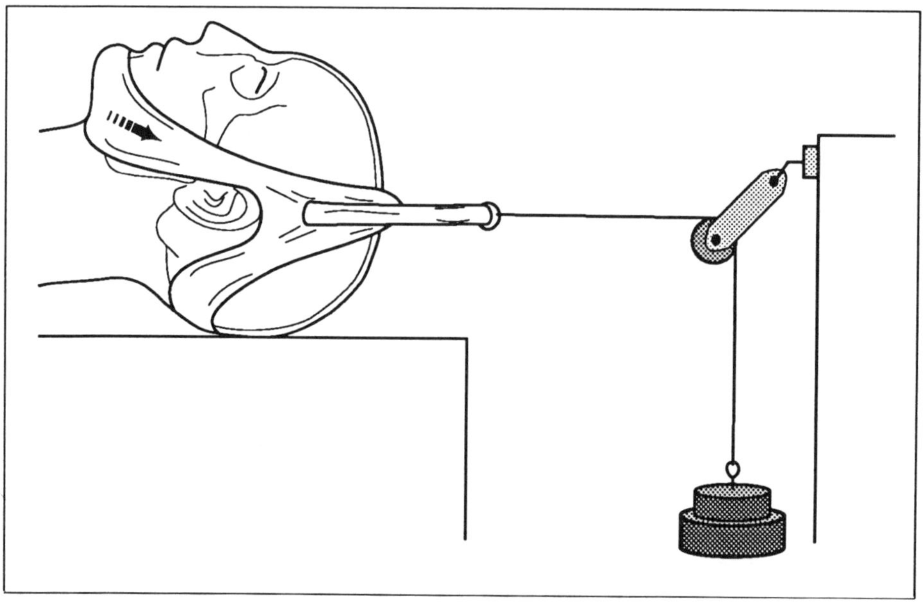

Figure 4-11. Precipitating TMJ-OSGS disorder by the use of improper cervical traction when pressure is applied to the mandible.

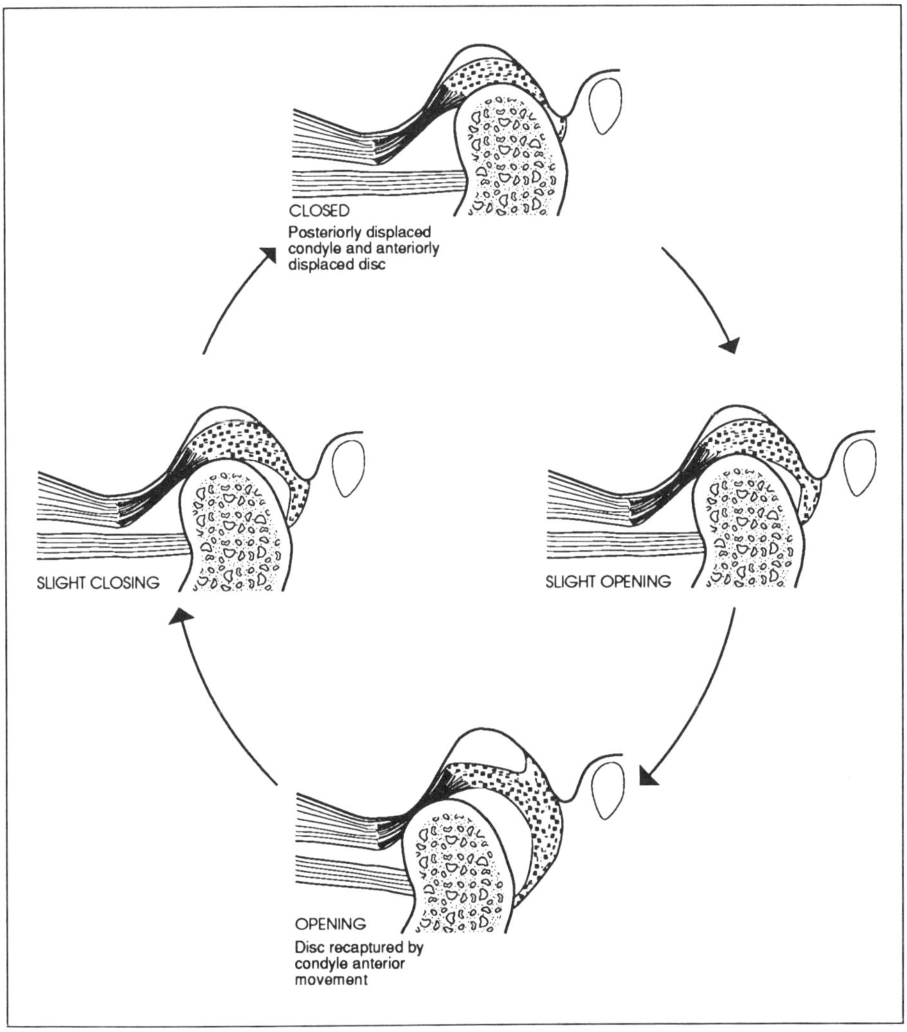

Figure 4-12. Anterior disc displacement with reduction—reciprocal click.

inflammation, is called *capsulitis*. The condylar displacement may put pressure on the retrodiscal tissue, and this is designated *retrodiscitis*. Patients with this condition present with stiffness and limited range of motion, or ROM, of the mandible and pain. The treatment of the reversible conditions capsulitis and retrodiscitis is rather simple.

Compression of the retrodiscal tissue by the posteriorly displaced condyle forces the articulating disc forward, causing anterior disc displacement. On opening the mouth the condyle moves down and forward, and the disc is recaptured, reduced, and placed on the condyle. Disc recapture makes a sound (snap) called an opening click. On closing the mouth the condyle moves posteriorly to a certain point beyond which the disc is displaced anteriorly. This displacement causes a snapping or clicking sound called a closing click. The opening and closing click cycle is termed reciprocal click, which is illustrated in **Figure 4-12**.

The patient experiencing these symptoms may or may not have pain, but if he does, it follows spasm of the muscle. The mandibular ROM may not be limited, however, the pattern of motion may be disturbed and resembles the letter Z, See **Chapter 5**. Treatment is mechanical: a mouthpiece, splint or

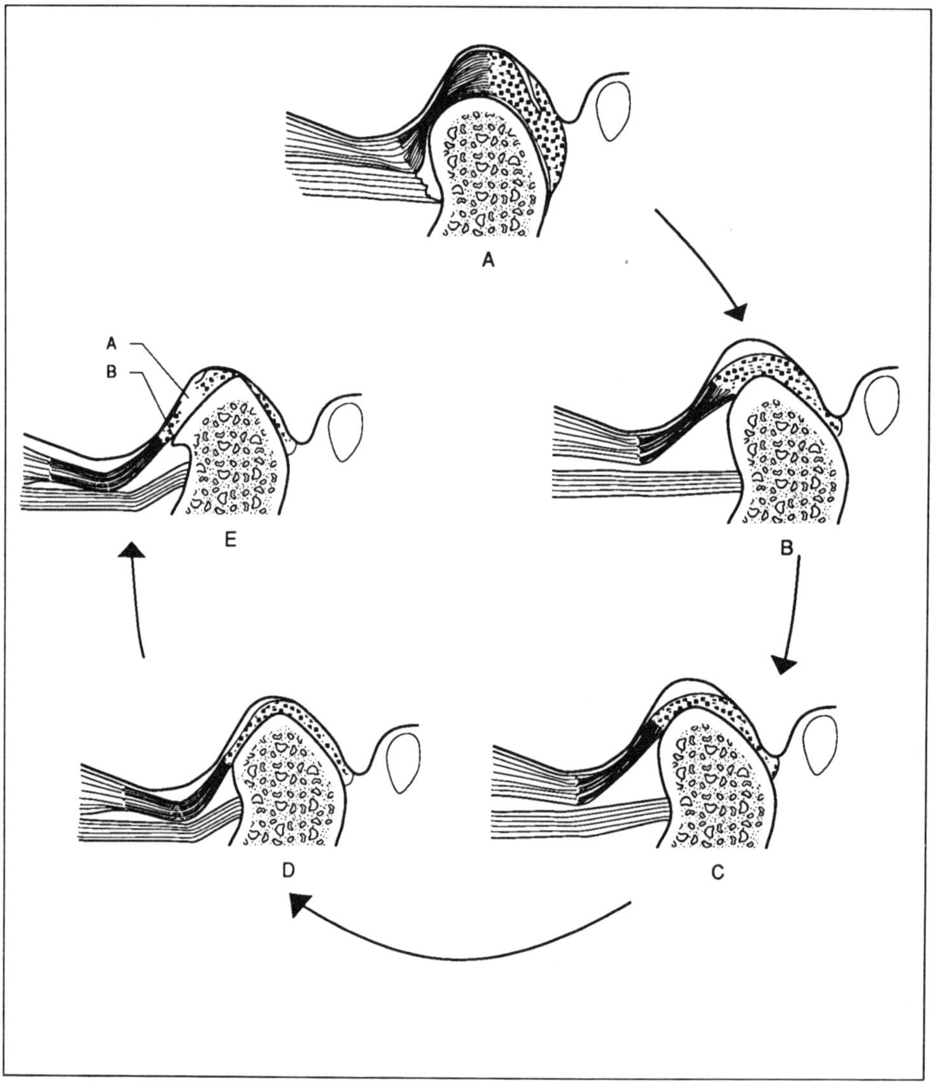

Figure 4-13. Pathogenesis of TMJ. (A) Normal joint. (B) Anterior disc displacement with reduction. (C) Thinning of the retrodiscal tissue. (D) Anterior disc displacement without reduction. (E) Osteoarthritis of the TMJ with (A) retrodiscal tissue damage and (B) osteophytes.

appliance, is worn between the upper and lower teeth, preventing posterior displacement of the condyle beyond the point of separation from the disc. The thickness of the dental appliance is usually determined by the point of disc displacement, i.e., early, moderate, or late.

If left untreated, the retrodiscal tissue becomes less elastic and it may be difficult for the tissue to reduce itself upon opening the mouth. There may be other contributing factors as well. This condition is called anterior disc displacement without reduction. *Reduction* is the return of the disc to its position on the condyle. The patient may or may not have pain. The mandibular ROM can be restricted, and the pattern of motion indicates a deviation to the affected side rather than following a Z shape. Early manual mandibular manipulation to decompress the joint may be successful in reducing the severity of the case; however, not all patients respond to such therapy. The clinician may then recommend arthroscopic meniscal release, an arthroscopic surgical procedure to unlock the nonreducing disc discussed in **Chapter 6**. Still other cases may require treatment *off the disc*, or management of condylar stability through the use of a dental appliance when the condyle is resting on retrodiscal tissue. A *pseudo-disc* may develop in place of the retrodiscal tissue.

Anterior disc displacement without reduction, shown in **Figure 4-13**, with other contributing or aggravating factors may result in the thinning and perforation of retrodiscal tissue, condylar remodeling, possible osteoarthritic changes with osteophytes (spur) formation, and in rare cases, avascular necrosis. Joint crepitation (the sound is like pieces of sandpaper being rubbed together) occurs and the patient may or may not experience pain. If this late stage is debilitating the patient may require open joint surgery to repair or replace discs, or to shave, recontour, or decompress the condyle.[10]

§ 4.5 Malocclusion

Malocclusion is an irregularity of the teeth beyond what is accepted by dental practitioners as proper arrangement, i.e., variations on the norm and representing biological differences.[11] The forms of malocclusion are shown in **Figure 4-14**. Generally malocclusion is either tooth malpositions or malformations or malrelationships of the dental arches. Tooth malposition may be one of four types:

1. Tilted: tooth that is angled abnormally.
2. Displacement: tooth that is displaced out of its normal position.

---

[10] D.M. Foreman & D.A. Rolfs, Whiplash and the Jaw Joint (1985); J.P. Okeson, Fundamentals of Occlusion and Temporomandibular Disorders (C.V. Mosby 1985).

[11] T.M. Graber, Orthodontics, Principles and Practice (W.B. Saunders 1961); R.E. Moyers, Handbook of Orthodontics (Year Book Medical Publishers 1988).

3. Rotation: tooth that has rotated in its socket.
4. Supereruption: tooth moved toward the occlusal plane.

Tooth malformation may be either a chipped tooth or a deformed tooth.

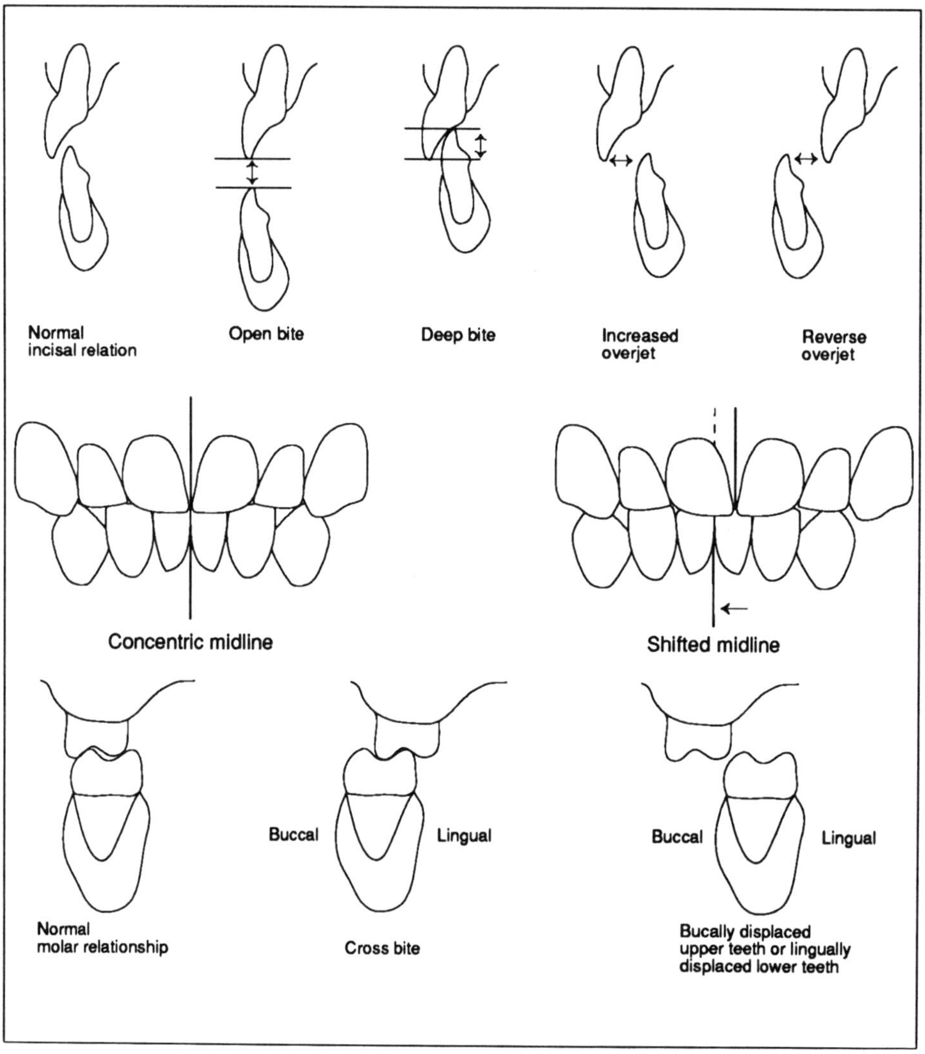

Figure 4-14. Forms of malocclusion.

Malrelationships of the dental arches have four categories:

1. Overjet: increase of the horizontal distance between incisors.
2. Overbite: increase of the vertical coverage of upper teeth to lower anterior teeth.
3. Reverse overjet: lower anterior teeth are anterior to the upper anterior teeth.
4. Crossbite: lower teeth are buccal, i.e. towards the cheek, to upper teeth.

Etiologic factors in malocclusion are considered general (extrinsic) or local (intrinsic) factors. General, extrinsic factors in addition to heredity include:

Congenital defects: cleft palate, mandibular hypoplasia, cerebral palsy.

Environmental factors: prenatal causes—trauma, dietary deficiency, infectious diseases, drugs; postnatal causes—birth injury (delivery by forceps), TMJ injury (falling from a bicycle).

Predisposing factors: endocrine or hormonal imbalances—disturbed growth hormone; metabolic diseases—malabsorption; infectious diseases—periodontitis.

Dietary problems such as calcium and vitamin A, C, or D deficiency.

Abnormal habits such as thumb sucking, tongue thrust, lip or nail biting, breathing through the mouth.

Poor posture.

Mechanical trauma.

Local (intrinsic) factors include:

Missing or supernumerary (excess) teeth.

Abnormal tooth size or shape.

Abnormal *labial frenum*, the mucous membrane fold extending from the alveolar ridge to the lip or cheek.

Early loss of deciduous or permanent teeth.

Retained deciduous or delayed eruption of permanent teeth.

Large dental caries.

Improper dental restorations.

Malocclusion is one of the causes of TMJ-OSGS disorder; however, the presence of malocclusion in the individual does not necessarily indicate the symptomatology of TMJ-OSGS disorder. Malocclusion often leads to the breakdown of soft and hard tissue in the oral and paraoral structures and influences such occurrences as adult tooth loss, periodontal disease, and

TMJ-OSGS disorders. Other catalysts may act in concert with malocclusion to manifest this breakdown.

One of the most widely used classifications of malocclusions is Angel's. Illustrated in **Figure 4-15**, it consists of:

Class I—Normal Molar Relationship. The mesial buccal cusp of the upper first molar occludes with the central fossa of the lower first molar.

Class II—Retroded Mandibular Molar. The mesial buccal cusp of the upper first molar occludes mesial (forward) to the central fossa of the lower first molar.

Class III—Protruded Mandibular molar. The mesial buccal cusp of the upper first molar occludes distal (backward) to the central fossa of the lower first molar.

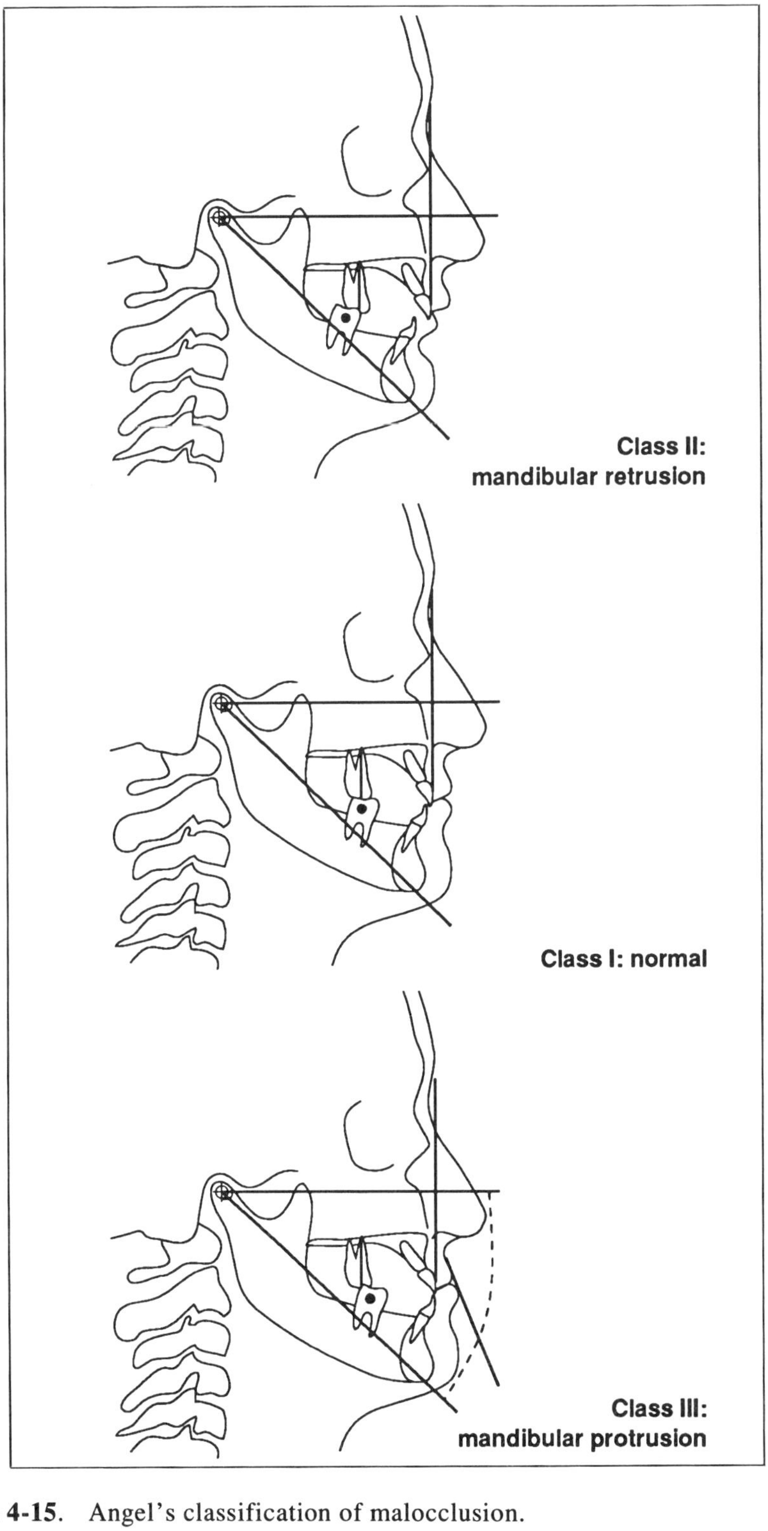

Figure 4-15. Angel's classification of malocclusion.

CHAPTER 5

EVALUATION AND DIAGNOSIS

§ 5.1 Classification

Disorders of the TMJ and the OSGS are classified as muscle disorders, ligament disorders, TMJ disorders, mandibular mobility disorders, maxillomandibular growth disorders, and neurologic disorders.[1&2] Additional problems are classified as systemic diseases and dental diseases.

Muscle disorders.

Myalgia: Localized tenderness to palpation. It can originate from local trauma, parafunctions, medications, stress, and other causes.

Splinting and spasm: Signals the presence of regional pain or the perceived threat of pain. The jaw muscles act to prevent movement and protect the body part.

Myocytis: Inflammation caused by an agent such as trauma or a biological factor such as bacteria.

Trismus: Significant mandibular restriction due to traumatic, chemical, bacterial, or psychological factors.

Dyskinesia: Simple incoordination or mild physiological tremor or movement usually result from side effects of medication. Proper training and exercise will help ameliorate this problem.

Contracture: Indicates significant muscle restriction following mechanical trauma.

---

[1] Sherry Rogers, The E.I. Syndrome: An RX for Environmental Illness.

[2] R.A. Abdel-Fattah, *Diagnosis and Prevention of Temporomandibular Joint (TMJ) and Odontostomattognathic (OSG) Injuries in Dental Practice*, 2 Today's Florida Dental Assoc. J. 50 (1990).

Hypertrophy: Identified by clinical observation and an indication of increased size of the muscles due to excessive function, or overuse of the mandible.

Bruxism: Unconscious grinding of the teeth, usually during sleep.

Tendonitis: Inflammation of a tendon, e.g., temporal tendonitis.

Ligament disorders.

Stylomandibular ligament syndrome (Ernest syndrome): Inflammation of the stylomandibular ligament. It may be due to injury and can refer pain to eye, ear, temple, TMJ, zygoma, molars, and the area of the neck behind the mandibular angle.

Stylohyoid ligament syndrome (Egel's syndrome): Elongation and calcification of the stylohyoid ligament associated with pain in the lateral pharynx, ear, temple, neck, and tongue, and difficulty in swallowing. Pain is the result of the hard styloid process impinging on the internal neurovascular structures. This is a chronic condition.

Hypermobility of TMJ capsule: An overstretched, loose capsule that cannot hold internal joint structures because of sudden trauma or long-standing overloading of the joint from clenching, bruxism, and similar activities. It manifests itself as joint popping upon opening the mouth wide and by increased range of motion to 60 mm or more.

Loose lateral TMJ ligament: An overstretched, loose lateral ligament that can be felt lateral to the TMJ during opening and closing the mouth. The articulating disc may be displaced laterally due to the lack of ligamental support.

TMJ disorders. These are disorders that occur within the joint vicinity usually resulting from either long or short term overloading the joint and can be called internal derangement or intracapsular disorders.

Disc-condyle incoordination: A disturbance of the disc-condyle-fossa relation such as disc or condylar displacement.

Restricted condylar translation: No translation of the condyle up to and beyond the condylar eminence. It may be a result of fibrous restriction, muscular restriction, anatomical restriction or disc displacement.

Open joint dislocation: The condyle is dislodged, placing stress on the muscle attachments as well as the ligament supports.

Arthralgia: Pain in the joint.

Osteoarthrosis: Asymptomatic condition of the joint causing some change in the bony structure.

Arthritis: Inflammation of the bony structure of the joint.

Traumatic arthritic disease: Arthritis in the joint as a result of chronic, long-standing or acute trauma.

Avascular necrosis: Aseptic or nonbacterial degeneration of condylar bone due to diminished blood supply.

Mandibular mobility disorders. This disorder is defined as a decrease in mandibular movement. The types of mandibular mobility disorders reflect the cause of decrease in mobility.

Fibrous or bony ankylosis: Can impair and restrict movement of the jaw due to excessive fibrous formation, bony fusion of the joint, and related problems.

Intracapsular adhesion: Collagenous adhesion from joint inflammation or injury that restricts disc movement. The condyle inhibits motion to a certain degree.

Contracture: Disturbs and prevents the mandible from achieving a total range of motion.

Skeletal obstruction: Elongated coronoid process can restrict movement of the mandible.

Internal derangement: Causes restriction of movement and disc displacement and inhibits condyle translation.

Osteoarthritis: Inflammation of the joint. Movement can be painful.

Maxillomandibular growth disorders. Mandibular growth disorder alters the symmetry of condylar growth, causing condylar displacement and subsequent TMJ-OSGS disorders. Mechanical trauma during childhood can lead to growth disorders leading to TMJ-OSGS disorders.

Benign muscle enlargement: Unilateral muscle enlargement due to hypertrophy causes muscle imbalance and subsequent TMJ-OSGS disturbances.

Other growth disturbance (hemifacial hypertrophy): Skeletal deformity influencing musculoskeletal problems.

Condylar hypoplasia: Decrease in condylar growth and size. Asymmetrical or unilateral hypoplasia causes mandible displacement with subsequent TMJ-OSGS disorders.

Condylar hypertrophy: Increase in condylar size due to neoplasm, which may also result in skeletomuscular symptoms as well as condylar and mandibular displacement.

Maxillomandibular or condylar neoplasm: Any neoplasm that changes condyle growth rate, especially unilaterally, causing TMJ-OSGS problems.

Neurologic disorders. Neuralgia is pain in the distribution of nerve. Neurologic disorders do not all emanate directly from the TMJ-OSGS, but may be induced by or be the result of disorders of other structures related to TMJ-OSGS.

Sphenopalatine neuralgia (Sluder's syndrome, lower-half headaches and lower facial neuralgia): Neuralgia in the sphenopalatine nerve, characterized by unilateral facial pain that never extends above the level of the ears.

Trigeminal neuralgia: Severe paroxysm affecting one side of the face supplied by the trigeminal nerve.

Reflex sympathetic pain: Does not conform to any segmented or peripheral nerve distribution or to any other recognizable pattern. It is associated with hyperalgesia, hyperesthesia, vasomotor, and trophic changes and usually occurs in surgical or traumatized anatomical sites.

Bell's palsy: Facial paralysis caused by lesions of the facial nerve.

Occipital neuralgia: Pain at the base of the skull, moving upward along the course of the greater and lesser occipital nerves to the top of the head.

Paresthesia: Altered sensation in the skin that causes numbness or tingling, usually due to nerve injury or pressure applied to the nerve root.

Causalgia: Persistent, burning sensation in an organ, visible in red, tender epidermis. Usually it is the result of deep injury to the nerve.

Glossopharyngeal neuralgia: Intense pain felt at the base of the tongue and in the throat and ear. It may occur spontaneously or via the motions of talking, eating, or swallowing.

Systemic diseases affecting the TMJ-OSGS.

Gout: Metabolic disorder in which uric acid is precipitated in joints, usually a single joint in the big toe. It can affect the TMJ. Affected joints become red, swollen, and tender.

Lupus erythematosus: Chronic disease of connective tissue. An autoimmune disease, discoid lupus erythematosus (DLE), affects exposed areas of the skin. Systemic lupus erythematosus (SLE) affects joints and kidneys and is fatal. Lupus erythematosus can affect the OSGs connective tissue.

Rheumatoid arthritis: Inflammatory disease affecting body joints. Pain, swelling, stiffness, and in severe cases, joint deformity, are the results.

Hormonal imbalance: Disturbed hormonal activities affect muscles and bones, leading to disturbed TMJ-OSGS.

Metabolic diseases such as diabetes mellitus: Vitamin deficiency, malabsorption, and similar problems can decrease tissue resistance to disease leading to disturbed TMJ-OSGS.

Dental diseases.

Malocclusion: Irregularity in tooth position, form, and skeletal relationships.

Periodontal disease: Inflammation of the gums and alveolar bone surrounding the teeth, which can cause resorption of alvealar bone and tooth mobility.

Dental caries (decay): A decalcification of the hard tooth substances.

§ 5.2 Evaluation and Diagnosis

Evaluation and diagnosis of TMJ and OSGS disorders should be based on a thorough history and systematic clinical evaluation.

History. The evaluation of an intensive medical history by an experienced therapist often indicates evidence of preexisting conditions.[3-5] The history as shown in **Figure 5-1** should cover the following points:

Personal data. Record the name, age, sex, race, and occupation of the patient. These data are important not only to the identification of the patient but also for possible prediction of disease prevalence in a certain sex, race, or age group.

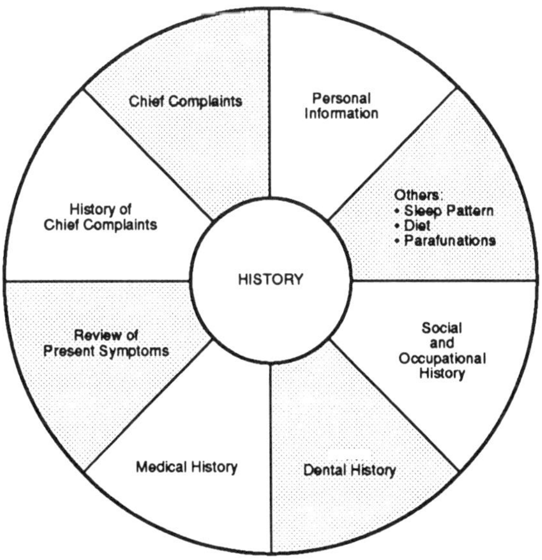

Figure 5-1. Patient history.

---

[3] Sherry Rogers, The E.I. Syndrome: An RX for Environmental Illness.

[4] R.A. Abdel-Fattah, *Diagnosis and Prevention of Temporomandibular Joint (TMJ) and Odontostomattognathic (OSG) Injuries in Dental Practice*, 2 Today's Florida Dental Assoc. J. 50 (1990).

[5] C. McNeill, Craniomandibular Disorders: Guidelines for Evaluation, Diagnosis and Management (Quintessence Publishing 1990).

Chief complaints and associated symptoms. The documentation of the character, severity, duration, onset and site of pain or dysfunction, and the precipitating, aggravating, and alleviating factors of any current complaints is vital.

Medical history. Taking a medical history (complete history of personal data, chief complaints, history of chief complaints, past and present medical condition) is essential and can greatly aid the clinician during the examination to causally relate the injury. It is also essential for review by the insurance adjustor or the attorney—a report without an adequate health history is worthless. It should be understood, however, that the history can be altered by the claimant and is therefore subjective.

The history must include previous systemic illnesses, traumas, surgeries, medications, diagnoses, and treatments, all of which are significant as possible initiators or aggravators of a TMJ-OSGS disorder. This may help in causally relating or refuting a particular cause for the disorder.

Dental history. The patient should be screened for previous TMJ therapy, orthodontic treatment, third molar or forcible extraction, extensive reconstructive dental work, dental occlusal equilibration, and periodontal treatment. As noted in **Chapter 4**, some dental techniques may suddenly alter the dental occlusion, subsequently overloading the TMJ, which usually precipitates a disorder.

Patient screening questionnaire. The history taker should include these specific questions:

1. Do you experience pain in the head, face, eyes, ears, jaw, neck, or back?
2. Does it feel unpleasant, uncomfortable, or painful when you chew, speak, sleep, swallow, or open your mouth wide?
3. Does your jaw make noise, get stuck, or deviate to one side when you open your mouth?

If the patient affirmatively responds to any or all of the above questions, clinical investigation must be undertaken to determine the source.

Present medications. Among the side effects of a number of medications is muscle spasm, the force of which may aggravate the TMJ. Medications taken and their side effects should be documented.

Occupational history. Physical activity required in the performance of a patient's occupation may initiate, precipitate, or aggravate a TMJ-OSGS disorder. Work that demands excessive changes in posture, e.g., computer operation, operating a motor vehicle, sewing, writing, and typing, places strain on the mandibular posture and sometimes initiates TMJ-OSGS disorders. Teachers, auctioneers, actors, and singers, in the performance of their jobs, must constantly manipulate the TMJ-OSGS. Musicians and some laboratory technicians hold instruments or tools in the mouth. These excessive and "unusual" oral activities disturb the condyle-disc-fossa assembly.

Social history. Social factors such as financial difficulties, sustaining injuries as the victim of a crime, disability, litigation, and secondary gain from sympathizers/empathizers are a great influence on the patient's perceptions and learned responses to pain, and should be recorded.

Parafunctions. Patients should be screened for clenching, bruxism, and excessive gum chewing or any "unusual" oral activity. These may demonstrate a propensity for or may precipitate dysfunction.

Behavioral history. Sleep patterns, dietary habits, jaw posturing, and sedentary lifestyle are behavioral factors that may predispose or aggravate the TMJ-OSGS.

Environmental history. The reversal of pathologic conditions require a healthy restorative environment. Evidence suggests that the pain involved in TMJ-OSGS disorders may, in part, have their genesis in chronic exposure to pollutants in water, food, or air. A thorough review of possible pollutants in the patient's environment may be helpful.[6]

Systematic clinical examination. Just as the history must cover a number of points, the clinical examination must be systematic to diagnose the problem. The points to be covered are diagrammed in **Figure 5-2**. The examination is of great value as it gathers objective findings.

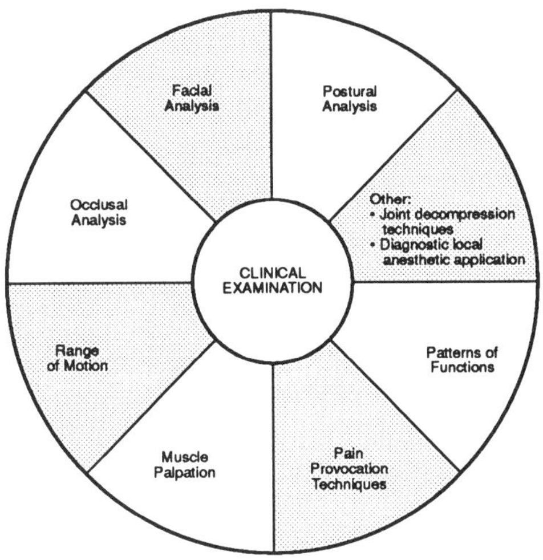

Figure 5-2. Systematic clinical examination.

[6] Sherry Rogers, The E.I. Syndrome: An RX for Environmental Illness.

Postural evaluation. The clinician should examine the patient for significant skeletomuscular dysfunctions such as a forward of tilted head position, a high or forward shoulder, a high iliac crest, or a short leg. See **Figure 5-3**.

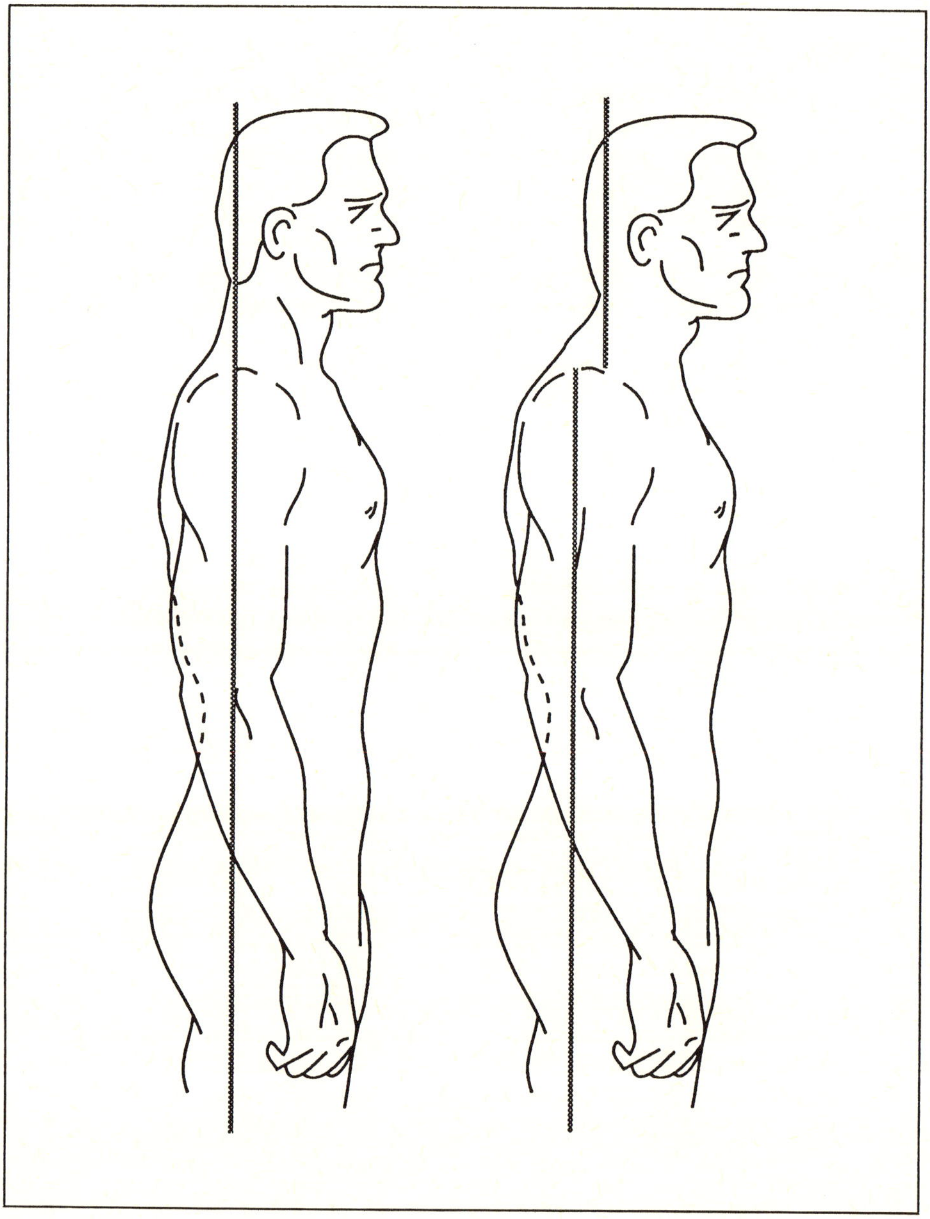

Figure 5-3. Postural evaluation, forward or tilted.

Facial analysis. The patient's face is inspected for any asymmetry. Asymmetrical eyes, ears masseter muscles, or zygomatic bone, or a deviation of the nose or chin to one side are indications of mandibular displacement and facial growth disturbances.

As shown in **Figure 5-4**, the facial analysis can be visually performed by looking at the facial profile with the forehead and lips on a vertical line. The

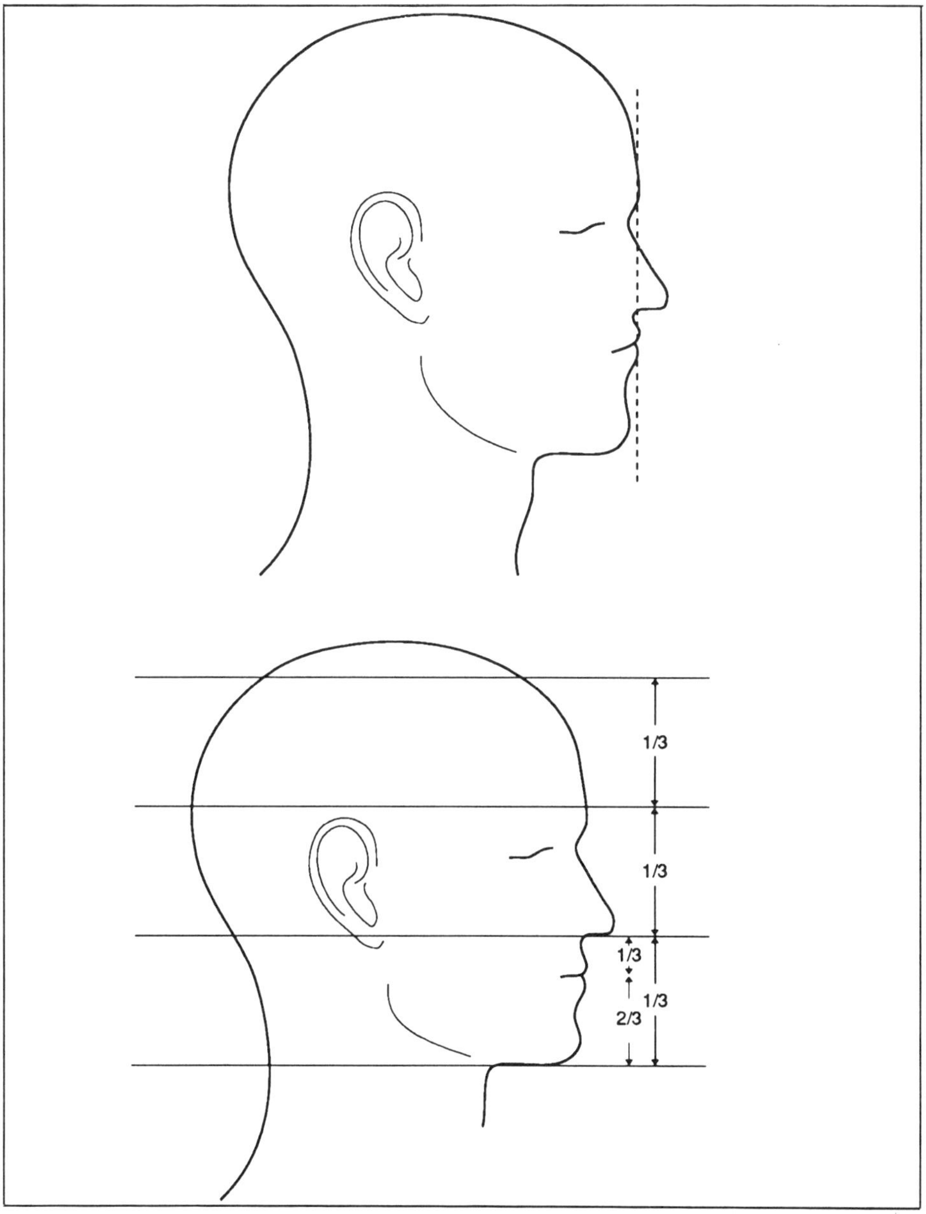

Figure 5-4. Facial analysis. Top: Facial profile should be near a vertical line. Bottom: Vertically, the face is divided into three equal thirds.

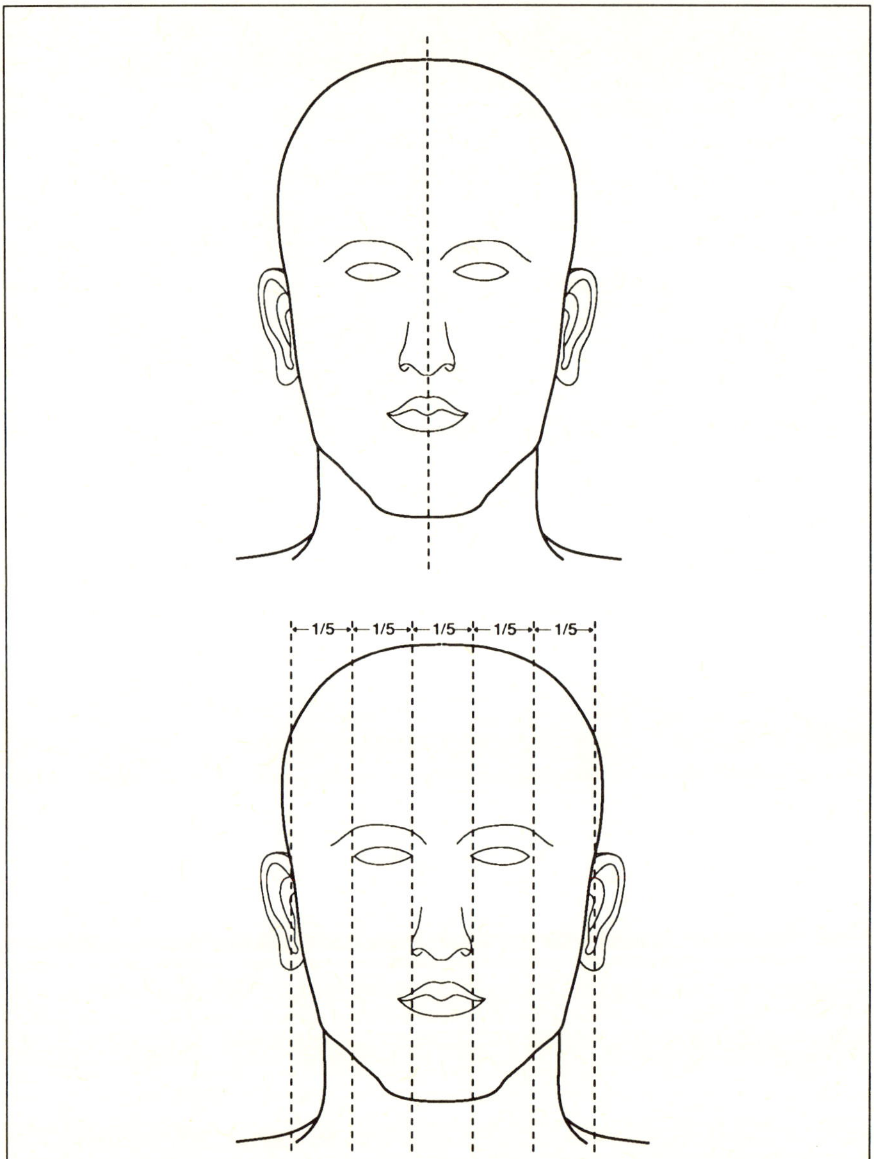

Figure 5-5. Frontal symmetry. Top: Face midline should divide face into two similar and equal halves. Bottom: Face should be divided into five equal fifths.

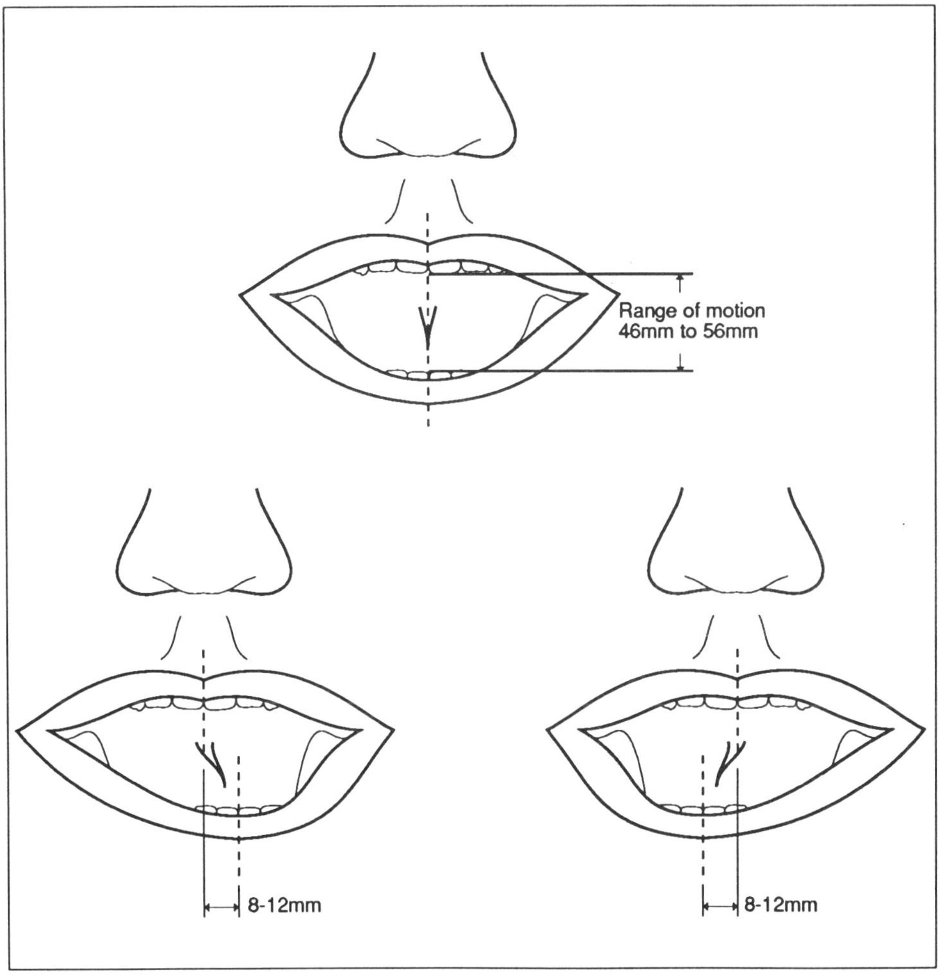

Figure 5-6. Mandibular ROM.

face can also be divided into three equal parts by horizontal lines into the upper, middle, and lower face. **Figure 5-5** shows the frontal view in which the face is divided into five equal or two equal parts. This way a comparison of the eyes, ears, and cheeks and their levels can be established.

Mandibular range of motion (*ROM*). The normal ROM distances are usually 46 to 56 millimeters vertical interincisal and 8 to 12 millimeters right or left from intermidline. These ranges may vary slightly according to the size and height of the individual. Reduction in ROM is generally indicative of a joint and/or muscle dysfunction; an increase can indicate joint laxity. See **Figure 5-6**.

Pattern of mandibular motion. Normal movement of the mandible is smooth downward, upward, and lateral, without deviation, hesitation, or audible sound. When disc interference, abnormal anatomical structure, ligament laxity, or muscle spasm (muscles overcompensating for other muscles) are present, the mandibular pattern of movement is disturbed, causing a deviant or Z-shaped opening. See **Figure 5-7**.

Occlusal analysis. Inspection of the dental occlusion should entail a search for chipped, cracked, broken, rotated, tipped, restored, or missing teeth. Any spaces should be recorded. Note must be made of midline deviation, crossbite, open bite, deep bite, group function, or any form of malocclusion, and dental caries, pulpal response, and periodontal diseases. Identification of the unstable occlusion—dual bite, large, retroded contact, or intercuspal position—is essential.

Figure 5-8 illustrates a frontal view of the upper and lower teeth indicating deviation of midline to the left (marked **1**), anterior cross-bite (marked **2**), space (marked **3**), missing tooth (marked **4**), and malposed tooth (marked **5**).

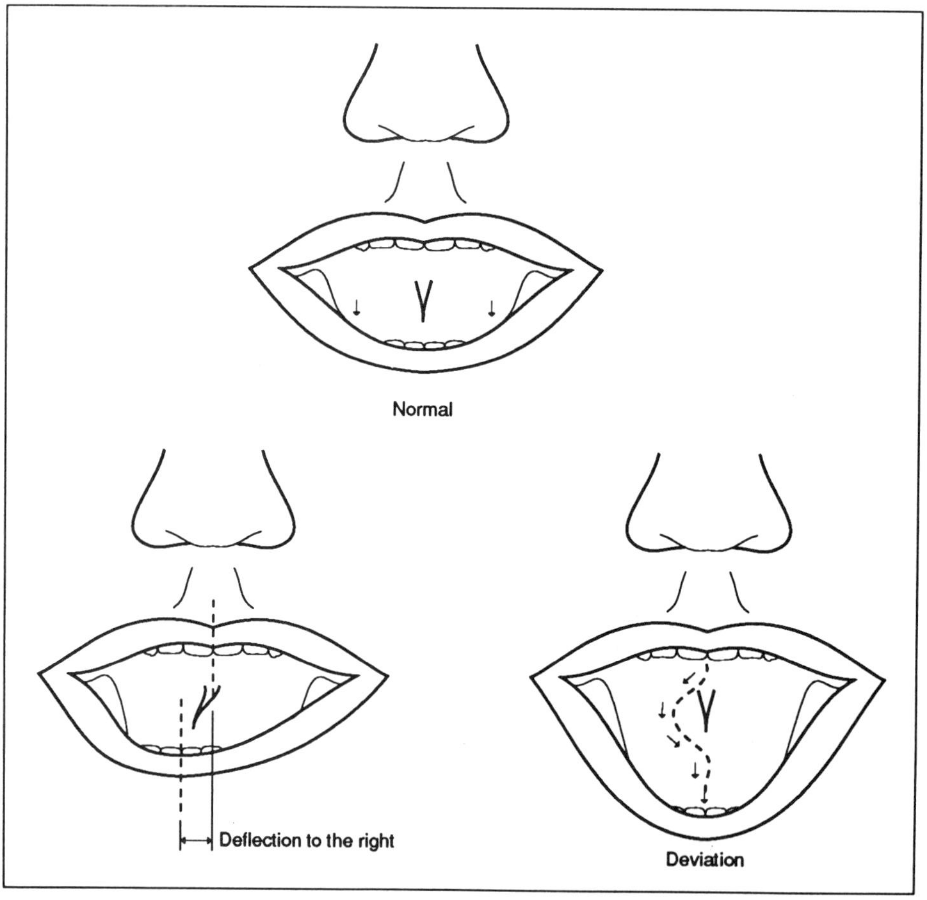

Figure 5-7. Pattern of mandibular motion.

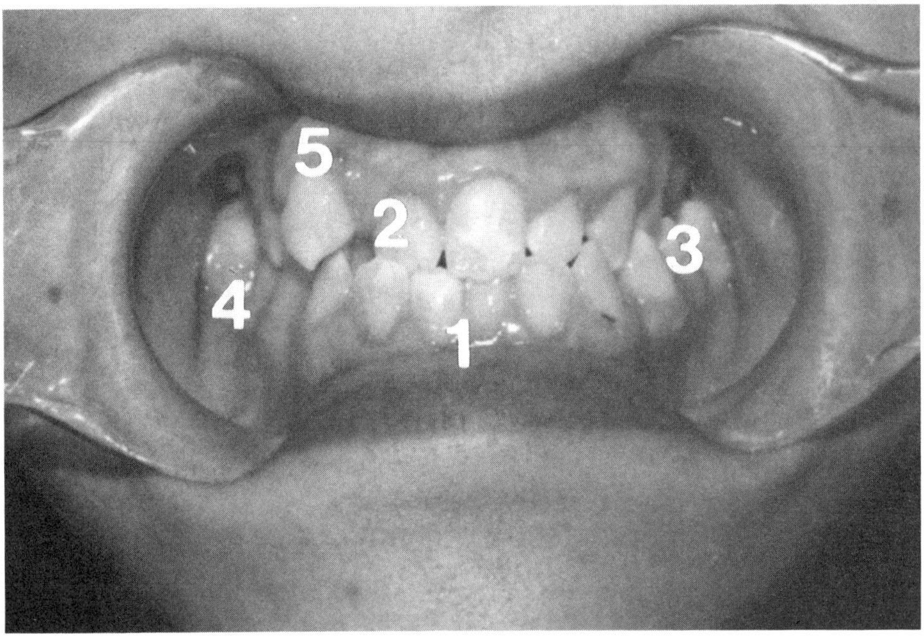

Figure 5-8. Occlusal analysis.

Tissue palpation. This technique detects tender, uncomfortable, and painful areas in the muscles of the patient. The examiner should exert gentle bilateral pressure digitally and systematically, while asking the subject to describe the sensation in each muscle of the head and neck. The emergent points of the nerves should also be palpated for possible head and neck neuralgia. This technique is shown in **Figures 5-9** and **5-10**.

Pain provocation. The source of pain should be determined, whether referred or localized to or from the area, upon palpation. This is done by attempting to reproduce the pain by asking the patient to open wide, move the mandible to right or left, to observe the indicated or affected muscle group. Pressure on certain areas may reveal sources of pain.

Examination of the TMJ. The physician should probe for swelling, bruises, erythemia, exudate, or other abnormal conditions. Sonic dysfunction should be determined by placing a stethoscope, without the membrane, in front of the ear of the patient, and asking him to slowly open and close his mouth. Recording should be made of any early, intermediate, late opening or closing click (snap) or crepitation (grating). Any tender or painful areas of the TMJ can be palpated by using gentle, bilateral digital pressure intra- and extrameatally. See **Figure 5-11** and **5-12**.

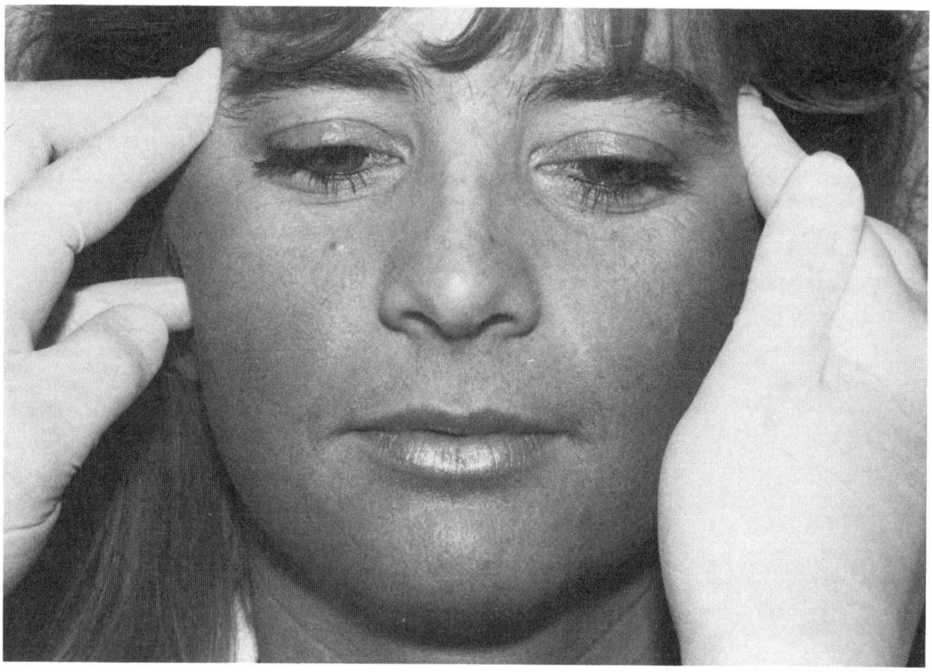

Figure 5-9. Palpation of the right and left temporalis muscles. Used with permission.

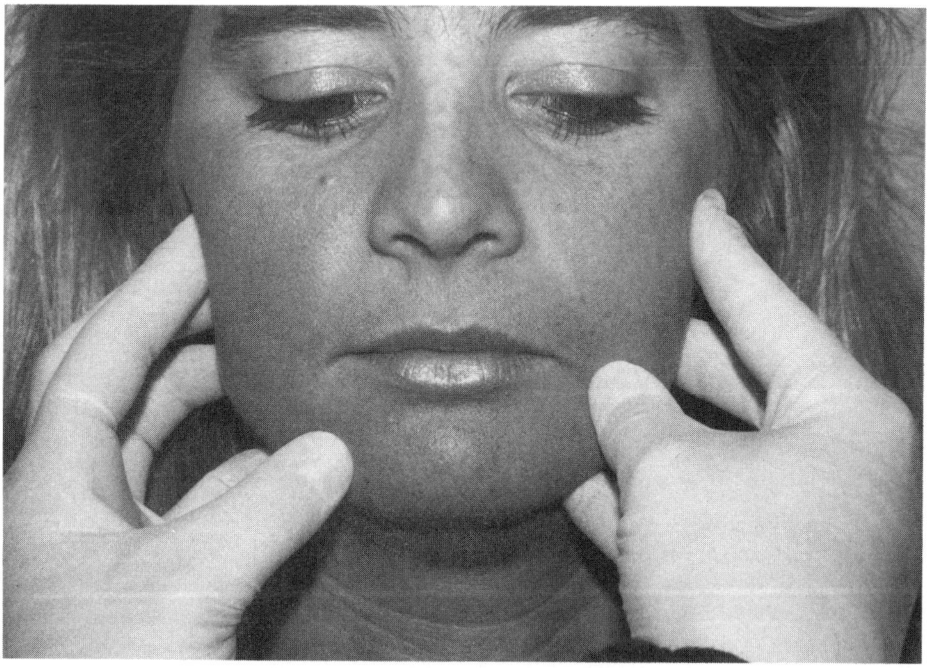

Figure 5-10. Palpation of right and left masseter muscles. Used with permission.

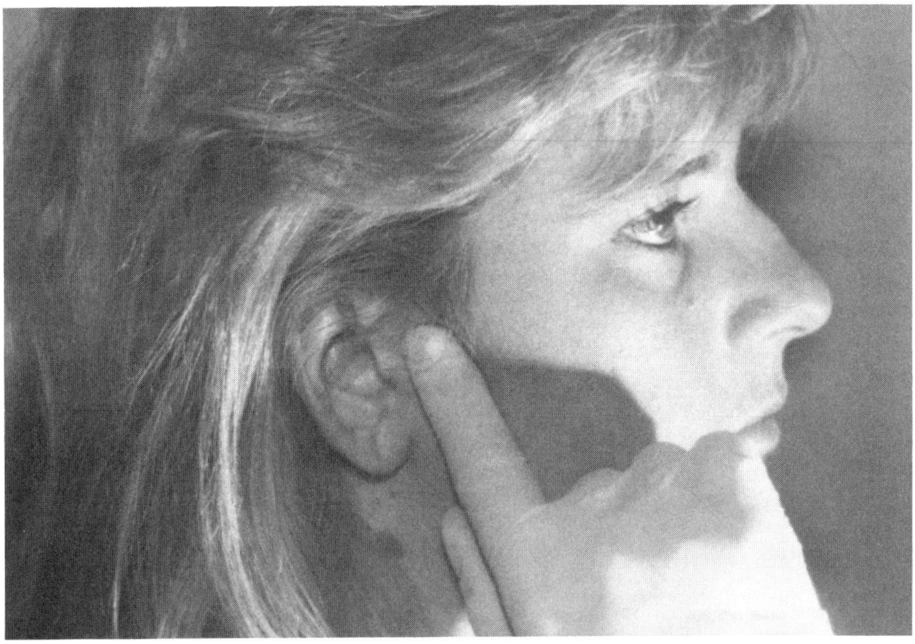

Figure 5-11. Examination for sonic dysfunction. Using a stethoscope to search for a click or abnormal noise. Used with permission.

Joint decompression. Allowing the patient to bite on cotton rolls in a slightly forward position will decompress the distally displaced condyle and may temporarily relieve pain. See **Figure 5-13**. If relief is obtained, it indicates the effectiveness of splint therapy, which decompresses the TMJ.

Bite wax block. Using a soft heated wax roll to reposition the mandible in an approximate centric position may decrease or eliminate the clicking sound caused by disc displacement in the joint. See **Figure 5-14**. This will indicate a high probability in reversing the disc displacement. Using the wax bite to rearrange the models can help in fabricating the splint or mandibular repositioning appliance.

Administration of local anesthetic. The topical application of *vapocoolants* or skin refrigerants such as ethylchloride or fluorimethane may decrease the pain in spastic muscles. Intramuscular injection of 0.5% procaine in an isotonic saline solution without a vasoconstrictor decreases pain in trigger points. These techniques localize the source of pain. See **Figures 5-15** and **5-16**. By reducing surrounding pain, this technique may make it possible to determine the source of pain.

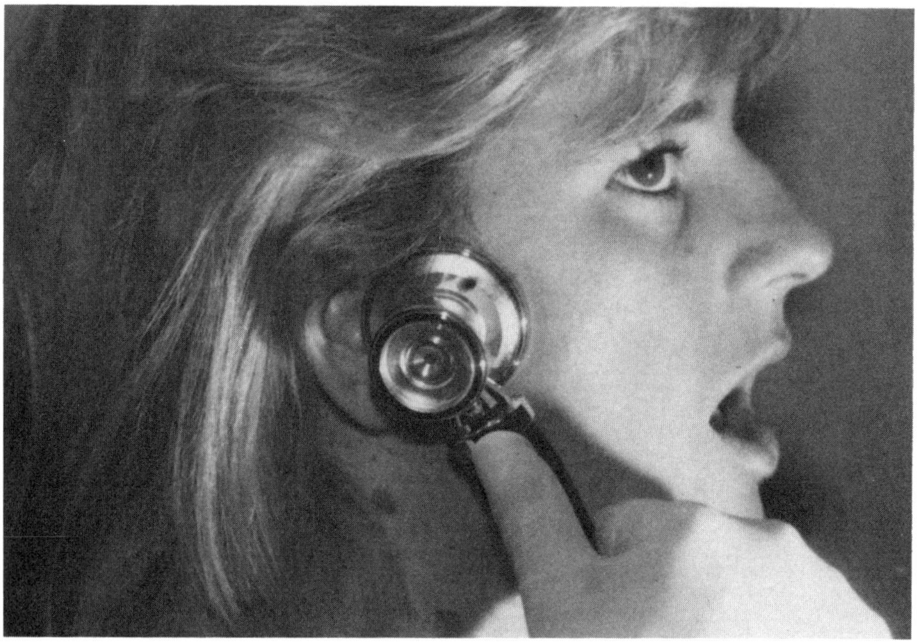

Figure 5-12. Palpating the TMJ searching for tenderness or pain which can indicate capsulitis. Used with permission.

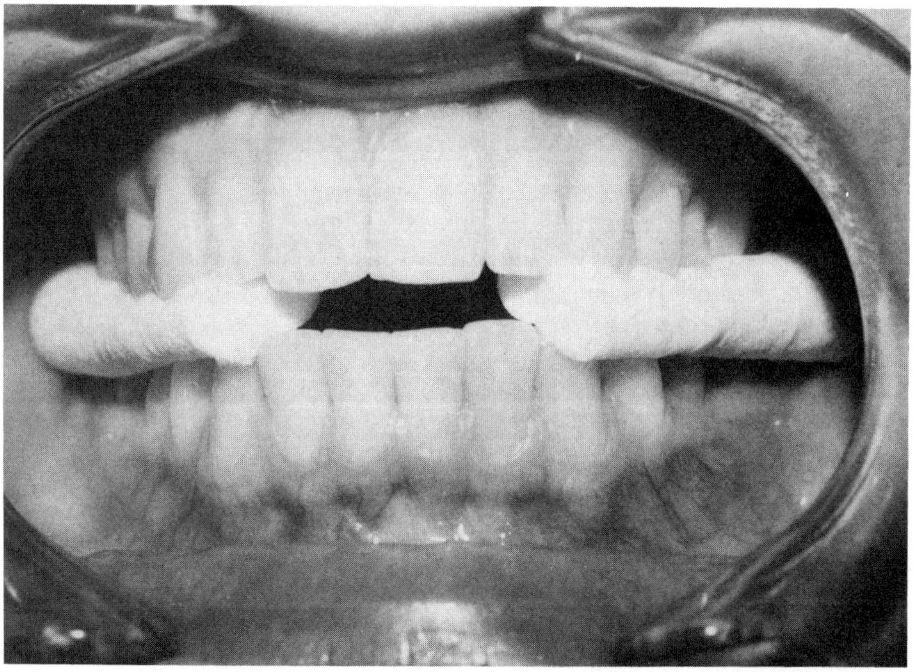

Figure 5-13. Joint decompression. Used with permission.

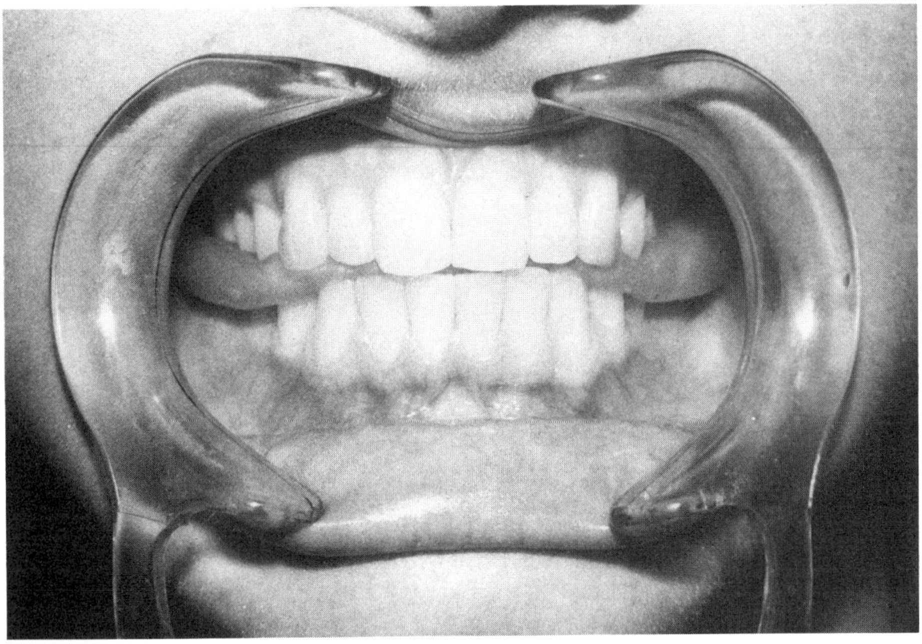

Figure 5-14. Bite wax block. Used with permission.

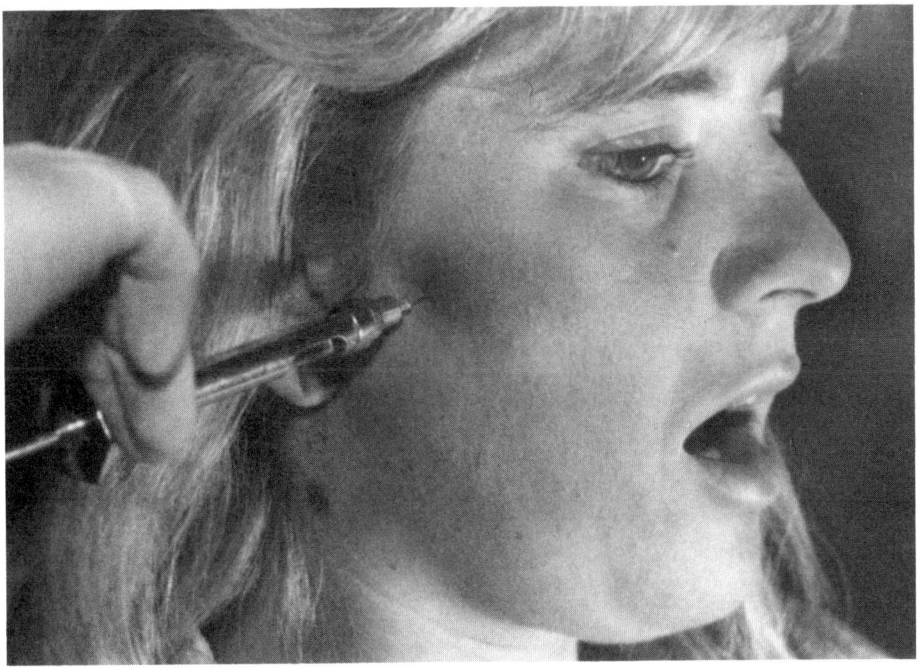

Figure 5-15. Intramuscular injection in trigger point: extra oral injection of the lateal pterygoid muscles with local anesthetic to reduce spasm. Used with permission.

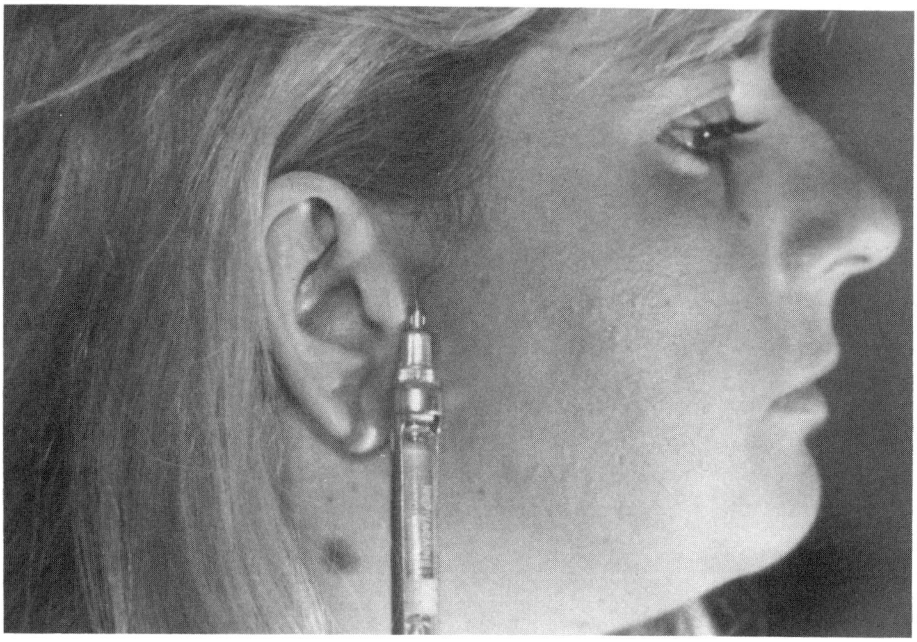

Figure 5-16. Extra oral injection, with local anesthetics, of the auriculo-temporal nerve to prove or rule out TMJ involvement. Used with permission.

§ 5.3 Establishing Adequate Records

As shown in **Figure 5-17**, there are a variety of diagnostic techniques which can create a record of the condition and help in both treatment and any related litigation.

Photography. Frontal and profile photography of the face, see **Figures 5-18** and **5-19**, itself is essential in documenting asymmetry and is used intraorally to record any occlusal or dental abnormality. These photographs should be reviewed in comparison with the symmetry diagrams shown in **Figures 5-4** and **5-5**.

Models. Accurate study models should be made for the maxilla and mandible to duplicate the teeth, arch, and alveolar bone forms. Models are valuable as records and allow the practitioner to study the occlusion outside the oral environment. See **Figure 5-20**, which shows the teeth occluding together ready for analysis.

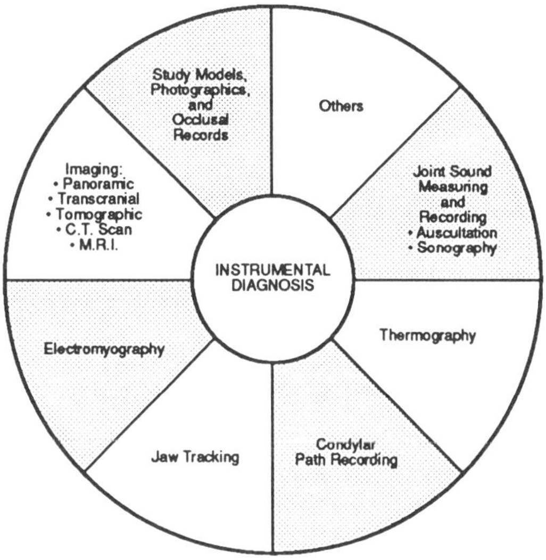

Figure 5-17. Instrumental diagnosis.

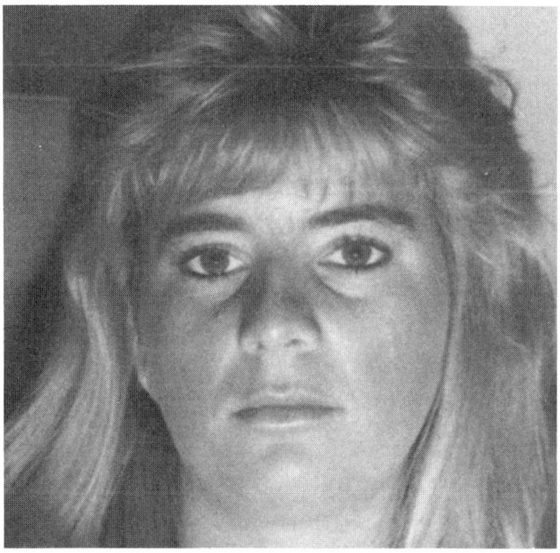

Figure 5-18. Frontal photograph. Used with permission.

Radiographic evaluation. Radiographic evaluation is absolutely essential to the diagnosis of oral and dental disease. Full-mouth radiographic periapical views are adequate for regular dental and periodontal evaluation, but not for the assessment of TMJ disorders. Panoramic views showing full condyles may be of value in the preliminary evaluation of the condylar structure and condylar and mandibular symmetry. In addition, they usually contain views of the maxillary sinuses and the coronoid and styloid processes; degenerative osteoarthritis of the condyle or condylar remodeling can also be seen.

Figure 5-19. Profile photograph. Used with permission.

Radiographs, or X-ray films, are necessary to determine the bony conditions of the mandible, maxilla, and the TMJ; however, they are limited in scope. Radiographs do not show the condition of the soft tissue, i.e., muscles nerves, discs, ligaments, and blood vessels, nor do they show bony destruction, except after 40 percent of the calcium in the specific part of the bone is removed. In addition, radiographs are only two-dimensional pictures, and in bones, which are plagued by several superimpositions, it is difficult to view many lesions or pathologies.

Panoramic radiographs are a method by which the clinician can screen the region of the oral and paraoral structures. It is a two-dimensional representation of the three-dimensional orofacial area, allowing visualization of the anatomy of the teeth, mandible, mandibular condyles, maxillae, sinuses, and other parts of the orofacial structures. Again, soft tissue cannot be visualized, but an indication of the soft tissue condition can be interpreted through an understanding of the reaction of the bone to the soft tissue pathology. Panoramic radiographs are not specific to TMJ pathology, but they are a screening factor, indicating osteoarthritis of the condyle and eminence, morphology of the condyle and eminence, the condition of the coronoid process, condylar hypo- or hyperplasia, the stylohyoid process, foreign bodies, the condition of antigonial notching, the symmetry of the mandibular body, tumores, condensing ostitis, periodontal disease, periapical involvement (abscesses), sinus cysts and sinusitis, and condition of the nasal septum. See **Figure 5-21**.

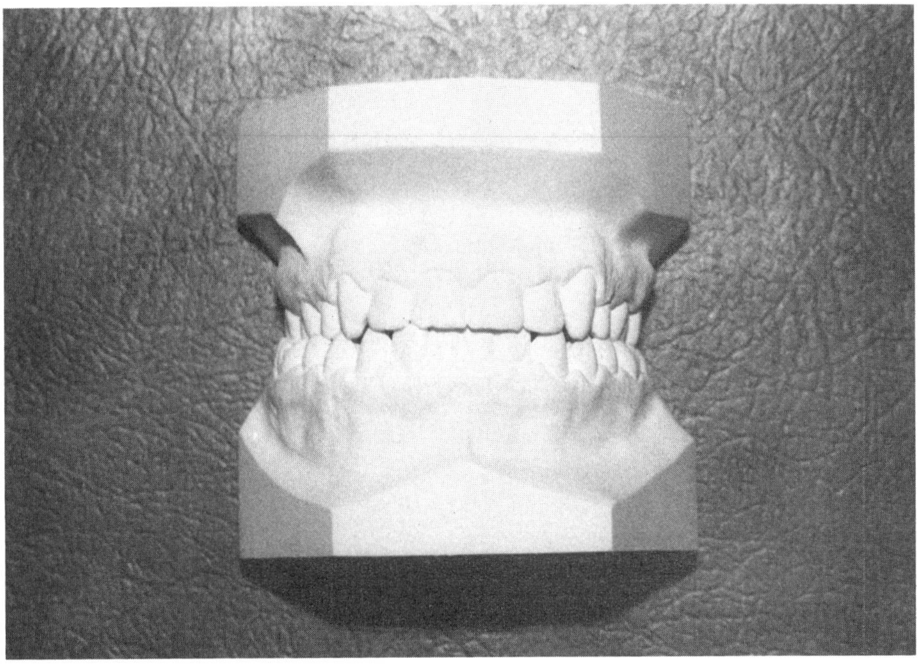

Figure 5-20. Model.

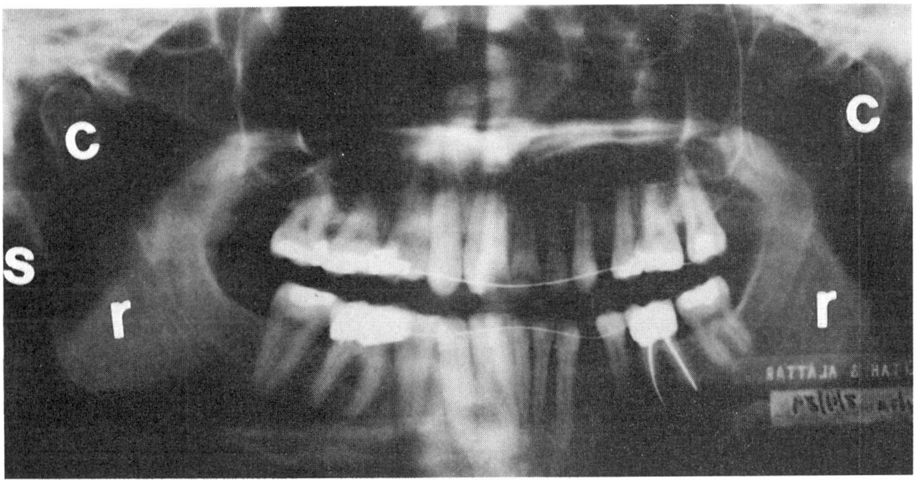

Figure 5-21. Panoramic view, showing condyles (c), mandibular ramus (r), and calcified stylohyoid ligament (s). Used with permission.

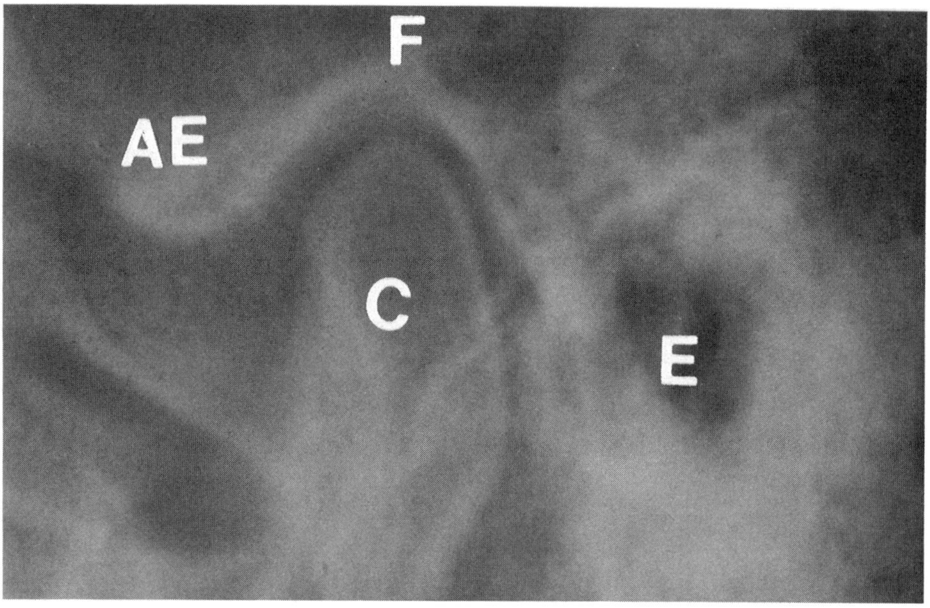

Figure 5-22. Transcranial view, showing condyle (c), external auditory meatus (E), fossa (F), and articulating eminence (AE). Used with permission.

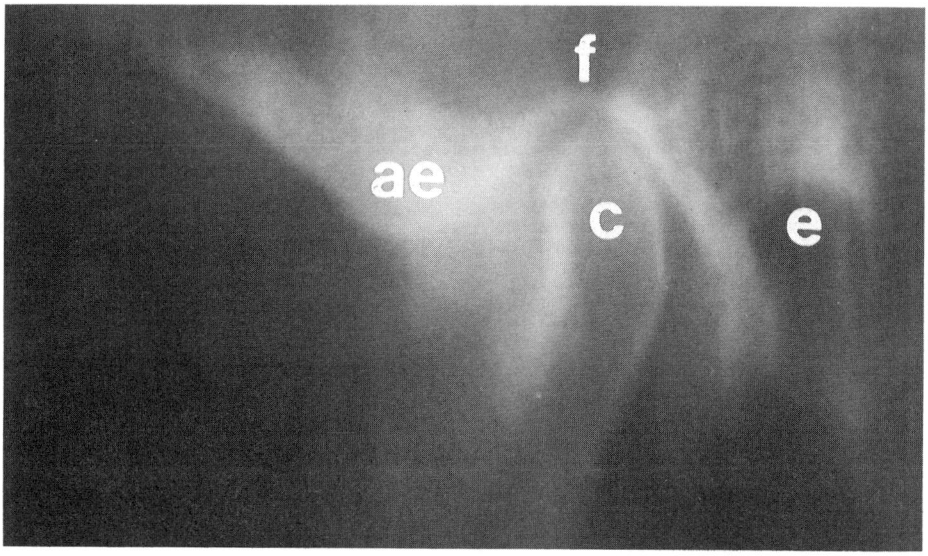

Figure 5-23. Tomographic view, showing external auditory meatus (e), condyle (c), fossa (f), and articulating eminence. Used with permission.

After establishing joint pathology and prior to treatment, it is advisable to employ more specific imaging techniques. Transcranial radiography may be helpful in discerning TMJ bony relationships, however, it does not provide an exact measurement of the reproducibility and precision of joint space. Tomographic views are essential to TMJ evaluation/diagnosis because of their accuracy in imaging both the bony relationships and joint space measurements. Tomography is valued over straight lateral transcranial radiography because the latter is seriously plagued by bony superimpositions.

Transcranial radiographs (see **Figure 5-22**) are an excellent screening device, although the clinician must focus his interpretive powers because of the large amount of superimposition of structures in this type of radiograph. These radiographs must be taken extremely carefully; if the angulations are not correct, the resultant film can give a deformed representation of the condyle and fossa relation. They can be useful in uncovering the condylar, articulation eminence, and articulating fossa morphologies; the structure of the condyle; and foreign bodies. They can also be useful after *arthrograms*, injection of certain radio-opaque dyes.

Tomography is the technique of taking radiographs from any part of the body in layers or sections. It is the most accurate radiograph for studying TMJ because it provides a true lateral or coronal view of the TMJ, and a precise joint space can be determined. Tomographs are good for determining the condylar position; eminence; condition of the articular surface; condylar head; bent angle of the condyle; remodeling process and calcification of the

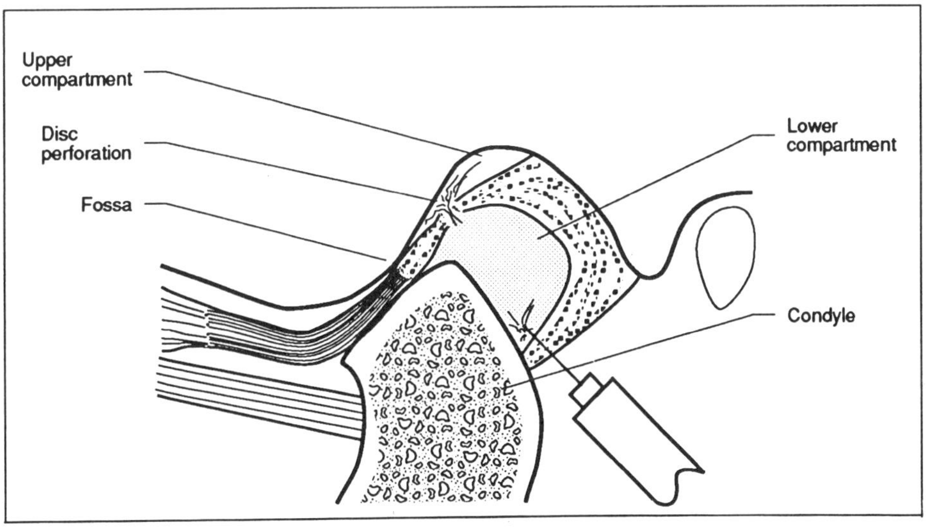

Figure 5-24. Arthrogram. Injecting a radioopaque dye in the lower compartment fills its space and determines its outline. In disc perforation cases, the dye travels to the upper compartment.

discs, fossa, or condyle; formation of the osteophytes; osteoarthritic changes; corticosteroid necrosis; and tumors. See **Figure 5-23**.

Arthrography is a method of imaging in which a fine needle is used to inject a radioopaque dye (seen as white material on x-ray films) into the lower or upper synovial compartment (see **Figure 5-24**). Regular transcranial radiographs, tomographs, or videofluoroscopy are used to image the joint in various opening or closing positions. Its advantage lies in the ability to produce a dynamic study of the joint while it is functioning. It can produce an image of the disc as well as its position. It should be understood that it is usually painful and invasive.

Magnetic resonance imaging (MRI) and Computerized Tomography (CT). CT, or CAT scan, is an ionizing radiation technique and MRI (also called nuclear magnetic resonance, although MRI is a more exact term) are the recording of radiowaves produced by body tissues. These newer techniques produce images of human tissue slices which demonstrate bony and soft tissues within a given dimension. MRI and CT primarily determine the articulating disc relationship to bony structures. See **Figures 5-25** and **5-26**.

Electromyography (EMG). EMG records muscle activity by measuring the facial and masticatory muscles while functioning and at rest. This

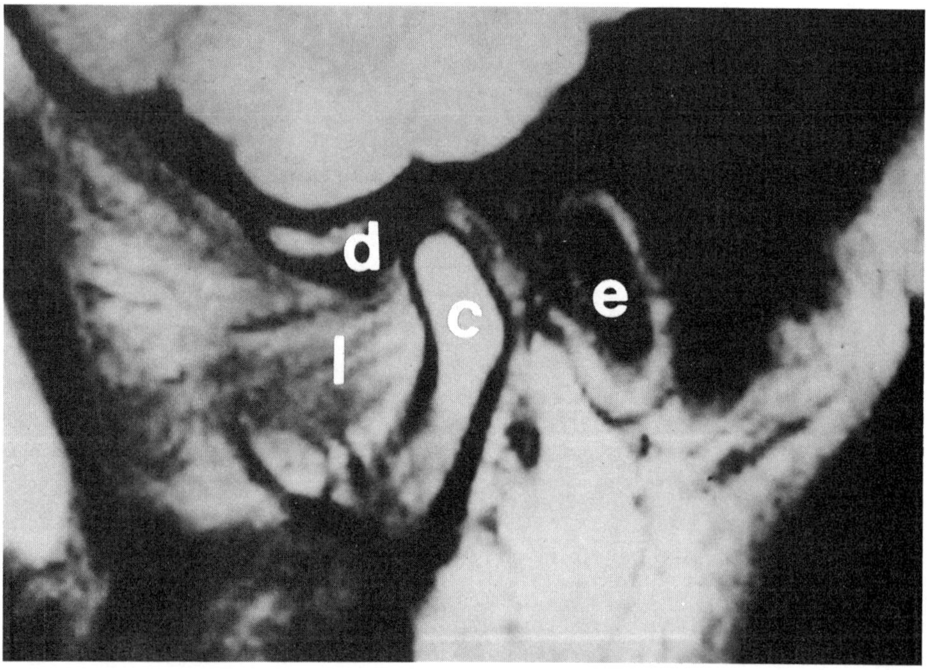

Figure 5-25. MRI of closed mouth (left) TMJ, showing external auditory meatus (e), condyle (c), and disc (d), and (1) lateral pterygoid muscle. Used with permission.

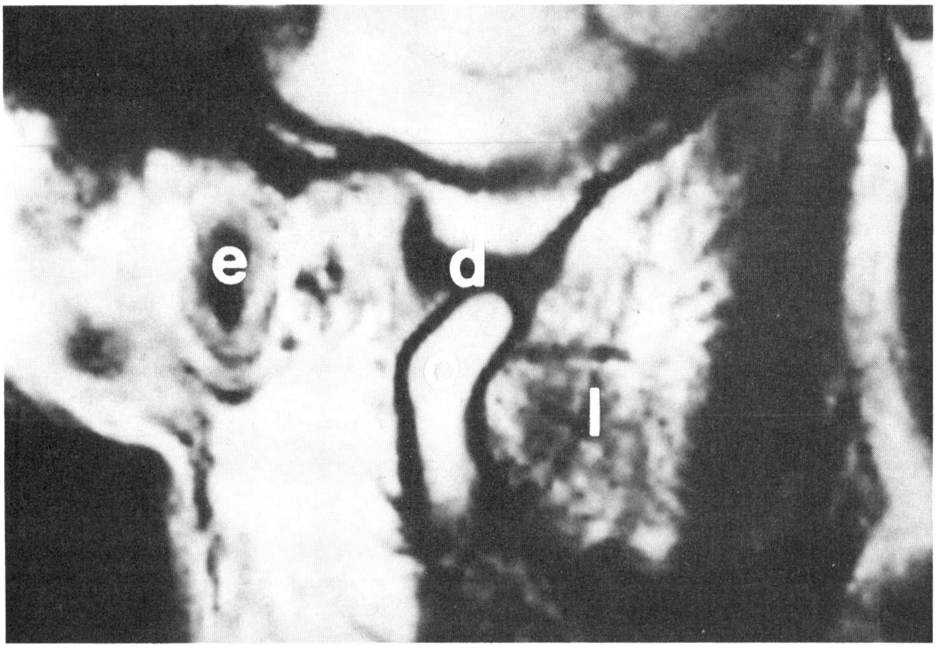

Figure 5-26. MRI of normal open mouth (right) TMJ, showing external auditory meatus (e), articulating disc (d), over the condyle (c) with an increased condylar angle bent, and (1) lateral pterygoid muscle. Used with permission.

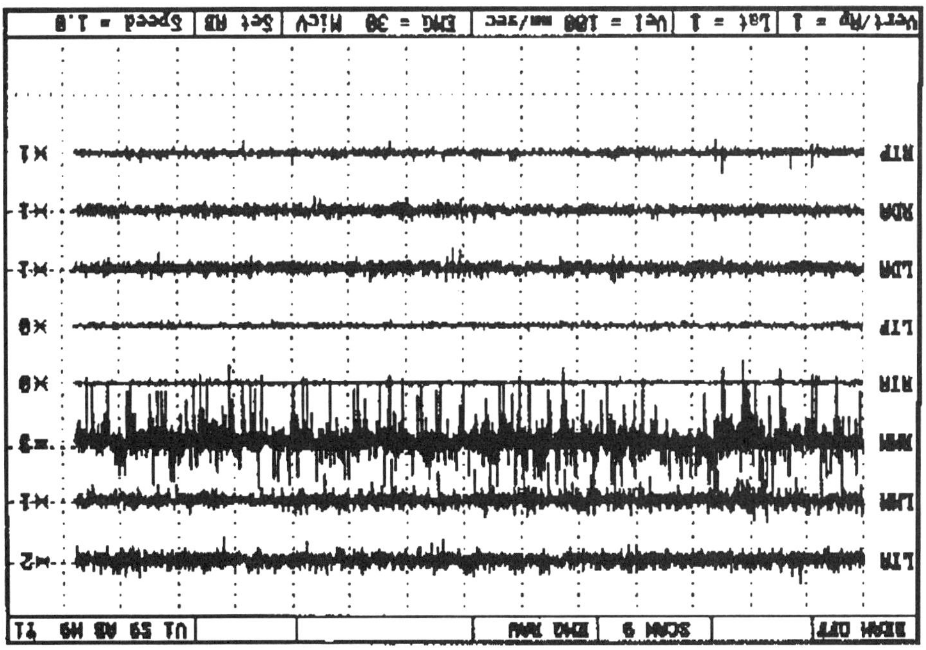

Figure 5-27. EMG graph

technique is capable of quantitatively indicating the electroactivity in a muscle spasm by recording the microvolts in a given muscle. See **Figure 5-27**. The increase of muscle activity is displayed on the graph as higher peaks.

Jaw tracking. Through the use of computerized mandibular scanning (CMS) devices, jaw movement is tracked and studied in sagittal, horizontal, and frontal planes to delineate the pattern and range of mandibular motion. See **Figure 5-28**. Mandibular muscle incoordination is shown as an irregular pattern rather than as a smooth curve or straight lines on the graph.

Joint sound recording. TMJ pathology is audibly indicated by joint clicks or crepitation. These sounds may be detected by listening to the joint while it is being opened or closed, using a stethoscope, doppler, or newer, more sophisticated electronic equipment. This is also known as sonography. See **Figure 5-29**. Increased noises in the joint will demonstrate higher peaks on graphs.

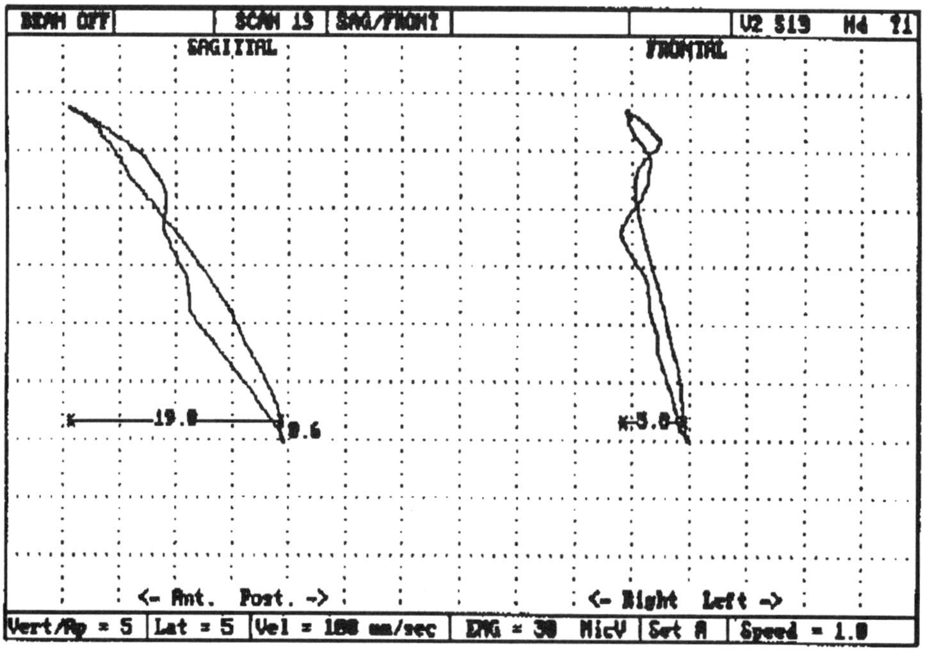

Figure 5-28. Jaw tracking.

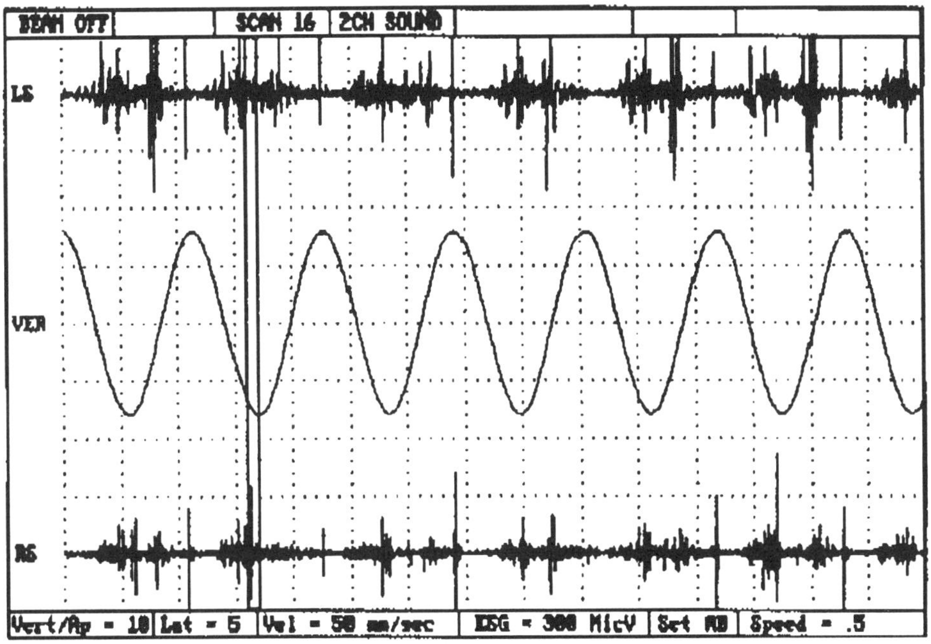

Figure 5-29. Joint sound recording (sonographic representation).

§ 5.4 Analytical Appraisal of Diagnostic Modalities

A large number of procedures exist that diagnose and document the TMJ-OSGS disorder. In the course of a case, insurance adjustors, attorneys, and experts are faced with either accepting or refuting a specific test.

The validity of a specific test should be questioned by using the following system:

1. Was it indicated? Why?
2. Was it done according to the recommended procedure?
3. Who performed the test? Was this person trained or untrained?
4. What factor(s) can affect the result of the test?
5. What was (were) the result(s)?
6. Interpretation of results.
7. Correlation of the results to other tests and clinical examination.
8. What is the value of the test results?

Not every test should be questioned, as most of the diagnostic procedures are valid when they are performed for the intended purpose; however, there is the possibility of abuse, overuse, or misuse of these tests. For example, a patient may provide an overly subjective history either consciously or subconsciously.

Clinical examination can reveal erythema, swelling, or any abnormality which cannot be manufactured, or faked by the patient. Muscle palpation, which can stimulate a patient's response by uncovering knots or bands, indicates muscle spasms. However, measuring the ROM clinically can be subject to claimant alteration. Many patients consciously reduce their ROM, hoping to receive greater financial compensation because the appearance of higher permanent impairment is given. A trained expert can perform certain tests to dismiss such a scam.

Doppler auscultation is an amplification of joint sounds that are louder than can be detected by the ordinary stethoscope. It enables the clinician to clearly listen to the minor and mild joint sounds. Mild sounds in many instances are considered normal. Doppler can also be used in detecting vascular blood flow in the superficial temporal artery and the vascular condition of the TMJ; however, its validity is unclear.

Lateral skull or cephalometric radiographs are good representations of the lateral side of the skull (although they are not good for determining the condition of the TMJ), the maxillomandibular relation, or the relation between the maxilla, the mandible, and the cranium. It is also valuable in determining the relationship of the hyoid bone to the mandible.[7]

Arthrography is an often painful, invasive method used to image the joint. Although it should not be used in the majority of nonsurgical, responding cases, it is an excellent diagnostic procedure that assists the clinician in deciding whether surgical intervention is necessary.[8]

MRI is a very good method for determining the condition of the soft tissue, i.e., discs, muscles, condylar morphology, and condylar position and adhesion. The problem with MRI is that it is static, and therefore does not uncover many of the dynamic forms of the mechanism of the motion of the joint, and muscle spasm and looseness of the ligaments cannot be evaluated. Also, some radiologists are not well versed in those dynamics. The new CINE-LOOP procedure allows videotaping the MRI and makes it suitable for studying the mechanism of joint motion.

Computerized mandibular scan (CMS) measures and records the movement of the jaw in all three dimensions. It is used to track the movement of the jaw, and this allows the clinician to precisely determine the correct jaw-to-skull relation. It does not record the condition of the TMJ, but does record and reflect the condition of the balance of the muscles and ligaments holding the mandible.

---

[7] R.A. Abdel-Fattah, *Diagnosis and Prevention of Temporomandibular Joint (TMJ) and Odontostomattognathic (OSG) Injuries in Dental Practice*, 2 Today's Florida Dental Assoc. J. 50 (1990).

[8] C. McNeill, Craniomandibular Disorders: Guidelines for Evaluation, Diagnosis and Management (Quintessence Publishing 1990).

Dysfunction in these muscles causes deviation of the mandible and subsequently an irregular pattern of mandibular motion can be recorded.[9]

Electromyography (EMG) is a process by which muscle activity is measured. When the occlusion is incorrect, the facial muscles subtly torque into a strained position which can cause muscle spasm. When this occurs, the muscles fire (or give off) electrical activity which may become excessive. These activities can be detected through surface electrodes. The EMG does not reflect the condition of the TMJ, but the condition of the muscles. As EMG uses surface electrodes, it does not reflect a specific muscle, but the condition of a group of muscles.[10]

Sonography is a method by which an electronic recording of the joint noises can be recorded on a hard copy. Through the use of transducers placed on the external surface of the TMJ, the sound can be recorded and reproduced. Sonograpy is useful in estimating the magnitude of the noise in the joint as well as its frequency. Magnitude indicates the loudness, which is not very significant. What is significant is the frequency. Disc interference or a click are common and records high magnitude or loudness. Crepitation increases the vibration and thereby the frequency.[11]

---

[9] R.L. Talley, G.J. Murphy, S.D. Smith, M.A. Baylin, & J.L. Haden, *Standards for the History, Examination, Diagnosis, and Treatment of Temporomandibular Disorders (TMD); A Position Paper*, 8 J. Craniomandibular Practice 60 (1990).

[10] *Id.*

[11] *Id.*

CHAPTER 6

TREATMENT AND MANAGEMENT CONCEPTS

INTRODUCTION

§ 6.1 Goals of Treatment and Management

Ideally, the practitioner takes a medical history, examines the patient, and identifies and confirms the disease with instrumental diagnostic aids, including models, radiography, sonography, kinesiography, magnetic resonance imaging, or computerized tomography. After a conclusion is reached, the practitioner creates a treatment plan specific to the diagnosis. In the case of TMJ-OSGS disorders, however, the practitioner, as one of the diagnostic procedures he will perform, may initiate treatments such as inserting a diagnostic splint to test the efficiency of mandibular repositioning or a myalgic splint in order to dismiss or confirm muscle dysfunction. Employing a treatment modality as a diagnostic aid usually occurs when an inconclusive diagnosis is reached.

The goals of TMJ-OSGS treatment or management in most cases are to

1. Relieve pain.
2. Restore function.
3. Avoid or eliminate the underlying causes.
4. Decrease or eliminate the predisposing factors.
5. Treat the pathologic effects.

Many clinicians believe TMJ-OSGS disorder to be a multifactorial problem; a multidisciplinary approach and the combination of several treatment modalities may be necessary in certain cases.

It should be understood that many patients can enjoy a satisfactory lifestyle with altered or partial function. In many instances, the goal of total elimination of pain and complete restoration of function is unrealistic.

§ 6.2 Phases of Treatment

Treatment of TMJ disorders proceeds in two phases. Phases I and II may overlap. In some cases phase II may precede phase I.

Phase I. A palliative stage in which pain relief as well as the orthopedic repositioning of the mandible and the TMJ are sought. This phase includes physical therapy, orthopedic repositioning, medications, nutritional supplement, and psychological counseling.

Phase II. A stabilizing stage in which the teeth are brought into proper occlusion in order that the mandible and TMJ may retain their new relation after phase I. Phase II includes orthodontics (braces), prosthodontics (crowns and bridges), equilibration (shaping of teeth), oral surgery (repositioning bone segments), or gradually decreasing the individual's dependence on a splint.

FIRST PHASE (PALLIATIVE) TREATMENT

§ 6.3 Rest

Resting the mandible by decreasing oral activity is vital to proper healing after injury or a disorder. Among the activities to be avoided are yawning, chewing hard food, extensive speaking, singing, shouting, fellatio, and other vigorous oral activities.

§ 6.4 Physical Medicine—Manual Therapy

Manual therapy may take a number of forms. It is effective in many cases in reducing pain and restoring ROM and muscle function. **Figure 6-1** illustrates different types of manual therapy.

Muscle manipulation. Digital pressure in the direction of the muscle fibers releases spasms and waste products, restores ROM, and normalizes muscle length.

Mandibular mobilization. Holding the mandible and helping the patient to open and close the mouth in a systematic manner can increase the ROM, reduce TMJ adhesion, and possibly reduce a displaced disc.

Mandibular manipulation. Holding the mandible and repositioning it to possibly unlock the joint.

Myofascial release. Manipulating the fascia, the superfacial layer of tissue surrounding the muscle, aids in reducing pain, excreting waste products, and restoring muscle function.

Myofunctional therapy (exercises). Passively or actively performing mandibular exercises can restore function and can stabilize the mandible by strengthening the weak muscles. Training to improve posture will decrease stress on OSGS musculature.

Cranial release. Digital, gentle, direct pressure can decompress cranial bones and decrease tension in the cranial structures, relieving pain.

Acupressure. Application of digital pressure on tender points, such as the back at the base of the skull, on the side of the face just below the TMJ area, or between the thumb and index finger may provide temporary pain relief.

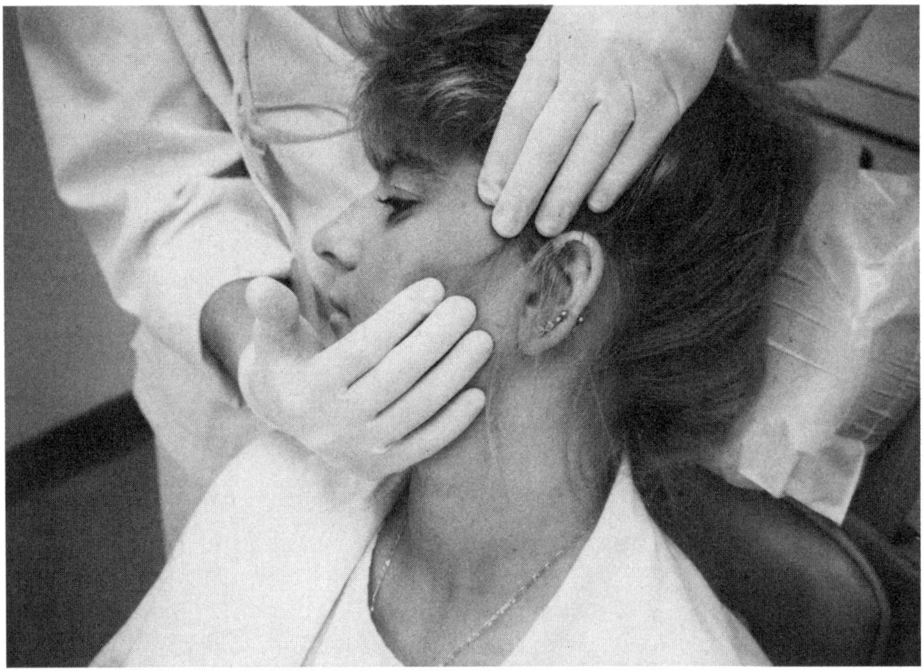

Myofascial release

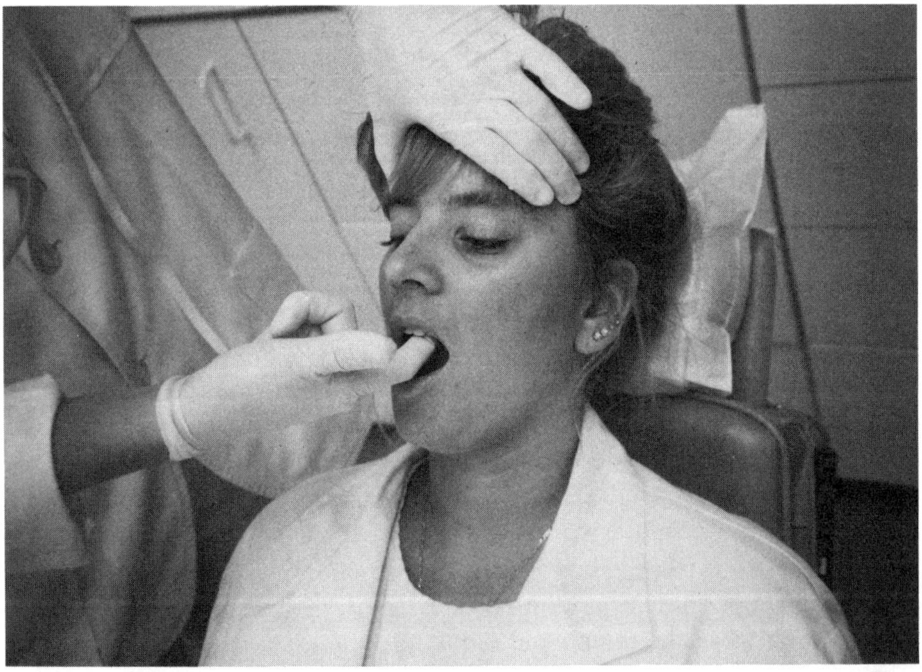

Cranial release

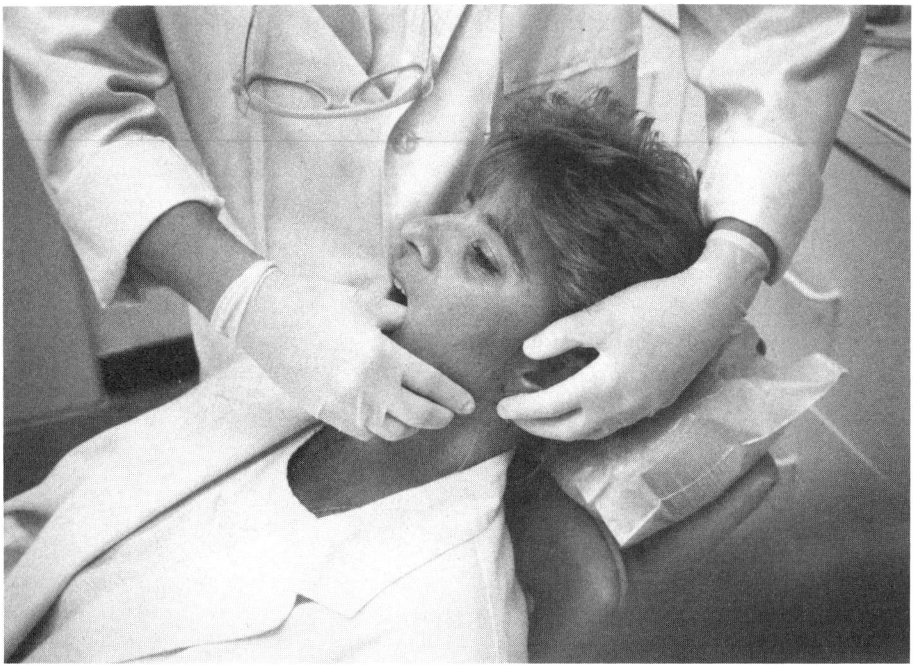

Mandibular manipulation

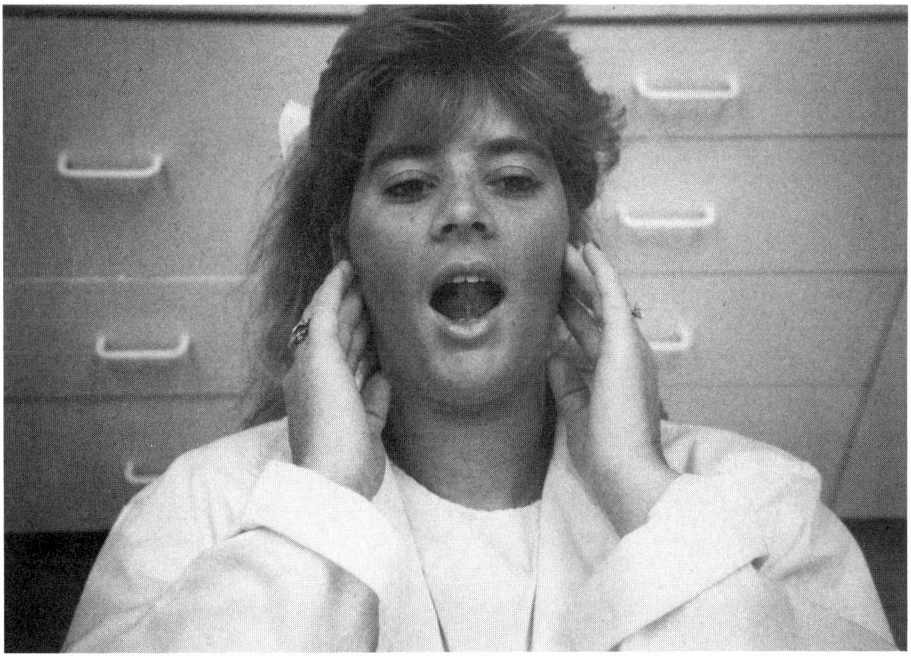

Myofunctional therapy (exercises)

Figure 6-1. Manual therapy. Used with permission.

§ 6.5 —Electromedicine

Electrical current may be therapeutic in treating pain. As shown in **Figure 6-2**, there are four primary types of electromedicine.

Transcutaneous electrical neural stimulation (TENS). A specific temporary treatment for pain. Although its mechanism is not understood, possible explanations are (1) when large, afferent fibers are stimulated, nociception (inhibition) occurs via activation of the gate mechanism in the dorsal horn of the spinal column; (2) TENS depolarizes the nerve; or (3) TENS enhances the secretion of endorphins, the body's intrinsic analgesics.

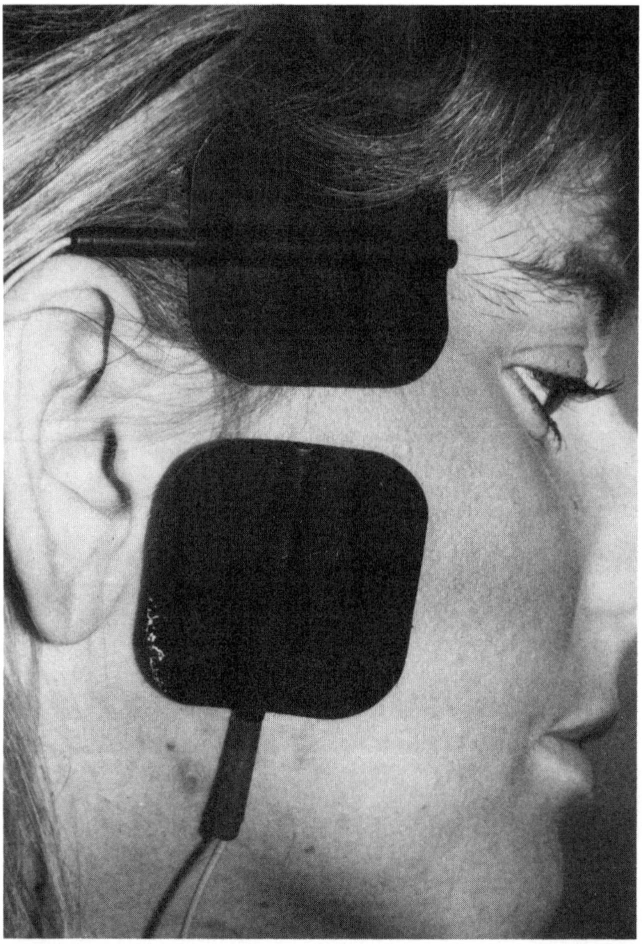

TENS application

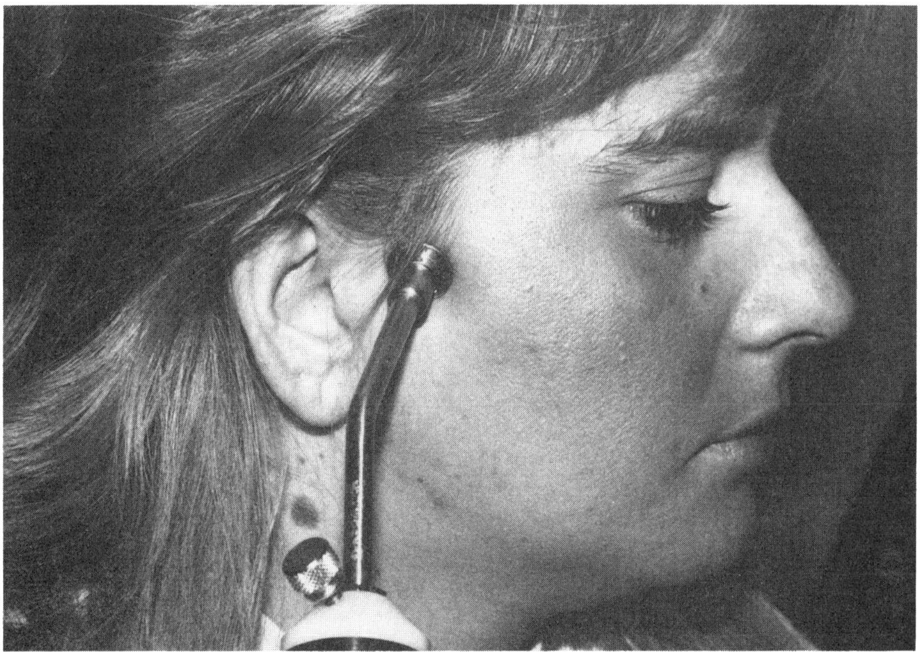

EGS application

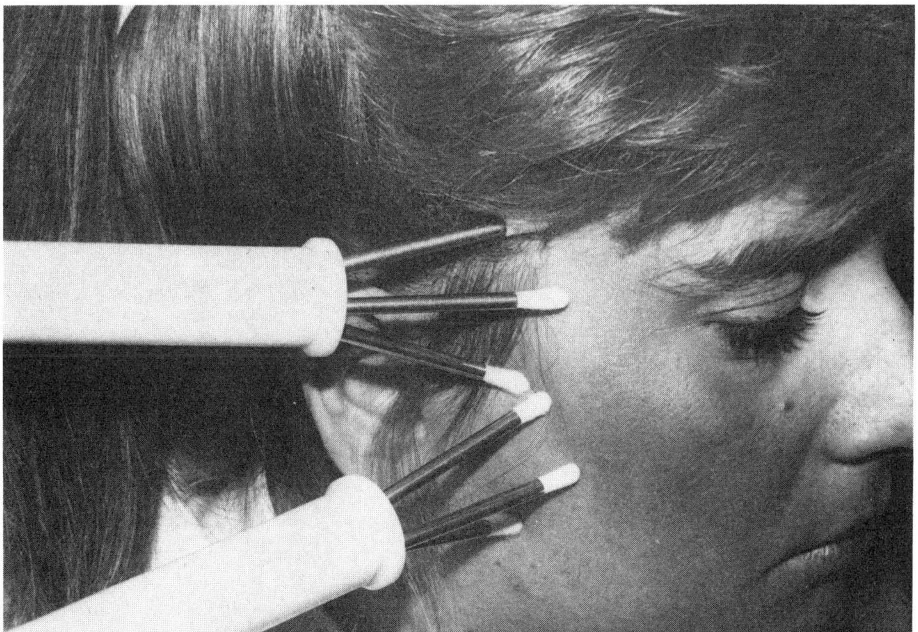

MENS application

Figure 6-2. Electromedicine. Used with permission.

Electrogalvanic stimulation (EGS). Most frequently used in treating muscle spasms, muscle splinting, trigger points (painful points in the muscle), and interstitial edema.

Microamperage electrical neural stimulation (MENS). Uses electrical devices against injured, inflamed, and painful tissue with the amperage set at the same level as that given off by the body. It reduces pain, promotes healing, and speeds recovery.

Iontophoresis. Transfers therapeutic drugs into tissue intradermally.

§ 6.6 —Thermal Therapy

Thermal therapy generally promotes healing and reduces pain. **Figure 6-3** illustrates common types of thermal therapy.

Heat treatment. May be successful in relieving pain and restoring flexibility. The most frequently used method is repeated application of moist heat on the face for 10 to 20 minutes. Blood flow is stimulated in a localized area and recovery from an injury is accelerated.

Diathermy. Shortwave devices used to increase blood flow and promote healing, restore function, and decrease pain.

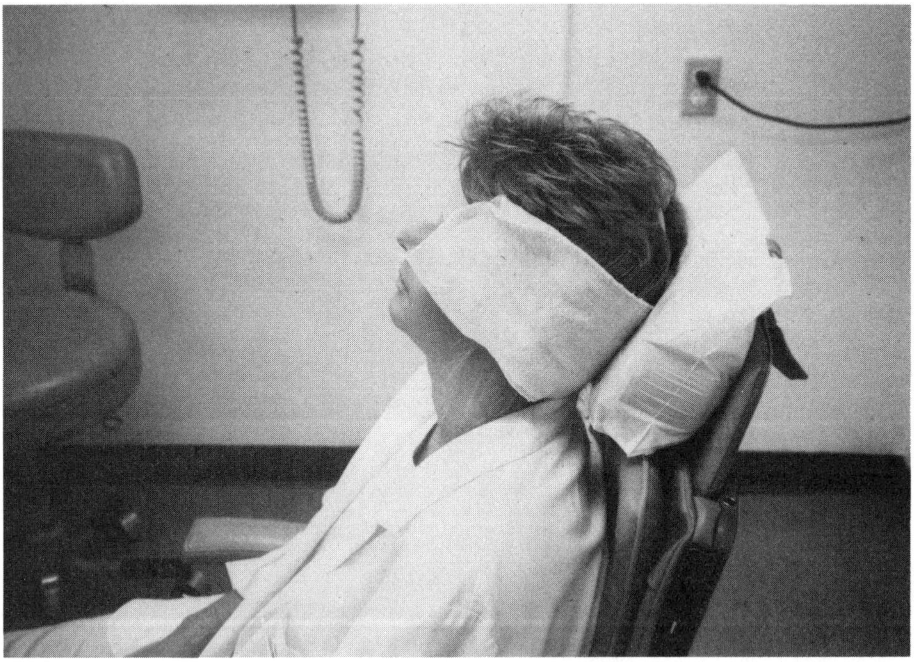

Heat application

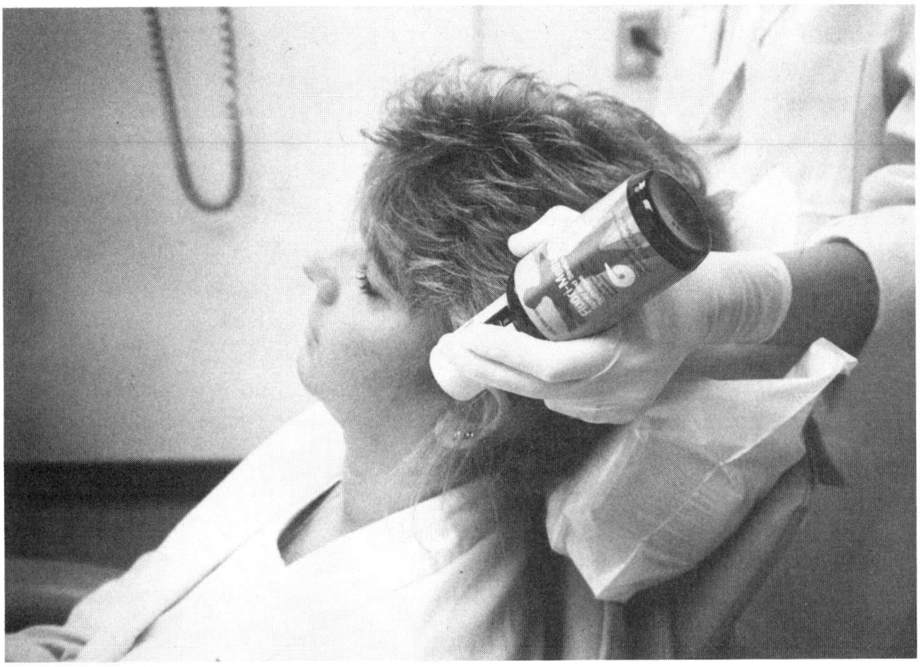

Vapocoolant spray application

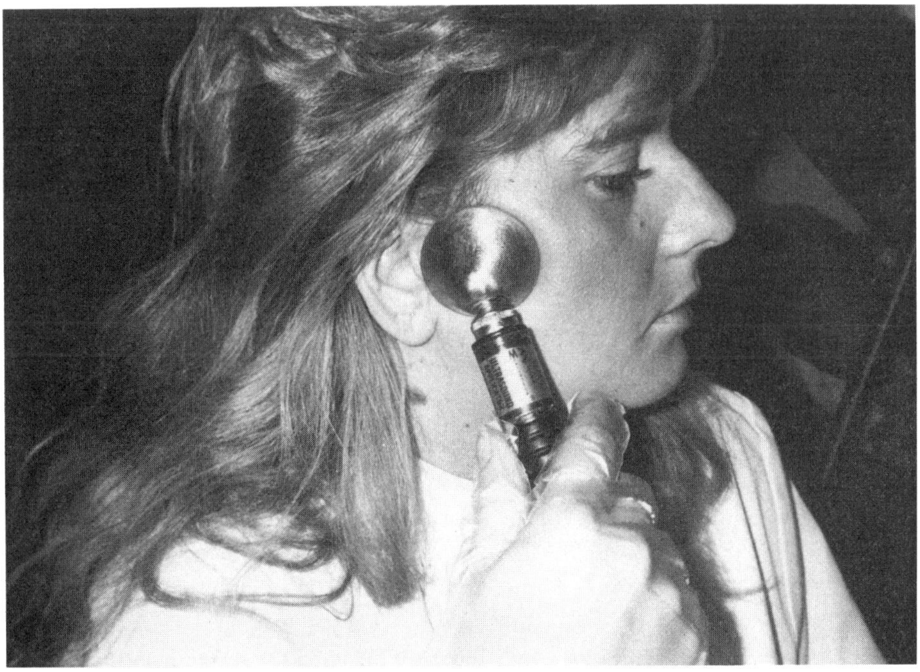

Ultrasound application

Figure 6-3. Thermal therapy. Used with permission.

Ultrasound. Production of acoustical energy in the ultrasonic range (1 million cycles per second). Therapeutic effects of ultrasound are twofold: tissue temperature is increased (thermal stimulation) and production of tiny air bubbles, or cavitation (mechanical stimulation). This promotes tissue healing, decreases pain, reduces edema, and increases the elongation ability of the tissues.

Vapocoolant sprays. Cold sprays or refrigerant agents, such as ethylchloride or fluorimethane. When sprayed on the skin they cause an inhibitory reflex that decreases muscle spasms and pain in the underlying muscles.

§ 6.7 —Acupuncture

Acupuncture is the insertion of needles at prescribed and mapped points on the body for the purpose of pain relief. Although not enough solid data exists, it can be considered a technique for temporary relief. As temporary relief, it should not be the sole treatment modality for TMJ-OSGS disorders.

§ 6.8 —Cold Laser

Cold laser, or light amplification by stimulated emission of radiation is a device that uses a helium/neon gas generator to emit a type of light in the red field of the spectrum. This light passes through silver mirrors and is transmitted through hand-held fiberoptics. It has a promising future in relieving pain and increasing circulation, collagen, and epithelial formation.

Currently the cold laser is available only for experimental use by dental and medical schools. Although the data are promising, it is not yet approved by the FDA.

§ 6.9 Oral Appliances (Splint Therapy)

Oral appliances, commonly referred to as intraoral splints, orthopedic repositioning, mouthpieces, night guards, orthotic or bruxism appliances are routinely used in the management of TMJ-OSGS disorders. These are removable acrylic resin appliances, shown in **Figure 6-4**, that cover the occlusal surface of the teeth in order that the relationship of the mandible to the cranium may be altered. Their purposes are

1. To diagnose or treat a masticatory muscle pain or dysfunction.
2. To diagnose or treat a displaced TMJ disc.

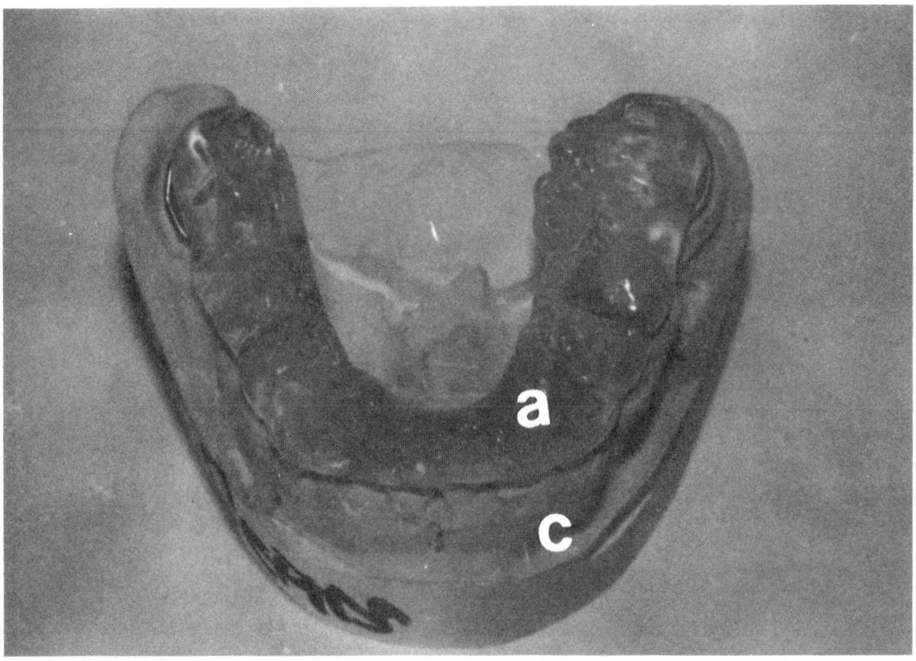

a: Mandibular orthopedic repositioning appliance (MORA), c: cast

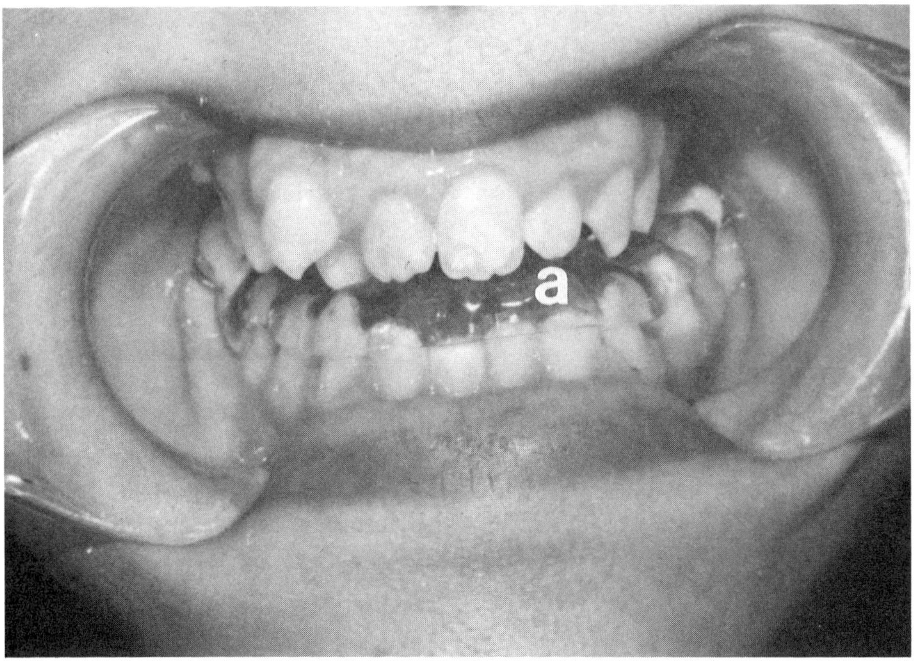

MORA placed in the mouth on the lower teeth

Figure 6-4. Mandibular orthopedic appliance. Used with permission.

3. To diagnose or treat oropharyngeal dysfunction, e.g., sleep apnea or dysphagia.
4. To diagnose or treat bruxism and protect the dental arches from extra forces applied during clenching or grinding of the teeth.
5. To replace missing teeth and/or bone structure.
6. To move teeth to a desirable position.

Different types of mandibular repositioning appliances exist for treatment of different problems:

Myalgic. For muscle dysfunction.

Repositioning. For the displaced mandible or condyle.

Stabilizing. For the unstable occlusion and for mandibular restriction of unnecessary movement.

Provisional. For bruxism.

Functional. For teeth repositioning and arch recontouring.

Deprogramming. For deprogramming muscle incoordination.

Prosthetic. For tooth and bone replacement.

Orthodontic. For tooth repositioning.

Deprogramming. For deprogramming muscle incoordination.

Use of these appliances may have these beneficial results:

1. Artificial decompression of the TMJ.
2. Limitation of TMJ function to promote healing.
3. Restore the foreshortened muscles to resting length.
4. Decrease of electrical activity of muscles.
5. Decrease of proprioception into the central nervous system.
6. Distribution of stress evenly on the dental arches.
7. Placebo effect.

Weaning a patient from a splint is a gradual process over a series of weeks or months, depending on the severity of the case. Each week the patient wears the appliance for an increasingly shorter duration. This process should occur only after the occlusion has stabilized. Some individuals may need to use splints for the rest of their lives.

§ 6.10 Pharmacological Therapy

Pharmacological agents can be used in the treatment of TMJ-OSGS disorder on a short-term basis and as an adjunctive therapy.

Local anesthetics. Xylocaine 2 percent, procaine 2 percent, and isocaine 3 percent can be injected at nerve or trigger points for temporary pain relief, removal of waste products, and to decrease muscle spasm. Surface topical skin refrigerants such as ethylchloride or fluorimethane can be used to break the cycle of pain-spasm-pain.

Analgesics. The use of nonaddictive analgesics such as aspirin or acetaminophen decrease pain perception. Moderately addictive analgesics such as codeine preparations should be reserved for difficult cases for which no other method exists for pain reduction. Morphine, meperidine, and fentanyl, the strongly addictive analgesics, are contraindicated in the management of TMJ-OSGS disorders.

Anti-inflammatory agents. Oral nonsteroidal anti-inflammatory drugs (NSAID), such as ibuprofen, naprosyn, and indomethacin, may be used to decrease pain and joint and muscle inflammation. They should be prescribed over a minimum of two weeks on a low-dose, rigid schedule of two to four times per day.

Steroidal anti-inflammatory agents such as glucocorticoids may be used orally for three days after surgical intervention. Corticosteroids can be used topically as a cream to decrease inflammation of the TMJ. Injection of intracapsular glucocorticoids relieved joint inflammation, however, it is no longer encouraged. Glucocorticoids may be combined with xylocaine for trigger point injections.

Anxiolytics or antianxiety agents. Drugs such as benzodiazepine (Valium) are used in the treatment of myofacial pain. They relieve early morning jaw stiffness when there is a nocturnal bruxing habit.

Antidepressants. Agents such as amitriptyline have analgesic as well as antidepressant effects and are prescribed for chronic pain patients to help reduce pain, improve sleep, and alleviate depression.

Anticonvulsants. Phenytoin (Dilantin) and Tegretol decrease the facial muscle pain found in tic douloureux (trigeminal neuralgia).

Muscle relaxants. Cyclobenzaprine (Flexeril), carisoprodol with aspirin (Soma Compound), methocarbamal with aspirin (Robaxisal), and/or phenadrine with aspirin and caffeine (Norgesic or Norgesic Forte) can be used to reduce muscle spasm and pain.

Antiarthritics. Indocin can be used to reduce the arthritic pain associated with TMJ-OSGS disorders.

Placebos. These can be effective in a large number of cases.

§ 6.11 Nutritional Support and Psychological Counseling

The body's natural or intrinsic healing cells require certain nutrients for optimum functioning in reversing pathological conditions. The patient's diet should contain or be supplemented by adequate amounts of vitamins, minerals, amino acids, and enzymes.

The use of progressive relaxation training, visualization, hypnosis, and biofeedback, among other techniques, are proven muscle relaxers/pain relievers. Research into such "New Age" stress reduction methods is ongoing. Many individuals feel better after settlement of the case, perhaps due to psychological or placebo effects.

SECOND PHASE (STABILIZING) TREATMENT

§ 6.12 Occlusal Rehabilitation—Occlusal Equilibration

Occlusal rehabilitation (bite restoration) can be accomplished through occlusal equilibration, prosthetic reconstruction, orthodontic therapy, orthograthic surgery, or a combination. Occlusal equilibration (coronoplasty or adjustment) is a procedure that reshapes the tooth surface for a better fit with the opposing tooth. Minor tooth adjustment may be indicated when there is a premature contact. Comprehensive occlusal equilibration may be needed after orthodontic repositioning or during restoration of teeth.

§ 6.13 —Prosthetics

Prosthetic restoration and/or replacement of missing teeth may be necessary to stabilize the occlusion when occlusal contact does not adequately hold the mandible in its normal physiologic position. Prosthetic restorations can be achieved by the construction of onlays, crowns (caps), fixed bridges, or removable partial denture overlays. **Figure. 6-5** illustrates a bridge and removable partial denture.

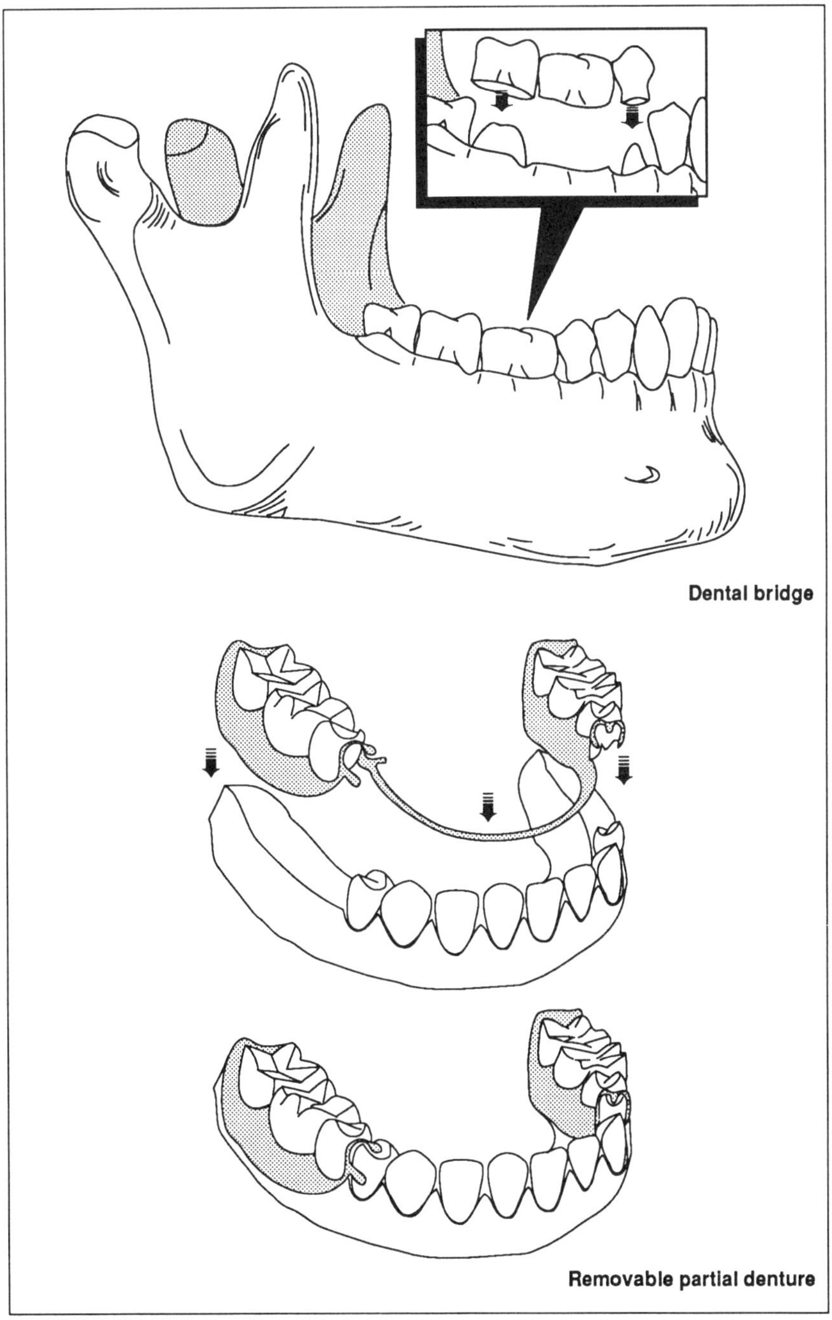

Figure 6-5. Prosthetics.

§ 6.14 —Orthodontics

Orthodontics, in the form of fixed appliances (braces) or removable appliances (mouthpieces with active components that move teeth, commonly known as retainers), can create a functional occlusion in harmony with the TMJ and the face and neck musculature by moving teeth to a position in which the mandible and TMJ become stabilized. This is indicated when there is a large gap, greater than 3mm, between upper and lower teeth. **Figure 6-6** illustrates this technique.

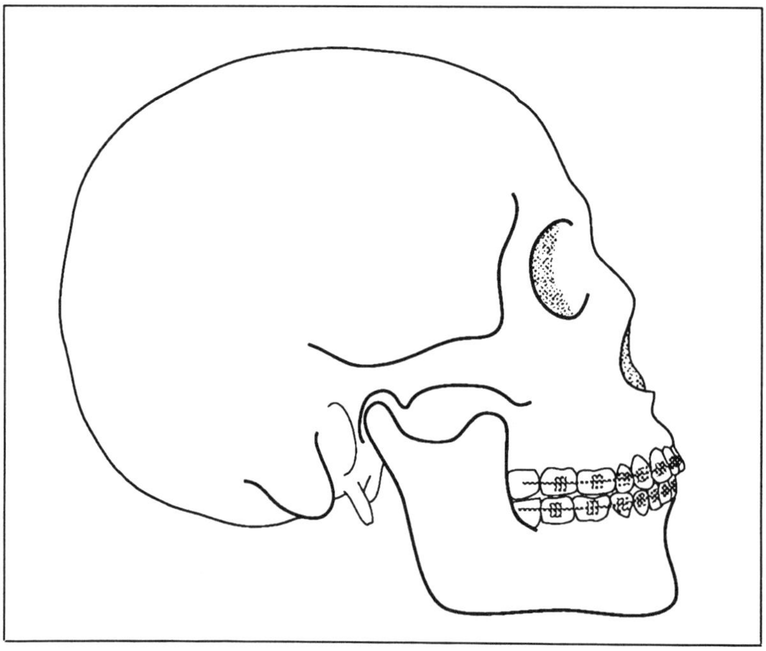

Figure 6-6. Orthodontics.

§ 6.15 Surgical Management

Its increased effectiveness has made surgery a more viable option for patients suffering from the most severe TMJ-OSGS disorders. However, the complexity of the surgical techniques, the possibility of major complications, the irreversibility of the result, and the availability of nonsurgical techniques must be considered before proceeding. The American Academy of Oral and Maxillofacial Surgeons has adopted certain criteria to be met before such a modality can be undertaken:

1. TMJ disc displacement or other structural disorder must be documented by an appropriate imaging technique.
2. Symptoms and objective findings must be proven to be the result of disc displacement or structural disorder.
3. Pain and/or dysfunction must be debilitating.
4. Prior unsuccessful nonsurgical treatment that includes orthopedic appliance, physical, and behavioral therapies.
5. Prior management of bruxism, oral parafunctional habits, other medical or dental conditions or contributing factors.
6. Written consent of the patient after discussing potential complications, goals of treatment, success rate, timing, postoperative management, and alternative approaches, including no treatment.

Based on these criteria, surgical management is contraindicated for

1. Inflammatory joint or muscle disorders such as muscle dysfunction, capsulitis, or nonpainful osteoarthritis.
2. When another nonsurgical modality or a combination of several intervention techniques can be used to produce reasonable results.

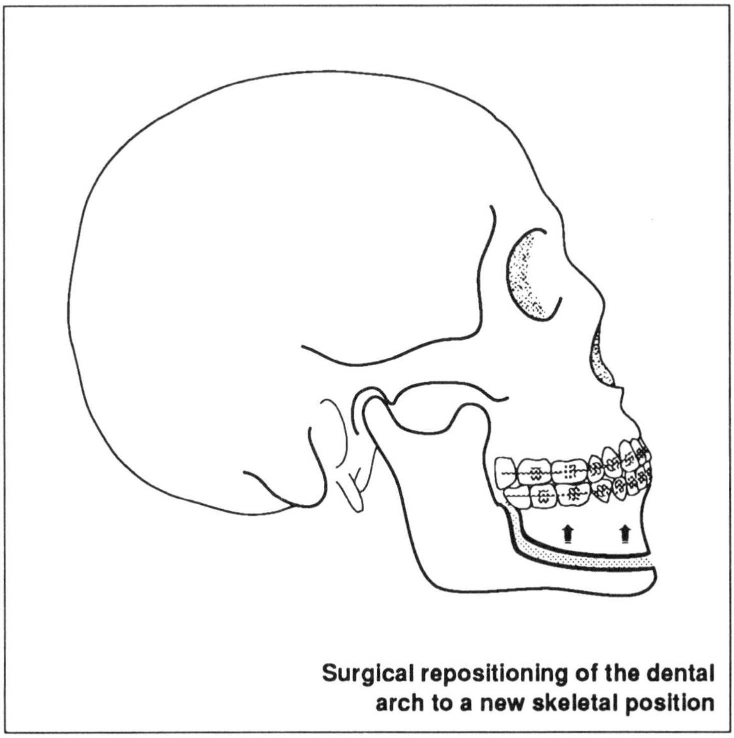

Figure 6-7. Orthognathic surgery.

Once the decision for surgical management is made, the following techniques are available:

Orthognathic surgery. A surgical procedure that is indicated only for severe skeletal dental malocclusion in adults: the jaw is fractured and reset in a new position in order to establish a stable occlusion. It is not recommended if a stable occlusion can be obtained by another method. See **Figure 6-7**. Usually the teeth are moved with braces before the surgery.

Arthroscopy. A wide needle containing a microscope is introduced into the TMJ for

1. Lysis and lavage (cleaning the adhesion materials) and debridement of foreign or loose bodies. See **Figure 6-8**.
2. Meniscal release to treat the persistent, nonreducing (displaced) disc. **Figure 6-9**.

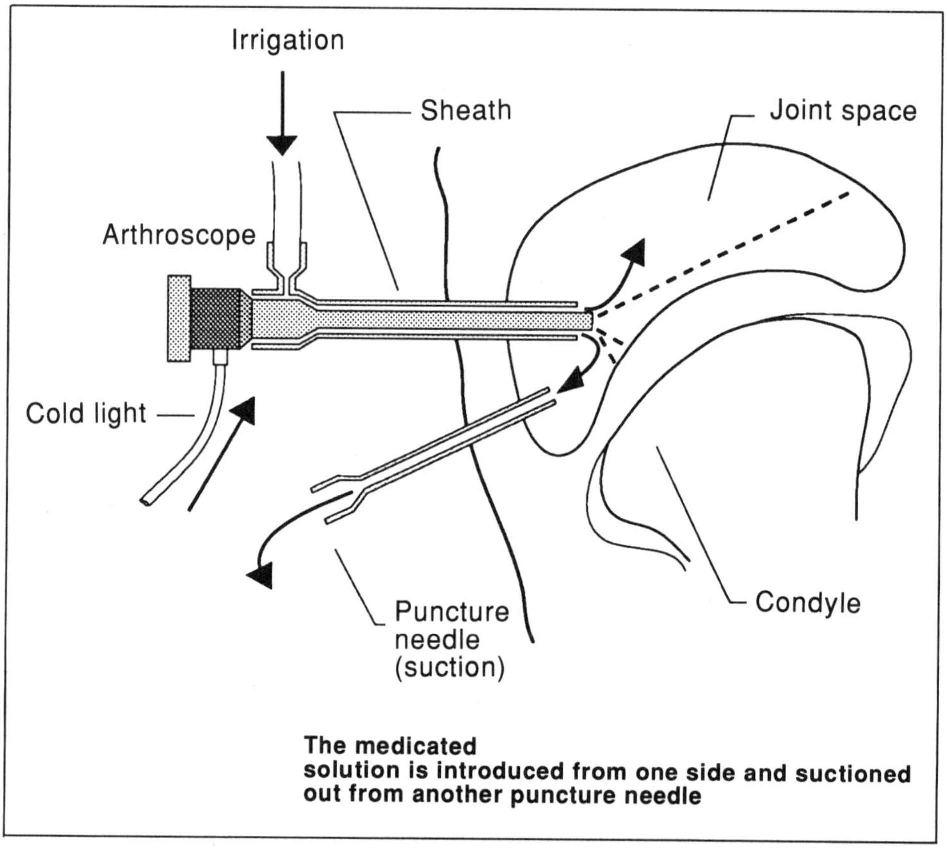

Figure 6-8. Arthroscopy (lysis and lavage).

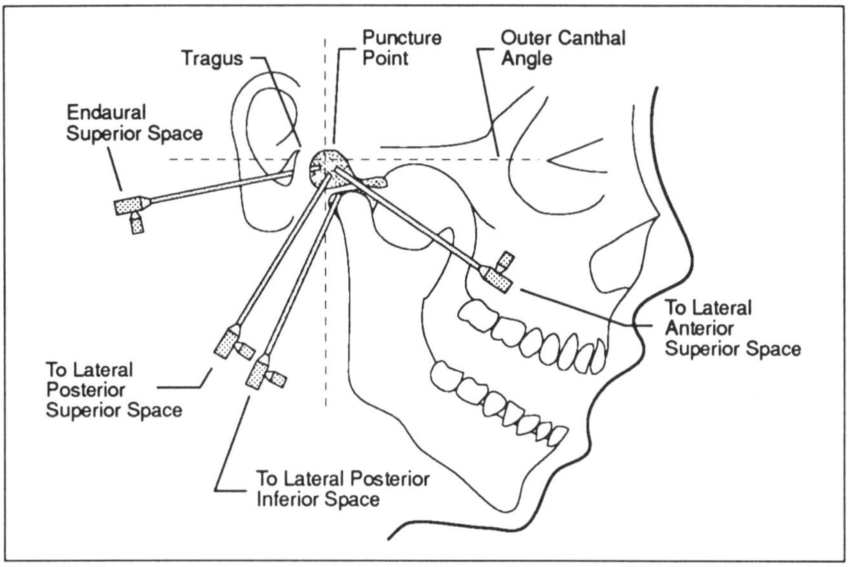

Figure 6-9. Arthroscopy (meniscal release).

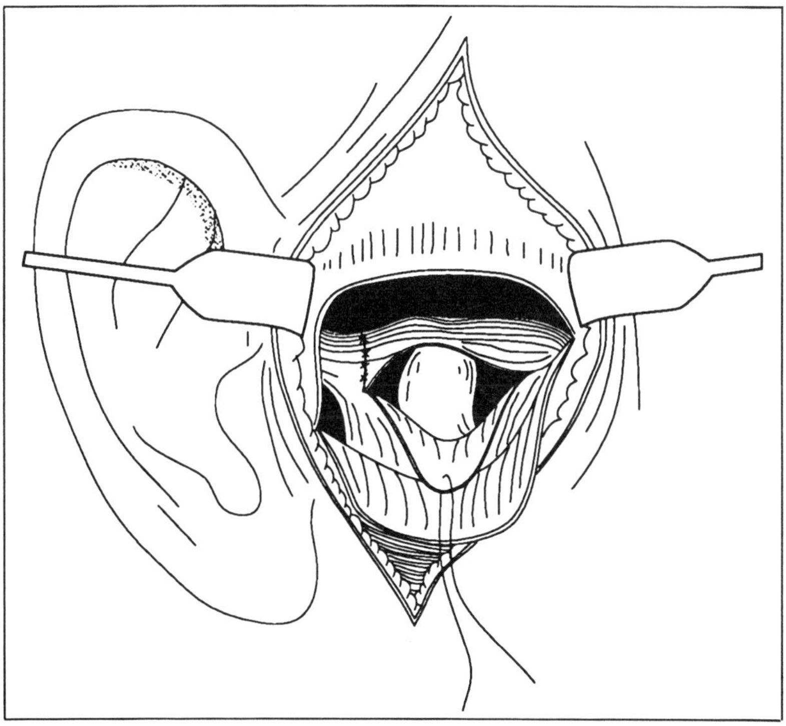

Figure 6-10. Arthrotomy.

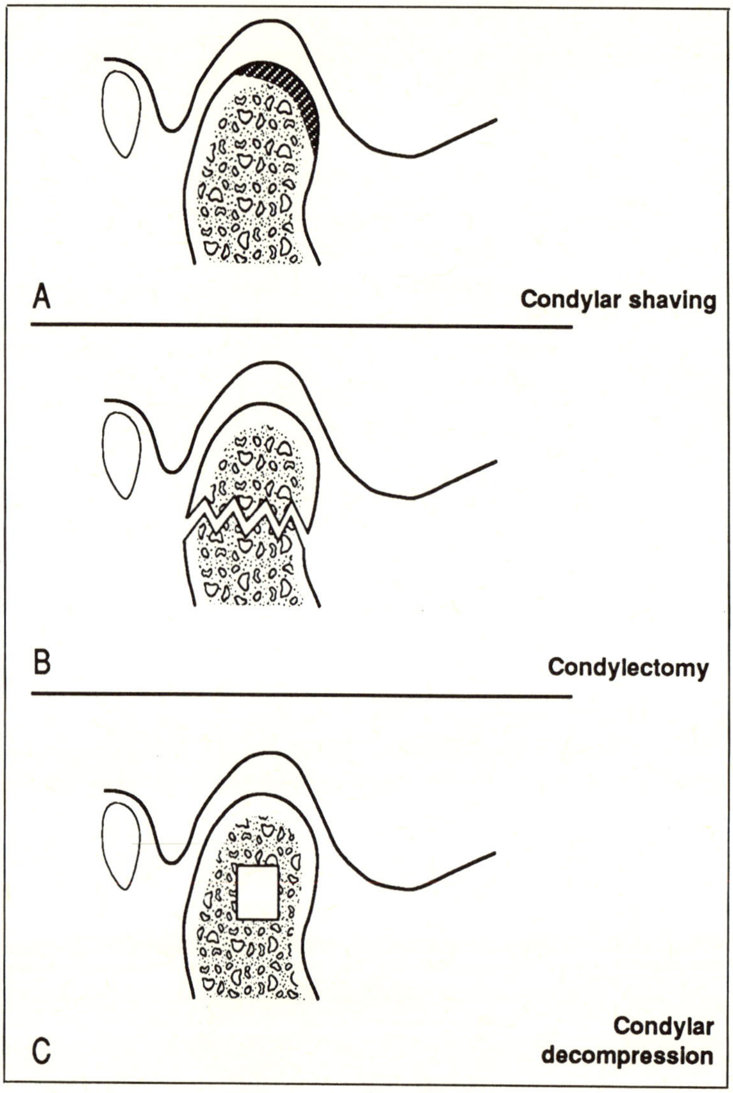

Figure 6-11. Arthroplasty.

Arthrotomy. The TMJ is exposed via an open flap in the skin, see **Figure 6-10**, for

1. Discoplasty. Repair of perforated disc or plication, reducing the slack, of discal tissue.
2. Discal repositioning with plication. Replacing the disc in normal relation to the condyle.

3. Discectomy (removal of the disc). Replacement of the disc by autogenous (to same patient's tissue), homologous (other human bank tissue), or alloplastic materials (silicon).

Arthroplasty. Condylar contouring to allow enough joint space or to treat osteoarthritic conditions. As shown in **Figure 6-11**, the condyle may be reshaped, removed, or decompressed.

1. Condylectomy. Condylar removal. This is done infrequently and indicated only for complex traumatic conditions.
2. Condylar decompression. A window is formed to allow revascularization in avascular necrosis.

The surgical results are based on many factors: proper case selection, medical condition and cooperation of the patient, postoperative follow-up, and others. In many cases the patient can resume a normal diet and functions; in others, further breakdown is expected.

§ 6.16 Success of Treatment

The level of success of the treatment and recovery phases depends on severity of injury or disease, extent of management or treatment, cooperation of the patient, and underlying predisposing, initiating, or aggravating factors.

Clearly, the complexity of the injury, financial interest, compensation neurosis, and conditioning of the injured patient may cloud the ability to estimate the success of a certain treatment.

Treating predisposing factors, avoiding aggravating factors, and prevention of new injury must be considered by the physician and then by the patient in order to avoid recurrence of the TMJ-OSGS disorder.

§ 6.17 References

R.L. Talley, G.J. Murphy, S.D. Smith, M.A. Baylin, & J.L. Haden, *Standards for the History, Examination, Diagnosis, and Treatment of Temporomandibular Disorders (TMD): A Position Paper*, 8 J. Craniomandibular Practice 60 (1990).

C. Craniomandibular Disorders: Guidelines for Evaluation, Diagnosis, and Management (C. McNeill, ed., Quintessence Publishing 1990).

R.H. Griffiths, Paper presented at the 1982 President's Conference on the Examination, Diagnosis, and Management of Temporomandibular Disorders, American Dental Association.

CHAPTER 7

MAXIMUM MEDICAL IMPROVEMENT AND PERMANENT IMPAIRMENT RATINGS

§ 7.1 Maximum Medical Improvement

Maximum medical improvement, or MMI, is defined as the point at which no further progress can be obtained in the management of an injury—a cooperative patient has spent a reasonable length of time under the treatment of an adequately trained therapist employing adequate diagnostic and treatment methods.

What is "a reasonable length of time"? The obvious answer is enough time to allow the traumatized or diseased tissue to heal properly; "enough" can vary greatly, depending on the amount of trauma received and the condition and tolerance of the individual. Management is generally conducted over a period of three to twenty four months,[1] with an average of six to nine months for moderate TMJ-OSGS injury cases.

A recommended standard of care exists for diagnosis and treatment of TMJ-OSGS disorders; the taking of a thorough medical history, thorough physical examination, and confirmation of the diagnosis by diagnostic aids.

[1] C. McNeill, *The Optimum TMJ Condyle Position in Clinical Practice*, 6 Int'l J. Periodontal & Restor. Dent. 52 (1985).

Ignoring this standard can have deleterious effects for the patients,[2] and for the physician as well, should he be sued for malpractice. Every avenue of treatment should be explored, not only one or two modalities. For example, in the reduction of pain, the therapist should initiate physical therapy to reduce muscle spasm in addition to the use of a splint to stabilize the TMJ. MMI can be achieved after applying several different courses of treatment to a correctly diagnosed problem.

An *adequately trained therapist* in TMJ-OSGS disorders may be a dentist having a strong postgraduate, professional, teaching, and research background. A few one- or two-day courses or seminars do not an expert make.[3]

§ 7.2 Permanent Impairment Rating

The basic terminology of permanent impairment rating is impairment and disability. *Impairment* is the loss of, loss of use of, or derangement of any body part, system, or function. It is usually divided into sensory impairment or dysfunction, indicating any change in the sensation in an organ, such as pain, numbness, tingling, or other effects; and motor impairment or dysfunction, the loss of moveability and strength of an organ. *Disability* is the limiting, loss, or absence of the capacity of an individual to meet personal, social, or occupational demands or to meet statutory or regulatory requirements.

The *Guides to the Evaluation of Permanent Impairment*[4] does not clearly identify the permanent impairment rating for TMJ-OSGS; however, an attempt is made here to clarify the rating.

§ 7.3 —Method I: The AMA Rating

Patients suffering from TMJ-OSGS disorders experience sensory as well as motor dysfunction. The sensory dysfunction of the TMJ-OSGS is usually the result of impairment of the trigeminal and facial nerves. Motor dysfunction can be viewed as hypoglossal nerve impairment.[5]

---

[2] R.A. Abdel-Fattah, *Diagnosis and Prevention of Temporomandibular Joint (TMJ) or Odontostomatognathic (OSG) Injury in Dental Practice*, 2 Today's Scientific Florida Dental Assoc. J. (1990); R.L. Talley, G.J. Murphy, S.D. Smith, M.A. Baylin, & J.L. Haden, *Standards for the History, Examination, Diagnosis, and Treatment of Temporomandibular Disorders (TMD): A Position Paper*, 8 J. Craniomandibular Practice 60 (1990); Craniomandibular Disorders: Guidelines for Evaluation, Diagnosis, and Management (C. McNeill, ed., Quintessence Publishing 1990).

[3] D.M. Foreman & D.A. Rolfs, Whiplash and the Jaw Joint (Book Publishing Co. 1985).

[4] Guides to the Evaluation of Permanent Impairment ch. 4 (A.L. Engelberg, ed., 3d ed. 1988).

[5] *Id.*

Impairment of the trigeminal nerve is classified as:

1. Complete unilateral sensory loss—3 to 10 percent impairment of the entire body.[6]
2. Complete bilateral sensory loss—20 to 35 percent impairment of the entire body.
3. Intractable typical trigeminal neuralgia or tic douloureux—10 to 50 percent impairment of the entire body.
4. Atypical facial neuralgia—0 to 20 percent impairment of the entire body.
5. Complete unilateral motor loss—3 to 5 percent impairment of the entire body.
6. Complete bilateral motor loss—30 to 45 percent impairment of the entire body.

Facial nerve impairment is classified as:

1. Complete loss of taste (rare)—3 percent impairment of the entire body.
2. Complete unilateral paralysis—10 to 15 percent impairment of the entire body.
3. Complete bilateral paralysis—30 to 45 percent impairment of the entire body.

Hypoglossal nerve impairment is classified as:

1. Unilateral paralysis—0 percent impairment of the entire body.
2. Bilateral paralysis (impairment of swallowing, for example)—diet restriction to semisolids, 5 to 10 percent; diet restriction to liquids, 20 to 30 percent; diet by tube feeding or gastrostomy, 40 to 60 percent of the entire body.

This rating is vague and wide-ranging. Because the diet is not restricted to liquids, tube feeding, or gastrostomy in TMJ-OSGS disorders, the minimal rating of 5 to 10 percent is an exaggeration for loss of motor function. The rating given to atypical facial neuralgia, 0 to 20 percent of the whole body, may also be applicable to TMJ-OSGS. The practitioner does not find severe, unexplained neuralgia for TMJ-OSGS disorder, nor a complete uni- or bilateral-paralysis in the facial area; therefore, the minimal rating of 10 percent is an exaggeration for facial pain and TMJ-OSGS disorder.

---

[6] *Id.*

§ 7.4 —Method II: The Phillips et al. Rating

This method of evaluation was compiled by the American Academy of Head, Facial, Neck Pain, and TMJ Orthopedics, using values outlined by the American Medical Association[7] for other discs in protected and functional joints, and was published in the Journal of Craniomandibular Practice.[8] The method does not exactly translate to the TMJ because the TMJ is not similar to other joints, but it is a good outline. It uses the following criteria:

Disc Derangement

1. Dislocated disc (closed lock) with no pain and no mechanical limitations—5 percent of whole person per joint.
2. A reducing dislocation or subluxation of one joint—5 percent of whole person per joint.

Range of Motion (ROM)

1. Normal. Considers 50 mm opening (from incisal edge of maxillary teeth to incisal edge of mandibular teeth) and 12 mm lateral movement to be normal.
2. Ankylosed. 25 percent of whole person per joint.
3. Hypomobility. Based on percentage of normal interincisal opening:

   0 to 10 mm opening—20 percent of normal—impairment of 10 percent of whole person
   10 to 20 mm opening—40 percent of normal—impairment of 8 percent of whole person
   20 to 30 mm opening—50 percent of normal—impairment of 5 to 7 percent of whole person
   30 to 40 mm opening—70 percent of normal—impairment of 3 to 4 percent of whole person
   40 to 45 mm opening—90 percent of normal—impairment 1 to 2 percent of whole person
   0 to 4 mm lateral excursion—60 percent of normal—impairment of 4 percent of whole person per joint
   4 to 7 mm lateral excursion—70 percent of normal—impairment of 3 percent of whole person

---

[7] *Id.*

[8] D.J. Phillips, P.J. Walters, O.J. Rogel, B.C. Stack, L.B. Weiner & I.M. Klemmons, *Recommended Guide to the Evaluation of Permanent Impairment of the Temporomandibular Joint*, 7 J. of Craniomandibular Practice 13 (1989).

8 to 10 mm lateral excursion—90 percent of normal—impairment of 1 percent of whole person

4. Hypermobility: no impairment designation.
5. Total condylar anterior dislocation, nonrecurrent: 15 percent of whole person per joint.

Arthroplasty

1. Repair of meniscus (disc)—5 percent of whole person per joint.
2. Meniscectomy (removal of the disc)—10 percent of whole person per joint.
3. Meniscectomy and alloplastic (usually silicone) implant—15 percent of whole person per joint.
4. Meniscectomy and soft tissue graft—15 percent of whole person per joint.
5. Total joint reconstruction—20 percent of whole person per joint.
6. Arthroscopic surgery—5 percent of whole person per joint.

This rating lacks a few necessary items, in the opinion of the author:

1. Pain as a sensory dysfunction and an impairment was not considered.
2. The mandibular ROM was considered to be normal at 50 mm vertical, 12 mm to the right or left. This is not true in many cases, as ROM varies according to the individual's size, height, etc. For example, a person with a 40-mm vertical opening can be considered to have normal function. According to these ratings, this individual experiences impairment over 3 to 4 percent of the body. Open bite or overbite measurements were not considered, which can affect the rating grossly. For example, when the interincisal distance is 40 mm, the Phillips group considers the patient's experience of permanent impairment to be 4 percent over the whole body; however, if an overbite of 10 mm is considered, the incisal points have traveled 50 mm (40 + 10), and this is accepted as normal.
3. The issue of hypermobility was not addressed.
4. The rating for permanent impairment of ankylosis and arthroplasty is too high in comparison to actual cases and needs to be reconsidered and re-evaluated.
5. The types of ROM were not considered, i.e, active (controlled by the individuals) or passive (guided by the examiner).

§ 7.5 —Method III: The Abdel-Fattah Rating

Based on the deficiencies of the AMA guidelines and the Phillips et al. systems, the author proposes his own recommended rating system, subject to updates, for permanent impairment.

Pain is an unpleasant sensory and emotional experience associated with actual or potential tissue changes.[9] It is always subjective, varies in frequency, intensity, cause of onset, and duration, and is usually associated with tissue damage or pathophysiologic causes. If pain is not associated with objective pathologic changes it is psychosomatic. Classifications of pain follow:

Onset of Pain

1. *Acute.* An unpleasant sensation provoked by noxious stimulation which is produced by an injury or a disease.
2. *Chronic.* An unpleasant sensation that persists one month or more beyond onset.

Frequency of Pain

1. *Constant.* Pain that occurs continually.
2. *Frequent.* Pain that occurs repeatedly.
3. *Often.* Pain that occurs repeatedly at short intervals two or three times per week.
4. *Occasional.* Pain that occurs at irregular intervals of some length, i.e., every week or every other week.
5. *Seldom.* Pain that occurs very infrequently.

Intensity (Quality or Magnitude) of Pain

1. *Severe.* Pain that causes the individual to avoid all activities and occupational pursuits.
2. *Moderate.* Pain that causes the individual to avoid some daily activities or occupational pursuits.
3. *Mild.* Pain that annoys the individual but does not cause him to avoid any activities or occupational pursuits.
4. *Minimal.* Barely perceptible pain or discomfort.

---

[9] J.J. Bonica, The Management of Pain 18, (2d., ed., Lea & Febiger 1990).

The classifications of frequency and intensity of pain are considered in conjunction to obtain a *sensory dysfunction* rating in terms of percentage of impairment of the entire body.

Intensity	Constant	Frequent	Often	Occasional	Seldom
Severe	6%	4%	2%	1%	0%
Moderate	4%	2%	1%	0%	0%
Mild	2%	1%	0%	0%	0%
Minimal	1%	0%	0%	0%	0%

Figure 7-1. Sensory dysfunction.

In patients suffering from *motor dysfunction*, consideration should be given to the ability of the individual to masticate foods. This ability can be classified according to food consistency:

1. *Soft.* White bread, mashed potatoes, spaghetti, etc.
2. *Semisolid.* Fresh fruits, chicken, fish, etc.
3. *Hard.* Nuts (peanuts, Brazil nuts), potato chips, vegetables, dried fruits, etc.
4. *Harder.* Bagels, steak, pork chops, hard potato chips, etc.

Motor dysfunction ratings are:

1. Inability to eat harder food 1—2 percent of the body as a whole.
2. Inability to eat hard food 2—3 percent of the body as a whole.
3. Inability to eat semisoft food 3—4 percent of the body as a whole.
4. Inability to eat soft food 4—6 percent of the body as a whole.

The combination of sensory and motor dysfunction ratings give a subjective impairment rating, or *Rating 1*. As this rating method is subjective, based upon the history given by the individual, we must assume that person's honesty. Potential for abuse of the system by malingerers, as mentioned earlier in the volume, runs high. Therefore, the author strongly recommends correlating subjective symptoms with objective findings discovered during the clinical and instrumental examinations within a reasonable degree of medical/dental probability.

Objective permanent impairment rating, or *Rating 2*, is the rating based on the objective findings.

Hypermobility. An excessive increase in the mandibular opening due to overstretched capsule or ligaments is indicated by this term. This increase can be measured through the study of patterns of mandibular motion. The pattern is usually disturbed and ROM increases. Instability of the ligaments leads to a decrease in the patient's ability to perform activities involving the oral cavity. The permanent impairment rating is 2 percent for each joint of the body as a whole.

Hypomobility. A decrease in mandibular vertical ROM is indicated due to dysfunction or anatomical interference. Passive ROM measurements (full extension of the mandible assisted by the examiner) are to be used.

1. Trismus. Muscle spasm that limits the mandibular opening about 5 to 10 mm can be documented through muscle palpation and measurement. It is usually treatable and the permanent impairment rating is 2 percent of the body as a whole for the small number of difficult to treat cases.
2. Anterior disc displacement with reduction in each joint (opening of about 20 to 40 mm) can be documented clinically (audibly observing click in the TMJ) or through magnetic resonance imaging (MRI). Permanent impairment rating is 2 percent of the body as a whole. This is assuming that the disc is not reducable by proper occlusal management.
3. Anterior disc displacement without reduction in each joint (opening of about 20 to 40 mm) can also be documented clinically and through MRI. Permanent impairment rating is 4 percent of the body as a whole.
4. Restricted lateral excursion has no specific rating, as it should be viewed through its cause: muscle spasm or disc displacement (rated above).

Ankylosis. Partial or complete loss of movement of the TMJ due to excessive fibrous or bony fusion. It can be mistaken for other functional disturbances, but is in reality quite rare. This can be documented through MRI or radiography. The permanent impairment rating is 15 percent of the body as a whole for each joint.

Arthroscopy. The permanent impairment rating should be based on the objective findings, i.e., hypomobility and remaining pain as well as functional restrictions imposed by the physician.

Arthroplasty. The permanent impairment rating should be based on the objective findings or on restriction of function Another method—5 percent for meniscus repair, 10 percent for meniscectomy and alloplastic implant, 12 percent for meniscectomy and soft tissue graft, and 20 percent for total joint reconstruction—can be used for each joint of the body as a whole. A combination table of impairment values of the AMA Guide may be used to produce the total one.[10]

In selected cases, the clinician may want to use both subjective and objective ratings and calculate the average of the two to obtain a single measure of permanent impairment.

[10] Guides to the Evaluation of Permanent Impairment (A.L. Engelberg, ed., 3d ed. 1988).

CHAPTER 8

CASE REPORTS

§ 8.1 Writing Case Reports

Medical narrative reports are written by clinicians for the purpose of clarifying a case to lawyers and insurance adjustors. The reports should be clear, accurate, and as complete as possible.

Initial reports. The initial report is written when a clinician first sees an individual and may include:

Personal history and data—name, age, sex, occupation, and marital status.
Chief complaints—pain or dysfunction, as described in the patient's own words.
Review of other symptoms—the patient's answers to questions about related symptoms.
Past medical history—accidents, injuries, traumas, illnesses, surgeries, and past and present medications.
Social history—marital status, social life, sexual habits, and so forth.

Occupational history—what duties does the patient perform during working hours and for how long.

Sleeping pattern—uninterrupted or interrupted, comfortable or uncomfortable, teeth grinding or clenching, condition upon awakening.

Diet—quality and consistency.

Clinical examination consisting of facial analysis, occlusal analysis, muscle palpation, TMJ auscultation, range of mandibular motion, pattern of mandibular motion, and postural analysis.

Diagnostic tests and results of radiographic evaluation, computerized electronic testing—sonography, craniomandibular scan, electromyography, and magnetic resonance imaging.

Diagnostic impression—initial or tentative diagnosis.

Recommended treatment—treatment plan.

Prognosis—prediction by the clinician of the outcome of a disease course.

Causal relation of the injury to the accident in question.

Progress or interim report. This report updates the patient's file on the progress of the treatment and may include:

Review of initial report.

Patient's response to the recommended treatment.

Restriction and limitation of the patient, if applicable.

Expected date of recovery.

Final report. This report is prepared after the patient reaches maximum medical improvement and may include:

Review of initial report.

Review of progress report.

Date at which patient reached MMI.

Patient's last subjective and objective findings (complaints, range of motion, muscle palpation, TMJ auscultation).

Special instructions to patient.

Future treatment or management, if applicable.

Permanent impairment rating, if applicable.

Overall report. The clinician writing this type of report is one who performs a single examination of the injured patient after that patient has spent a certain length of time under treatment. This report is similar to a final report with detailed history, clinical examination, results of instrumental diagnosis, progress of treatment, future care, and permanent impairment rating if applicable.

When any type of report is required, the inquiring party is advised to compose a list of items necessary to insure completeness of the report. Some reports also require a follow-up letter for further explanation.

The balance of this chapter contains reports seen by the author with his comments. Please note that many of these reports were not cases treated by the author.

§ 8.2 Case Report 1

Doctor's Name Date
Address
Re: Patient

Dear Doctor:

The above mentioned patient visited our office on (date) with specific complaints of neck pain, arm pain, and pain in his elbow. The patient stated that he was involved in an automobile accident on (date). He described it as he was rear ended by three cars in a chain accident. He was looking left when he was struck from behind. His head snapped backwards while looking in the left sideview mirror. He also stated that immediately following the accident his neck and left elbow were painful. Symptoms present since the accident now include:

Swollen, stiff or painful joints.
Muscle soreness or stiffness.
Neck injury or operation.
Twisting neck quickly makes noise.
Numbness of shoulder, arms, hands, and fingers.
Shoulder pain.
Neckaches.

Clinical examination revealed:

There is a possible anterior derangement of the discs of the left and right temporomandibular joints.
There is a strain of the temporomandibular joints bilateral.
There is forward head position of 6.6 cm. This figure should not exceed 6 cm.
There is Trapezius Muscle Syndrome with entrapment neuropathy of the greater occipital nerve on the left.

Range in motion is as follows: 45 mm opening, 12 mm left lateral, and 12 mm right lateral. Normal range in motion is as follows: 44-51 mm opening, 12 mm left lateral, and 12 mm right lateral.

The following muscles are in spasm:

Levator Scapulae Inferior and Superior Trigger Point Bilateral.
Upper Trapezius Bilateral.
Semispinellus Capitus Bilateral, most prominent on the left.
Sternocleidomastoid Bilateral.
Posterior Belly of the Digastric Bilateral.
Middle Fibers of the Temporalis Bilateral.
Posterior Fibers of the Temporalis on the left.

The following area is tender to palpation:

Greater Occipital Nerve on the left.

In my opinion, to a reasonable degree of medical probability, this myofacial pain/temporomandibular joint dysfunction disorder is the result of the automobile accident of (date). Patient presents with mandibular whiplash.

Treatment will include:

Modify existing splint into a Gelb splint adjusted to reflex swallow.
Treatment of Trapezius Muscle Syndrome with entrapment neuropathy to Greater Occipital Nerve.
Trigger point therapy including injections and spray and stretch on the left Splenius Capitus muscle.
Continuation of chiropractic care.
Check with Chiropractor about possibility of a rotated atlas.
Orthopedic stabilization will be accomplished by restorative dentistry.

The prognosis is guarded. There is, within a reasonable degree of medical probability, permanent impairment due to the type of injury sustained by the automobile accident of (date).

Thank you again for referring the patient to our office. Your confidence is greatly appreciated. If there are any questions or comments or alternative programs you care to discuss, please do not hesitate to call.

Sincerely,
Signature

Comments on Report 1. It is computer generated. Chief complaints written in the doctor's or the computer program language, not the patient's own words. There was no indication of medical history. Although there is a good explanation of clinical examination, there was no basis except the clinician's opinion for causation of an injury to the accident in question. Also, the treatment, plan appears excessive for the clinical findings and the report predicts permanent impairment too early.

§ 8.3 Case Report 2

Doctor's Name Date
Address

Re: Patient

Dear Attorney:

The above mentioned patient is a 34 year old white female who was presented on (date). The patient was accompanied by one of her attorneys, (name of attorney), a court reporter, and a video technician. This crowd made it very inconvenient and influenced this examination.

The patient complained of the present chief complaints:

(1) Very bad headaches, and when it is bad she throws up
(2) Neck pain
(3) Sensitive to light
(4) Constant leg pain and back pain
(5) Constant weakness

She claimed that her headaches occur during cold weather, rainy days, driving, or stressed.

The patient related the above symptoms to an alleged accident of (date). She was a driver, and did not remember if she had her seat belt on, she did not know what happened, how she was hit, and did not recall what people told her about what happened. She said she was hospitalized at the (name of the hospital) for two weeks. She did not remember what happened there, she said she had a lot of anesthesia, x-rays, physical therapy, and hot packs. The patient said that she has seen different doctors to deal with her pain. She saw an orthopedic surgeon, neurologist, and a dentist. She did not remember the neurologist or the dentist's name. She visited the dentist only one time on (date) who according to her did not tell her anything.

Past medical history:

Medications: Currently she is taking Prozac, pain medications?, before (date) she was taking aspirin and Tylenol for pain and she did not remember how much.

Previous surgeries: Surgical treatment of a broken nose when in high school, and a c-section on (date).

Previous injuries: She did not recall.

Occupation: She is currently unemployed. She used to be in the armed forces and she was put out after her accident on (date).

Socially: She is married with a (age) old child.

Diet: She claimed to basically eat healthy food. For breakfast she takes coffee and juice. For lunch, she takes soup or a sandwich of peanut butter. For dinner she eats chicken, vegetables, and salad. She claimed that she did not like to eat meat.

Stress: She claimed to have stress before (date) due to her moving down to (location) and now due to money problems.

Chiropractic treatment: The patient admitted to a history of chiropractic treatment before (date) and did not know or remember for what purpose.

Drinks: She claimed to drink no alcohol, no sodas, she said that she drinks juices.

Daily activities: Takes care of her (age) child, walks, walks the dog, pays the bills, and makes the budget. She lives in a one-story two-bedroom house.

Limitations: She claimed to be limited in sitting for a long time, lifting her body, and sleeping due to her constant pain.

Sleep: She claimed to sleep from 11 p.m. to 7 a.m. and sleeps on her left side.

Dental history:

When the patient was asked about clenching her teeth she admitted that she did it. After looking to her lawyer she said that she does not remember when she did it.

History of three wisdom teeth extraction sometime during (date).

No history of braces.

The patient did not recall if she had any trauma to her jaw.

She claimed that she gets cracking of her jaw and her jaw gets stuck especially in the morning.

Clinical examination revealed:

Face:

Slightly elevated left eye.

Slightly elevated left ear.

Slightly flattened right cheek bone.

Retrognathia

Accentuated mental angle.

Nose slightly deviated to the left.

Occlusion:

Poor oral hygiene.
Periodontitis
1 mm midline shift to the right.
4 mm overbite.
2 mm overjet.
Wear facets in teeth #23, 24, 25, and 26.
Tooth #26 chipped.
Fine cracks in teeth #26 and 23.
Multiple restorations.
No contact of teeth #20 and 21, they are lingually inclined.
Interference in tooth #14.
Irregular curve of spee on right.

Pattern of mandibular motion is straight down and up without deviation.

Range of mandibular motion:

The patient opened 25 mm vertical, 3 mm to the left, and 4 mm to the right. When asked to put her fingers in her mouth, she placed 2+.

Digital muscle palpation of the oral-facial musculature revealed no bands, no knots, or trigger points. The patient only made facial expression upon touching the lateral pterygoid. There was no withdrawal reflexes.

TMJ auscultation: Using a stethoscope there was no noise or clicks.
Posture evaluation: Mild forward head position.
Panoramic radiographic evaluation:

Asymmetrical mandibular rami and condyles.
Elongated calcified right stylohyoid ligament.
Slightly accentuated right antigonial angle.

In conclusion, and it is my opinion based on the patient's history given to me by herself, review of provided records, and panoramic radiographs I can see the subjective findings are not consistent with objective ones.

Thank you, and please don't hesitate to contact me for any questions you might have.

Sincerely,
Signature

Comments on Report 2. This Claimant was well coached for "I don't remember" answer. The report has a good medical history and good clinical examination. However, the very short conclusion is not helpful. An attorney would want an explanation of how the subjective findings are not consistent with the objective ones. An opposing attorney would inquire about the inconsistency at deposition.

§ 8.4 Case Report 3

Attorney's Name Date
Address

Re: Patient

Dear Attorney:

This is an addendum to my previous report on the above named individual.

The patient's progress was steady and successful. On the last appointment on (date) he had no complaints.

The range of mandibular motion was 48 mm vertical, 10 mm to the right, and 10 mm to the left. There was no muscle tenderness during palpation and there were no clicks or obvious abnormal sounds when T.M.Joints were auscultated.

The patient was released to return to our office as needed. He was also advised for continuous routine dental care.

At this time the patient has reached maximum medical improvement and with no obvious impairment in the T.M.J. area.

Thank you, and please don't hesitate to contact me for any questions you might have.

Sincerely,
Signature

Comments on Report 3. This is an honest final report by an honest clinician for an honest patient.

§ 8.5 Case Report 4

Attorney's Name Date
Address

Re: Patient

Dear Attorney:

As per your request this is a progress report for the above named individual.

As you are well aware the patient is under my care for the treatment of the anterior disc displacement of the temporomandibular joints as well as myofacial pain dysfunction. The patient related this disorder as a result of the auto accident she allegedly sustained on (date). Recommended treatment was given and the patient showed no significant progress. Range of motion was restricted and the pain was still present.

In September I requested a Magnetic Resonance Imaging examination and the patient was referred to (location) which is an affiliate with (hospital's name). The result was a bilateral fixed anterior dislocation of the menisci with significant decrease in excursion. The report also indicated flattening of both mandibular condylar surfaces. This means that the discs of the joints were displaced anteriorly without any recapture. On the visit of (date) the patient was given choices or options; surgical consults, continue the same plan for the treatment of the disc hoping to stabilize the bite as it is without invasive procedures, or mandibular manipulation with intense muscle therapy in the hope of reducing the discs non-surgically. The patient expressed her desire not go to surgery at this time.

I have injected her with 3% mepivacaine in the right and left lateral pterygoid muscles and manipulated her mandible. As a result the range of mandibular motion increased to 40 mm. On (date) the patient came with less headaches in frequency and severity. We continued the same non-surgical treatment. The patient reported on (date) an improvement in symptoms and an increase in the range of motion to 50 mm vertical, 6 mm to the right, and 7 mm to the left (still restricted laterally).

I am planning to continue the same muscle manipulation as well as non-surgical techniques to help this lady. I will be more than happy to provide you with further progress.

Thank you, and please don't hesitate to contact me for any questions you may have.

Sincerely,
Signature

Comments on Report 4. In this case, the practitioner treated a case which had been referred for surgical intervention by non-surgical manipulative methods. This report explained the patient's condition, her response to treatment, and gave a short future treatment plan. It is a good interim report.

§ 8.6 Case Report 5

Attorney's Name Date
Address

Re: Patient

Dear Attorney:

As you are well aware the above named patient is under my care for the treatment of anterior disc displacement, myofacial pain dysfunction, and ligament laxity of her temporomandibular joint.

The patient was suffering the above mentioned diagnosis due to an alleged auto accident on (date). The recommended treatment was progressing significantly and the last time I saw her was on (date). The patient complained of no headaches at this time. She complained of jaw pain when performing her work as a (job description). This jaw pain limits her performance and sometimes she is unable to perform her job. The jaw pain also increases when stressed.

Clinical examination revealed:

Mandibular range of motion: 65 mm vertical opening (hyperextension), 10 mm to the right, and 8 mm to the left (slightly restricted).
Muscle palpation elicited pain and discomfort in the following muscles: right and left anterior, medial, and posterior Temporalis; right and left deep and superficial Masseters; right and left Lateral Pterygoids; right and left Trapezius; and right and left Paracervicals.

TMJ auscultation and examination revealed: Popping and laxity in the temporomandibular joints bilaterally which increased when the splint is removed out of the mouth.

The patient was released with instructions to return to the office when needed. The patient was also given instructions to be careful when chewing hard food, getting involved in any vigorous oral activities in which her mandible has to move excessively.

At this time the patient has reached maximum medical improvement with a permanent impairment rating of 5% of the body as a whole (2% motor dysfunction and 3% sensory dysfunction). This impairment rating is based on the American Medical Association Guidelines for Permanent Impairment and modified according to my experience with similar cases. Surgery in forms of disc plication is possible, however, there is no need for it at the present time. The patient has to be continuously monitored.

Thank you, and please don't hesitate to contact me if you have any questions.

Sincerely,
Signature

Comments on Report 5. This is a final report which explained the patient's condition in the last visit following a significant improvement. It contains good explanation of the clinical findings and instructions to the patient at the time of release. Future care was only vaguely explained. Permanent impairment was mentioned without detail.

§ 8.7 Case Report 6

Attorney's Name Date
Address

Re: Independent medical examination
Patient Name
Claim #
Date of accident
Date of examination

Dear Attorney:

As you requested on (date) I did an I.M.E. on the above named individual. I also reviewed his x-rays, video, and records which you sent. He also completed a TMJ scale which is enclosed. He was a pleasant individual that appeared to give straightforward answers.

On (date) the patient was rear ended in an MVA. When the cars collided he was looking out his outside rear view mirror with his elbow leaning on the window.

Upon impact his neck turned hyperextended backwards.

Immediately, his neck and elbow were sore and he went to his chiropractor, (doctor's name). He administered physical therapy for five months and then on (date) referred him to (doctor's name), another chiropractor for a second opinion. He referred the patient to (doctor's name), a radiologist, for a cervical MRI exam. (Doctor's name) reported that there was pathology at the level of discs C5, C6, and a small anterior herniation and C6 and C7.

Two or three months later on (date), (doctor's name) referred him to (doctor's name), a dentist, for an occlusal splint to relieve symptoms created by the herniated disc (tingling fingers). The splint apparently gave some relief.

On (date) approximately eight months after the accident, (doctor's name) began seeing the patient. Apparently, the patient felt that it was too far to travel to (location). (Doctor's name) and his partner (doctor's name) made him an upper right temporary bridge to enable them to make a splint, and in the future plan to make him a new splint because three weeks ago, the patient developed frontal headaches and pressure behind his left eye. Following this, they plan to stabilize this jaw with ($) worth of crowns.

His chief complaints today in the order of severity were:

(1) Pain around and behind the eyes
(2) Sore left neck
(3) Numb and sore right leg whenever he drives more than three or four hours
(4) Uncomfortable when sleeping

Significantly medical history includes a skiing accident when he was younger which resulted in dental injuries. An excision of fibrous nodule in the area of the back of the neck on (date), earaches prior to the accident, a motorcycle accident on (date), a job related accident on (date) where an object hit the top of his head and left jaw and neck and another accident on (date) where he injured his right hip and knee.

My examination reveals no numbness, tingling, or facial muscle tenderness. His range of jaw opening is normal (51 mm) and he can move his jaw to the left 14 mm and to the right 16 mm and thrust his jaw 5 mm without pain. This means that his jaw functions normally and is consistent with measurements by (doctor's name).

My orthopantomograph x-rays showed no temporomandibular joint pathology nor did (doctor's name) tomograms.

On auscultation, there were no sounds in either joint other than very mild crepitus which is not abnormal for a man his age. (Doctor's name), on the other hand, heard clicks and pops. It should be noted, that over 50% of our population has some clicking, and it alone is not an indication for treatment.

His temporomandibular joints and masticatory muscles were not tender to palpation and he did not complain of temporomandibular joint pain. This is consistent with the history records of (doctor's name), i.e., no TMJ symptoms were mentioned. (Doctor's name) history form indicated that he had a neck problem only. In addition, (doctor's name) pain drawing chart indicated no TMJ pain.

Dental casts indicate that he has a narrow maxillary arch with malocclusion. There is evidence of a new temporary right maxillary bridge. (Doctor's name) justified this new bridge by stating that it was necessary to stabilize an occlusal splint. I disagree with this because there are ample teeth to have good splint stabilization.

My diagnosis is a normal temporomandibular joint without significant pathology except for the faint crepitus. This differs from (doctor's name) diagnosis where he suggests the possibility of internal derangement and permanent injury to the joint. There was no evidence, including his video, that justifies his diagnosis. (Doctor's name) referred the patient to a dentist because the patient had tingling fingers, not TMJ disease.

The use of splints to treat this condition is not supported by the scientific community. Even (doctor's name) mentioned in his letter to (doctor's name) that "only one or two in the entire country would have referred this patient" for splint therapy.

I don't believe that there is permanent damage to his TMJ's, and therefore crowns to establish a new occlusion is inappropriate. Any change in occlusion will ultimately settle back anyway because of muscle forces.

His past medical history indicates other possible causes for his disc injury and the tingling besides the MVA of (date). I believe he did sustain a cervical whiplash injury and it is possible that he had a mild strain in his temporomandibular joint ligaments. When (doctor's name) videotaped his examination there was no indication of temporomandibular joint problems.

(Doctor's name) diagnosis of an impaired circulation of the superior temporal artery is questionable and could be investigated with Doppler studies. The sonogram that (doctor's name) took on (date) revealed some crepitus, however, it is unlikely that the accident caused it because there were no other symptoms.

Regarding future treatment, I disagree that there is a need for constructing the right maxillary bridge. Further, there is no indication for any phase II treatment for jaw stabilization.

This case might be reviewed by the State Board of Dental Examiners or the Pain Clinic at the University of (state name) Dental School because it is questionable whether the treatment plan is suspicious. It may be simply a lack of knowledge, or it may be fraud because there is no scientific body that I am aware of, or literature that supports the use of splints for cervical nerve root irritation.

The idea to change his bite to stop tingling and headaches with thousands of dollars worth of crowns is ridiculous. There are millions of people without teeth with overclosed bites, that don't have headaches or tingling fingers. To conclude that an unusual jaw position cause these symptoms is without foundation.

I don't think the patient sustained permanent injury to his temporomandibular joints. Since the first day of the accident until today he never had any dysfunction. The jaw opens normally and he has never complained to anyone about joint discomfort. I do believe, however, that the patient still needs physical therapy for his sore neck and hopefully his irritated cervical nerves will eventually calm down.

Thus, the MVA of the patient did not cause direct damage to his TMJ's and no insurance should exist to cover reconstructive dentistry.

Further, the bio-electronic instrumentation applied by (doctor's name) was medically unnecessary and not supported by the scientific literature which concludes that it lacks the sensitivity and specificity for diagnosis or treatment of TMJ disorders. For further information please call or write me.

Sincerely,
Signature

Comments on Report 6. This patient seems to be shopping for a different practitioner who will help increase the value of his case. The examiner defamed other colleagues: a better way to handle disagreement with treatment is to state the treatment given is not consistent with the guidelines set for treatment of this disorder or that this examiner would recommend a different approach or alternative modality. He also left himself open to a lot of attacks as he might be impeached due to opinion on the relation between the cervical problems and the bite. He wrote wrong information because these signs and symptoms indicate an abnormal rather than normal temporomandibular joint. The issue in this case is not the TMJ disorder but the causation. Based on the information given here, the TMJ disorder seems pre-existing and was aggravated in the accident.

He mentioned that 50 percent of the population has some clicking without listing a reference. He mentioned that any change in occlusion was restored properly but then he stated that phase II occlusal stabilization is not indicated, which is not correct. He misinformed the attorney about the relation between the neck (posture) and the bite. He mentioned no permanent impairment while acknowledging previous injuries to the neck and TMJ.

The examiner seemed to be seeking more business from the law firm by denying the existence of the disorder. This actually hurt the case and can be a ground to attack his credibility at trial.

§ 8.8 Case Report 7

Insurance Adjustor's Name Date
Address

Re: Patient

Dear Adjustor:

I have examined the above named individual on (date) in (location) and reviewed the provided records on the same day. Her examination took 65 minutes during which she was coughing excessively due to her smoking habit.

The patient is a 69 year old white female who presented the following chief complaints:

Jaw pain on the right side.
Neckache on the right side.
Left eye pain.
Soreness behind her right ear and at the base of the skull on the right side.
Backaches.

The patient claimed to have none of these symptoms before an alleged auto accident on (date). She was a passenger in the back seat of an automobile driven by her son. She claimed to have the seat belt on and was rear ended. Her body was moved upward, her head hit the roof of the automobile and was rolled over to the right side. She felt head and back pain. She felt neck swelling on the right side. She went to (name of the hospital) where she was examined, had x-ray films taken, and hospitalized for a two-day observation. She was released then and a given a cervical collar and a prescription of Darvocet medication for the pain. She was seen by (doctor's name) at the hospital and for neurosurgical follow ups. She also went to (doctor's name) for physical therapy and was referred to (doctor's name) for T.M.J. disorder treatment. The doctor examined the patient, took x-ray films, and fabricated a mouth piece. She also had physical therapy for the T.M.J. area. She said that the treatment gave her a lot of relief and she will be evaluated on (date) by (doctor's name). These days she is using the mouth piece only at night.

Past medical history revealed the following:

The patient had thumb surgery on (date).

The patient takes Synthroid medications for the hypothyroidism for a long time. She uses Motrin for headaches since the (date) accident. She also admitted to the use of Motrin for headaches before the (date) accident.

History of tonsilectomy in her childhood, two vaginal deliveries, thyroidectomy about (date), and dental extractions, and foot surgery.

The patient's diet consists of cheese sandwich for lunch, chicken soup, potato, spaghetti, or steak with gravy for dinner. She claimed to seldom eat breakfast due to loss of appetite.

The patient drinks coffee in the morning, no alcohol, no beer, a lot of water, and juice.

The patient admitted to the dental neglect. She did not have a dentist and last time she has seen a dentist was for extractions (# of years ago).

She also admitted to clenching and grinding her teeth for a long time, and snoring.

Hysterectomy (# of years ago).

Socially: The patient is married to the same husband for (# of years).

Occupation: The patient works (location). She does (job description) and other activities.

Habits: The patient is a smoker (10 cigarettes a day).

Clinical examination revealed the following:

Left Temporalis muscles
Left Masseter muscles
Right Diagnostic muscles
Right Suboccipital area

Posture evaluation:

Elevated left shoulder
Head tilt to the left
Mild forward head posture

In conclusion, and based on the history given to me by the patient, clinical examination, and review of the provided records I can see a pre-existing condition of T.M.J. disorders (signs and symptoms). However, it seemed that the (date) accident may have aggravated it slightly. It is also important to mention that this aggravation was treated and the patient has no or minimal residuals.

Thank you, and please don't hesitate to contact me if you have any questions.

Sincerely,
Signature

Comments on Report 7. This report shows good history taking and a good clinical examination with an honest conclusion.

§ 8.9 Case Report 8

Attorney's Name Date
Address

Re: Patient

Dear Attorney:

As per your request, this is a preliminary report for your client and my patient (patient's name) medical condition.

I have seen the patient in my office on (date). The patient came with chief complaints of:

(1) Headaches of dull continuous nature
(2) Inability to open mouth wide
(3) Swelling on the left side of the jaw
(4) Jaw pain
(5) Inability to chew food
(6) Neckaches
(7) Shoulder pain
(8) Depression
(9) Back pain

The patient stated that his neckaches started on the second day after an automobile accident he sustained on (date). This neck pain was so severe that he could not move his neck. He further stated that his headaches started the second month after the accident and his jaw pain and swelling came one month later.

As you are well aware the patient has been seen by (doctor's name), Neurologist, (doctor's name), Orthopedist, (doctor's name), Otolaryngologist, (doctor's name), Chiropractor, (doctor's name), Dentist/TMJ, (doctor's name), Oral Surgeon, and (doctor's name), Physical Therapist. The patient came to my office with a T.E.N.S. unit attached to his shoulders and back. He claimed that he was in severe pain.

Clinical examination revealed:

Muscle palpation of the following muscles elicited pain:

Right and left Temporalis muscles x3
Right and left Masseter muscles x3
Right and left Sternocleidomastoid muscles x3
Right and left Trapezius muscles x3
Right and left Paracervical muscles x3
Right and left Lateral Pterygoid muscles x3
Right and left Scaleni muscles x3
Right and left Infraspinatus muscles x3
(0=no pain, 1=mild pain, 2=moderate pain, 3=severe pain)

Range of mandibular motion: 38 mm vertical, 10 mm to the right, and 8 mm to the left.
TMJ auscultation: Reciprocal click on the left side.
Pattern of mandibular motion: Opening with deviation to the right and then to the left side.
Dental occlusion examination:
Anterior deep bite.
Anterior overbite 4 mm.
Anterior overjet 1 mm.
Missing teeth #3, 4, 18, 32 with a bridge replacing teeth #3 and 4.
Right excursion interference of teeth #2 with #31 and #6 with #27, and left excursion showed canine guidance.
Wear facets in teeth #7, 8, 9, 10, 11, 21, 22, 23, 24, 25, 26, 27, and 28.

Radiographic evaluation:

Panoramic views: asymmetrical condyles, asymmetrical rami, accentuation of left antigonial angle, and irregular mandibular angle bone surface (left).
Tomographic views: bilateral steep posterior slope of the articular eminence.
Other tests: stretch and spray reduced pain and trigger point injections eliminated pain.

Cause relation of the injury to the accident: Cervical muscle spasms and pain were felt by the patient on the second day after the accident. Muscle spasms of the neck caused postural changes with anterior head position. This put too much pressure on the hyoid bone which in turn put pressure on the mandible and caused its retruder position. This is reasonable to happen in two to six months.

When the mandible is in a retruder position it is most likely that the mandibular condyles move or displace the articulating discs anteriorly and causing both muscle spasms as well as internal derangements of the joints. Furthermore, the steep slope of the posterior surfaces of the articulating eminences is causing a great difficulty in repositioning the mandibular condyle and disc assemblies.

References

1. Bell, W.E. Clinical Management of Temporomandibular Disorders (Chicago: Year Book Medical Publishers, 1982), pp. 53 and 66.
2. Mannheimer, J.S. and Gerald, N.L. Clinical Transcutaneous Electrical Nerve Stimulation (Philadelphia: F.A. Davis, 1986), pp. 138—139.
3. Okeson, J.P. Fundamentals of Occlusal and Temporomandibular Disorders (St. Louis: C.V. Mosby, 1985), p. 115.

Initial Diagnosis:

Bilateral anterior disc displacement with reduction.
Myofacial pain dysfunction.
Cervicalgia.
Cephalgia.

Recommendations:

Intensive physical therapy in forms of vapocoolant, trigger point injections, electromedicine, manipulations, etc.
Mandibular orthopedic repositioning appliance.
Maxillary orthopedic repositioning appliance.
Continue orthopedic observations.
Others when necessary.

Conclusion: Based on the information given to me by the patient, clinical, and radiographic evaluation, it is reasonable to say that the chief complaints of the patient are consistent with an injury caused by a whiplash, hyperextension and hyperflexion trauma.

Thank you, and please let me know if I could be of further assistance.

Sincerely,
Signature
cc: Patient

Comments on Report 8. This report has good causation of injury to accident. It is a detailed explanation of the patient's history, clinical examination, radiographic interpretation, diagnostic impression, and treatment plan. References can be particularly useful to support points and provide further explanation. Here the references relate to causation and the delay between the accident and the report of TMJ symptoms.

§ 8.10 Case Report 9

Attorney's Name Date
Address

Re: Patient
Your File #

Dear Attorney:

Craniomandibular examination was performed for the above captioned patient on (date). The patient's history details a chief complaint of severe complicated migraines, the ears feeling plugged-up, catching and popping in the jaws and hyperesthesia of the face coinciding with migraine headaches. She reports pain present in the head, face, ears, left shoulder, there is weakness in the hand and pain in the left leg. She reports increasing severity of the headache approximately six months ago. These above symptoms are noted subsequent to a fall the patient experienced on (date). She reports falling backwards on a slippery tiled floor, hitting her lower spine on a step. She further reports a fracture of the lower spine. When questioned as to the frequency of the symptoms she was not certain. An influencing factor listed is tension. Prior therapies administered are manipulations of the body by (doctor's name), and craniomandibular splint treatment by (doctor's name). Medication taken is amitripetyline, Motrin, Inderal, and Midrin. Regarding (doctor's name) treatment she reports starting lower splint therapy on (date), she feels the splint has improved her symptomatology and has not had the severe migraine headaches that she has suffered prior to initiating splint care. Significant medical history reports this patient to suffer from an ulcer.

Physical examination reveals the following: Auscultation is silent bilaterally. Maximum opening is 30 mm with a soft end point, on a scale of 50 plus or minus 3-4 mm. Lateral translation is right 10 mm and left 5 mm. The mandibular midline is not determinable due to the wearing of an upper and lower complete denture. Palpation reveals a response at the joint capsule bilaterally. No opening deviation is noted. Muscle palpation further reveals hypertonicity bilaterally in the sternocleidomastoid on the left side only in the trapezius. Painful response is noted on the right in the deep belly of the masseter and the left at the insertion of the temporalis. The patient also responds to pain from palpation at the left lip. Joint mobility testing could not be executed. The above palpatory findings and joint mobility testing were accompanied by extreme histrionic behavior. There is absolutely no anatomical basis for the response to left lip palpation. Joint capsule palpation was instituted with extremely minimal pressure and accompanied by dramatic response.

Facial examination reveals a symmetrical face. The lower 1/3 facial height is approximately 2 mm deficient. This is noted in the lower plane of occlusion. The lip form is poor due to this vertical dimension deficiency. The masseteric form is normal. The profile is retrognathic. The facial form is brachyfacial. The dentition is class I with a normal overbite which is non-restrictive. The teeth show normal wear. The mouth appears to be neglected evidenced by the fit of the dentures and the diminished vertical dimension. All teeth are missing and replaced with a complete upper and lower denture as noted above. The patient reports this denture to be approximately twelve years old.

At the time of this examination the patient is wearing a lower heat-cured splint which restores the vertical dimension approximately 3-4 mm. With the splint in place the vertical dimension is slightly excessive. It is a flat, stable heat-cured splint. At this time the patient does not report any further therapy indicated by (doctor's name). She has been advised to continue to wear the splint.

Transcranial radiographic examination reveals a concentric position of the condyle in the fossa in maximum intercuspation. Cortical detail of articular components is well defined. With the splint in place condylar movement does not occur. In repose the condyle postures slightly anteriorly in the fossa. The left joint reveals a concentric location of the condyle in the fossa. In repose the condyle postures slightly anteriorly in the fossa. With the splint in place condylar position remains the same as in maximum intercuspation. The angle of the eminence is steep bilaterally with a noted convexity on the distal slope. Cortical detail of articular components is good bilaterally.

Clinical impression by patient response is a bilateral capsulitis and myalgia. The histrionic behavior of the patient during the examination lends considerable question to the validity of this aspect of the examination. Although the patient reports popping and catching in the jaw joints this could not be demonstrated at the time of my examination. Opening is limited but accompanied a noticeable soft end point. At the time of this examination the patient did not appear entirely cogent to me. Although this is a subjective evaluation the patient appeared to me to be under the influence of pharmacological agents. Due to my physical findings and the character of the patient's behavior, I do not feel there is a permanent injury present.

If I can be of any further assistance, please do not hesitate to advise me.

Sincerely,
Signature

Comments on Report 9. The examiner gave a good history, good clinical examination, and an adequate interpretation of the transcranial radiograph. He left himself open to attack by stating the patient appeared to be under the influence of pharmacological agents. He also based the existence of permanent impairment on the patient's behavior rather than on objective signs.

§ 8.11 Case Report 10

Attorney's Name Date
Address

Re: Patient

Dear Attorney:

The above mentioned patient is a (age) year old white female who came to my office on (date) with the following chief complaints:

(1) Severe headaches which exist all the time. She takes aspirin all the time. These headaches involve the entire head.
(2) Dizziness and sometimes fainting.
(3) Jaw pain when eating, talking, or using the phone
(4) She felt soreness under her jaw

The patient denied any symptoms of this nature before the accident of (date). She was a driver with a seat belt on and was hit from the passenger side by another automobile. She went to the right, her chin hit the dashboard, and had a cut on her right lip. She also had a bruise on the right side of her chin. The patient went to the emergency room of the hospital where she was x-rayed and released. She has been seen by a chiropractor (doctor's name), a neurologist (doctor's name), and a dentist for TMJ therapy (doctor's name). The patient found that she did not have any relief.

Past medical history: Non-contributing.
Past dental history: History of orthodontic treatment.

In addition, the patient complained of frequent headaches on the right and left side of her head, soreness of the T.M.Joint areas on the right and left side, limited jaw opening, jaw locks open, bad sinus allergies, pain ringing and fullness in the right ear, difficulty swallowing and lower back pain.

Clinical examination on (date) revealed:

Face:

Higher left eye level.
Chin deviated to the right.
Right cheek bone was flatter.
Left ear with higher level.

Occlusion:

4 mm overbite.
0 mm overjet.
Missing teeth #1, 5, 12, 16, 17, 21, 28, and 32.
Group function on the right and left side.

Mandibular range of motion: 27 mm vertical, 7 mm to the right, and 7 mm to the left.
Muscle palpation elicited pain and tenderness in the following muscles:

Right and left Temporalis.
Right and left Masseters.
Right and left Lateral Pterygoids.
Right and left Medial Pterygoids.
Right and left S.C.M.'s.
Right and left Trapezius.
Right and left Posterior Cervicals.
Right and left Splenius Capitus.
Suboccipital areas.

TMJ findings:

Mandible deviates to right when opening.
Tenderness in the T.M.Joint.
Palpation on the right and left.
Slight clicking, opening and closing on the left side.

Posture evaluation:

Mild forward head posture.
Head tilt the left.
Left shoulder with higher level.

Vapocoolant test: Decreased pain.
Radiographic examination revealed:

Asymmetrical mandibular condyles.
Slight right condyle with osteoarthritic changes.
Left condyles with osteoarthritic changes.
Severe left condyle posterior displacement.
Hypoplasia of the right condyle.

Magnetic resonance imaging (MRI): The patient was sent to (location) department of imaging for bilateral sagittal MRI of the T.M.Joints. The result which was concluded by (doctor's name) was fixed bilateral closed lock. This means that the patient is suffering from anteriorly displaced T.M.Joint discs without reduction.

Diagnostic impressions:

Bilateral anterior disc displacement without reduction.
Myofacial pain dysfunction.
Trauma to T.M.Joint.

Recommendations:

Continue medical supervision.
Mandibular orthopedic repositioning appliances.
Physical medicine to facial musculatory musculatures.
Oral maxillofacial surgery consultation for possible arthroscopic surgery.
Others when needed.

Prognosis: Guarded

The planned treatment was delivered in a timely manner and the patient showed significant improvement concerning the pain aspect of her problem. The mandibular range of motion is not improving and the manipulative therapy to unlock the locked jaws was not successful. Therefore, arthroscopic surgery was recommended to recapture the displaced disc. The patient did not prefer at this time to pursue a surgical consult or any kind of surgical intervention. Therefore, I will continue treating her with non-surgical, conventional method in order to further reduce the pain. This treatment should be concluded within a few weeks. The patient will be released with instructions to return to the office as needed.

Permanent impairment rating: It is my opinion that the permanent impairment rating for this condition would be 8% of the whole body. This rating is based on a 3% sensory dysfunction in forms of facial pains and headaches, and 5% motor dysfunctions in forms of limitation of chewing, talking, and mandibular movement. It should be understood that this rating is based on non-surgical treatment, if there is a need for surgical intervention this rating will definitely be altered.

The patient was instructed to limit her eating to semi-solid food, avoid hard foods, avoid excessive talking, avoid excessive activities with her mandible. Due to the fact that she has a fixed closed lock bilaterally which was documented by the MRI study, there is a probable chance of the need for surgical intervention.

Thank you, and please don't hesitate to contact me for any questions you might have.

Sincerely,
Signature

Comments on Report 10. This is a detailed final report giving a good explanation of the chief complaints, an inadequate medical history, but excellent clinical examination supported by a thorough interpretation of MRI and radiographs. The diagnosis and treatment plans were carefully explained. It should have included a projected cost of future care.

§ 8.12 Case Report 11

Attorney's Name Date
Address

Re: Patient

Dear Attorney:

The above mentioned patient is a (age) year old white female who came to my office on (date) with the following chief complaints:

(1) Facial and headaches, mostly on the right side.
(2) Neck and shoulder pain.

In addition to the above mentioned complaints, the patient complained of:

(1) Right and left frequent headaches.
(2) Right and left facial pain.
(3) Right and left soreness in the TMJ area.
(4) Right and left clicking and grating sound in the TMJ area.
(5) Limited jaw opening.
(6) Stiffness in the neck.
(7) Right and left restricted neck movement.
(8) Right and left fullness in the ear.
(9) Right and left pain behind the eyes.
(10) Right side visual disturbances.

(11) Right and left shoulder pain.
(12) Right and left upper back pain.

The patient denied any of the above named symptoms before the alleged accident of (date). Patient was the passenger in a vehicle driven by her husband with her seat belt on. Their car was rear ended by another driver. During the accident, her head moved forward and backward. Two hours later she started experiencing symptoms. The next morning the patient was not able to move her head and that morning she went to (doctor's name), a chiropractic physician in the (location). In addition to the chiropractic physician, the patient also went to (doctor's name), a neurologist and (doctor's name), an orthopedic surgeon. All three of these recommended seeing a TMJ practitioner.

Past medical history:

Over the counter medication to help sleeping (Sominex).
No previous accidents.
No recent surgery.
Previous surgeries: appendix, and tubal ligation.

Medical examination revealed:

Face:
Higher level of right eye.
Asymmetrical face—Chin slightly deviated to the right.

Occlusion:

2 mm midline shift to the left.
5 mm overbite.
Closed anterior bite.
Crowded lower anterior teeth.
Upper anterior teeth with worn facets.
Fine vertical cracks.

Range of motion:

56 mm vertical.
8 mm to the right.
8 mm to the left.

Muscle palpation revealed pain and discomfort in the following muscles:

Right and left Temporalis.
Right and left Masseter with a trigger point on the left.

Left Lateral Pterygoid.
Right and left Sternocleidomastoid.
Right and left Posterior Cervicals with a trigger point on the left.
Left Suboccipital area.

TMJ findings: Bilateral reciprocal click.
Cervical evaluation:

Mild forward head posture.
Mild tilt of the head to the left.
Right shoulder slightly higher.

Radiographic findings:

Panoramic view showed asymmetrical mandibular rami and condyles and elongated calcified stylohyoid ligaments on the left side.
Submental vertex views showed asymmetrical condylar form.
Tomographic view showed right condyle posterior surface flattening right displaced mandibular condyle.

Sonography: Abnormal bilateral joint sounds.
Kinesiography: Abnormal mandibular movement in three dimensions.
Diagnostic impressions:

Anterior disc displacement.
Myofacial pain dysfunction.
Trauma to mandible.
Dyskinesia.

Recommendations:

Medical supervision (neurological, orthopedic, internal medical evaluation).
Continue gentle non-traumatic manipulating therapy.
Mandibular repositioning appliance.
Physical medicine to the OSGS.

Prognosis: Guarded.

Thank you, and please don't hesitate to contact me with any questions you might have.

Sincerely,
Signature

Comments on Report 11. This report has a good explanation of clinical examination; however it is lacking causal relation of the injury to the accident.

CHAPTER 9

THE LEGAL CASE

§ 9.1 Initial Claimant Interview

TMJ-OSGS injury may be suspected in cases of a direct blow to the mandible, mouth, head, or neck, if accompanied by the pertinent symptoms, although it is also possible for an indirect trauma to be named as the cause. Because of the answers given during the initial interview with the claimant, the attorney for the plaintiff may with the help of a TMJ practitioner form an opinion as to the validity of the injury or may decide that the client is a malingerer.

Malingering is the intentional production of false or grossly exaggerated physical or psychological symptoms, motivated by external incentives, such as gain of financial compensation, avoidance of work, and gaining sympathy. The number of TMJ-OSGS cases generated by malingerers is myriad and often successfully litigated. These items characterize a typical malingerer:

1. Marked inconsistency between the symptoms and signs claimed by the client and his actual condition—client complains of severe pain in his jaw but is loquacious during the deposition or is observed by surveillance personnel/equipment to feel no discomfort while eating.
2. Client refuses to cooperate during diagnosis and treatment—refuses radiographic evaluation, refuses to wear the splint, will not show up for scheduled medical appointments.
3. Unusual reaction to examination or treatment procedure—the client claims that muscle palpation caused severe pain, client claims that the use of the splint is painful and/or inconvenient.

The attorney should then refer the client to a TMJ practitioner familiar to counsel for confirmation or contradiction. This referral may arise from concern for the health and well-being of the client and/or the financial outcome of the case. While the author believes there are many attorneys who are motivated by humanitarian reasons, he believes most referrals stem from a financial base.

An attorney should not refer indiscriminantly. He should be wary of unusual complaints and consult with a TMJ practitioner when in doubt of the validity of a claim. A practitioner who may be motivated in the same manner as the unscrupulous attorney may cause harm to the client as well as the case. It is vitally important that a lawyer knows that what is good for the case may not be good for the client—many treatment courses could be focused non-surgically when, in fact, a greedy practitioner performed surgery. By the same token, no attorney should accept a case generated by malingering because of the cost to reputation and finances.

In the course of the author's practice, he has found it inconvenient for persons other than the examiner, the dental assistant, and the patient to be present during the clinical examination. The author has conducted examinations in which the attorneys, paralegals, court reporters, spouses, parents, and video technicians were present. He feels that a large audience influences the patient as well as the examination. For instance, the presence of a court reporter can be fatal to the case should be courtroom testimony of the plaintiff differ from the transcript of the clinical examination.

After an initial referral pointing to a valid TMJ claim, the attorney should request copies of all medical and dental records, models of teeth, photo- and radiographs, magnetic resonance imaging films, and the reports attached to them for the last five years. A detailed narrative report from treating doctors is useful in determining the extent of injury while pre-accident medical and dental records are essential in the evaluation of any preexisting condition of the client. The defense should request the same items, and neither side should skimp on the expense involved in obtaining these records. Every detail counts.

§ 9.2 Initial Case Preparation

A thorough reading of the records can assist the attorney for the plaintiff in the establishment of signs and symptoms; causal relation of the injury to the accident; whether the tests administered were valid and whether they prove damage; validity of the provided treatment; and the monetary value of permanent impairment and the future treatment. These points are usually determined by the physician or dentist of record, and corroborated via a second opinion.

Attorneys for the defense evaluate the records for

1. All factors that may possibly cause TMJ-OSGS disorders before and after the accident such as other accidents, other traumas, medications, iatrogenic factors, and so forth.
2. Whether all injuries relate to the accident being litigated.
3. The possible invalidity of the diagnostic modalities used, e.g., transcranial radiographic views alone cannot prove disc displacement, clinical examination alone cannot prove internal derangement, tests in which standard operating procedures are not followed, and false positive results of some diagnostic tests.
4. Adequacy of the treatment provided.
5. Minimal or no permanent impairment.

The report of the independent medical/dental consultant/examiner (IME) should be thoroughly analyzed and evaluated by both sides. In many cases, rejection of the case, settlement, mediation, or arbitration may be reached at this point.

If the decision is made to proceed to deposition or trial by jury, the advocate must prepare a strong defense of his position, whether plaintiff or defendant; this includes an effective examination of the expert(s) and a case construction that is convincing to the jury.

During the deposition, the advocate for the plaintiff must query the client in the manner described in the Initial Case Evaluation section. He must also qualify his expert witness and attempt to discredit or impeach the testimony of the IME. Obviously, the opposing attorney wishes to establish just the opposite.

There are problems inherent in trial by jury. Jurors often do not understand the subject of TMJ-OSGS. A competent attorney can forestall this by calling on his expert witness to provide anatomical models, demonstration charts, illustrations, or projector slides to facilitate the jurors' knowledge and thereby help them to arrive at a fair decision. The expert witness may also aid in the preparation of opening and closing statements to the jury and the line of questioning to be directed at the opposing counsel's expert witness.

§ 9.3 Postlitigation Treatment

Most cases are not so complex that they require the services of a vocational rehabilitation consultant to determine the economic damages that will finance future treatment. A simple report compiled by the practitioner of record may be sufficient to outline the postlitigation courses(s) of medical/dental care. In some instances, the patient may need continuous physical therapy to the face and jaw, dental office visits, and appliance adjustment (a new appliance may be needed every two to three years) to reduce periodic exacerbation of the TMJ-OSGS disorder. Outpatient care in the home using hot and cold packs, message therapy, and transcutaneous electrical neural stimulation may also be adequate.

A large number of patients involved in lawsuits discontinue treatment after settlement of the suit or when the patient realizes that he must pay future medical fees out of pocket. Other cases require lengthy and expensive postlitigation treatment plans and unfortunately not all lawsuits are settled for fair financial rewards.

§ 9.4 Expert Witness

The most important factor in case preparation and success could well be the selection of a good expert witness. The expertise of such a consultant is helpful in the following areas:

1. Case review and evaluation. A thorough review of the records of a case is made by the expert witness-consultant and an opinion is rendered as to the viability or importance of the case, the chances for success, and factors that weigh favorably or unfavorably against the case. This may assist the attorney in his decision to accept or reject the case and in his accounting procedures—billable hours, percentage of the potential damage award collectable, etc.
2. Examination of the plaintiff. A physical examination of the plaintiff by the expert witness-practitioner avails the attorney of a postexamination report on the medical condition of the plaintiff. The examining TMJ-OSGS practitioner must be capable of answering the following questions for the attorney:

   What are the diagnostic findings?
   Did patient reach maximum medical improvement?
   Is there any needed further treatment? If so, what is the possible cost?
   Was the injury related to the alleged accident?
   Is past medical history of any significance?
   Is past dental history of any significance?
   Is there any medical impairment? If so, what percentage?

3. Litigation assistance and preparation. An expert witness-consultant may be asked by the attorney to prepare a list of questions for the plaintiff and the opposing expert witness aimed at either proving or disproving the relation of the alleged TMJ-OSGS injury and its residual symptoms to the accident.

4. Consultation. A lawyer may use an expert witness to explain to him particular points of the theory or reports generated by the opposition. These points are often couched in unusual or unfamiliar terms and may intimidate or confuse the counselor. A simple telephone call or note from the expert witness to explain or refute these points is often all that is needed for clarification.
5. Providing knowledge and references. The clinician can provide the attorney with references, articles, demonstration aids, and common knowledge to educate him regarding certain aspects of the personal injury case. For example, in the TMJ-OSGS injury field, books and articles abound and a literature search can be confusing or too time consuming for the lawyer. An expert can supply a concise, brief, complete review, along with a demonstrable reconstruction of the alleged accident and its effects.

§ 9.5 —Selecting an Expert

As TMJ-OSGS conditions are greatly affected by the health of the teeth, qualified dentists provide the best primary health care. A Doctor of Dental Surgery (D.D.S.), Doctor of Dental Medicine (D.M.D.), or their equivalent is the basic requirement. However, a dental degree by itself does not reflect the level of training or expertise in the TMJ-OSGS field. Unfortunately, TMJ training is little or not at all emphasized by schools of dentistry. Degrees obtained in a foreign country does not mean inferior training—it may mean superior training.

Specialty training in fields such as oral-maxillofacial surgery, orthodontics, prosthodontics, periodontics, does not translate necessarily to specialty training in TMJ-OSGS disorders. Extensive postgraduate training in the fields of oral-facial pain and TMJ disorders (at least 600 hours in recognized TMJ educational programs) is preferable. These programs are numerous in the U.S.

In order for dentists in general and TMJ-OSGS experts in particular to keep current, they are required to continually supplement their education. Because of the rapid developments in diagnosis and treatment in this field, the average TMJ-OSGS practitioner should spend at least sixty hours per year in study; more hours would obviously benefit both the therapist and his patients.

A private TMJ-OSGS practitioner who sees twenty to forty patients per day and has a 30 percent trauma case load will make a better expert witness than a university professor who spends 50 percent of his time in administration work or other miscellaneous duties that take him away from hands-on experience with TMJ-OSGS disorders patients. The attorney should select a practitioner who is involved in the day-to-day diagnosis and treatment of TMJ-OSGS cases.

An expert who claims to have proveable, extensive experience in handling TMJ-OSGS disorder cases must have treated at least 250 cases and have devoted at least 50 percent of his work experience to the management of TMJ-OSGS disorders.

The expertise of any practitioner, TMJ-OSGS therapists included, is usually recognized by their peers and colleagues. The lawyers should telephone the city or county dental society, local dentists, chiropractors, or physicians to learn the reputation of the expert in question. The true expert is known in his geographical area and usually has a reputation of fairness and independence. Neutrality is of particular importance; the expert witness should always render an independent opinion based on the information given him by the patient, his own clinical examination, and the confirmation of laboratory tests.

Membership in major TMJ organizations should indicate to the attorney that the dentist is interested in sharing knowledge and participating in the advancement of his field. Several organizations such as the Academy of Craniomandibular Disorders, International College of Craniomandibular Orthopedics, American Academy of Head, Facial, and Neck Pain, TMJ Orthopedics, American Equilibration Society, and the International Association of Orthodontics are among the many respected groups in the TMJ-OSGS field.

Many expert witnesses lecture and conduct seminars on a continuing basis for professional organizations. Often, these experts are more aware of the state of the art in the TMJ-OSGS field and should be solicited first by the attorney. Publications in the field of TMJ-OSGS disorders will increase recognition and thereby the value of the expert as they indicate his participation in the advancement and thorough understanding of his subject.

It is essential that the expert witness be available for questions, comments, or a review of the records of the case, although prominent experts are more difficult to pin down. Cooperation between attorney and expert witness in case preparation and presentation is helpful. A humble, articulate, and logical clinician is far desirable than one who is arrogant and antagonistic.

To summarize, the lawyer must research the field of expert witnesses prior to hiring one. An expert witness, carefully selected, makes a good teammate and sometimes wins the case for the attorney.

§ 9.6 —Dealing with Expert Witnesses

Numerous legal texts discuss this issue; however, the author disagrees with the majority because they are written from the attorney's point of view. This section provides the reader with recommendations based on the author's experience as an expert witness.

Your expert witness.

1. Ask him to testify truthfully. It is unprofessional, unethical, and disrespectful to ask your expert to do otherwise.
2. Educate your expert in the salient aspects of the case. An expert well versed in protocol during the deposition or trial strengthens your case, the value of the expert witness, and reduces the possibility of embarrassment.
3. Educate your expert in his legal rights on the stand, such as whether he must answer certain personal questions such as income, private life, referrals, and so forth.
4. Be available to answer the expert's questions, such as is it permitted to bring charts and models to court?
5. Be prepared to go to trial. Know your case well, understand the sequence of events of the accident, study other opinions, and so forth.
6. Ensure that your expert is the stronger of the two. An advantage is gained from having an expert who has experience in similar cases and has testified as an expert witness both for the defense and the plaintiff.
7. A contract for the expert's compensation should be prepared. An expert with no concern about compensation is more cooperative.
8. Remember, you need your expert's services, attention, time, knowledge, and cooperation.

Opposing expert witnesses.

1. Be professional—a disrespectful attitude may create unnecessary animosity.
2. Discounting the testimony or attempting to discredit the expert altogether should be avoided. Your case will usually be the one to be hurt.
3. Have a working knowledge of the oppposing expert's credentials, background, and style of presentation. Review previous testimony he has given in other litigation.
4. Remember, the expert for opposing counsel is not a part of the lawsuit; treat him as such.

APPENDIXES

A. Sample of Patient's Questionnaire
B. Sample of Clinical Examination
C. Sample of Direct Examination of Plaintiff's Expert by Plaintiff's Lawyer
D. Cross-Examination of Plaintiff's Expert by Defendant's Lawyer
E. Sample of Redirect Examination for Plaintiff's Expert by Plaintiff's Lawyer
F. Sample of Direct Examination of Defendant's Expert by Defendant's Lawyer.
G. Cross-Examination of Defendant's Expert by Plaintiff's Lawyer

APPENDIX A

SAMPLE OF PATIENT'S QUESTIONNAIRE

SECTION I: QUESTIONNAIRE

Date:______________

Name: ____ Age: _____ Date of Birth: _________

Home Address: ________________________________ Phone: ________________________

Business Address: _____________________________ Phone: ________________________

Occupation: _________________________________

Sex: ❒ Male ❒ Female Race: __________ Marital Status: ______________

What are your present specific complaints? List from most to least important.

____

____

____

____

When did you first experience the problem for which you are here for? Date: _____________________

How did you experience these symptoms? (Do you associate this problem with any incidence(s)?)

____

____

In order list all physicians, therapists, or health care providers you have consulted for this problem:

- Emergency Room of ____________________
- Neurologist ____________________
- Physical Therapist ____________________
- Orthopedic ____________________
- Chiropractor ____________________
- Dentist ____________________
- Rheumatologist ____________________
- Others ____________________

Did the symptom(s) start after any particular incidence?

____

____

DENTAL TREATMENT:

Did you have any of the following?

If so give date:

Grinding on teeth: ______________________

Orthodontics: ______________________

Irregular or raised dental filling: ______________________

Oral Surgery: ______________________

General Anesthesia ______________________

Did you have injury to:

❒ Jaw ❒ Neck ❒ Head ❒ Back ❒ Other ______________________

What do you think is the cause of your problem?

____

____

What aspect of your condition concerns you most?

____

____

SECTION II: MEDICAL HISTORY

1) What medications are you presently taking?
(A) ____________ for ____________
(B) ____________ for ____________
(C) ____________ for ____________
(D) ____________ for ____________
(E) ____________ for ____________
(F) ____________ for ____________

2) What medications have you taken in the past?
(A) ____________ for ____________ from ________ to ________
(B) ____________ for ____________ from ________ to ________
(C) ____________ for ____________ from ________ to ________
(D) ____________ for ____________ from ________ to ________

3) Have you had any injuries?
Date: ____________
Date: ____________
Date: ____________

4) Have you had any illnesses?
1. ____________
2. ____________
3. ____________
4. ____________
5. ____________
6. ____________

5) Have you had any surgeries?
If so, with general or local anesthesia and give the date.
1. ____________ Date: ________
2. ____________ Date: ________
3. ____________ Date: ________
4. ____________ Date: ________

6) Have you had any of the following?
1. Dental extractions (pulling of the teeth) Dates: ______ ______ ______
2. Orthodontics (braces) Date: ______ from ______ to ______
3. Grinding of teeth by a dentist Dates: ______ ______ ______
4. Crowns, bridges, or dentures (false teeth) Dates: ______ ______ ______
5. Fractures of the jaw Date: ______
6. Oral surgery Date: ______

7) Do you do any of the following? (Check as many as you do)

- ❐ Read in bed
- ❐ Clench your teeth
- ❐ Chew gum
- ❐ Bite on pencil
- ❐ Bite your nails
- ❐ Cheek biting
- ❐ Sing frequently
- ❐ Yawn frequently
- ❐ Chew ice
- ❐ Speak frequently
- ❐ Phone cradling
- ❐ Carry shoulder bag
- ❐ Lean on your chin or hand
- ❐ Wear high heels
- ❐ Lift heavy objects
- ❐ Play a musical instrument
- ❐ Any other oral activities

8) Diet:

What do you usually eat for breakfast? ______________________________
____

What do you usually eat for lunch?
____
____

What do you usually eat for dinner?
____
____

Do you drink any of the following? (check)

- ❐ Coffee regular or decaf, if so how much? ____________________
- ❐ Tea regular or decaf, if so how much? ____________________
- ❐ Soda regular, decaf, or diet, if so how much? ____________________
- ❐ Juice, if so how much? ____________________
- ❐ Alcohol, if so how much? ____________________

9) Do you smoke? ❐ Yes ❐ No

If yes, how many packs per day? ____________________

10) How many fingers width can you open your mouth? ____________________

11) Touch your head and jaw and write what you feel.
____
____

12) Did you have any of the following?

If so, give date.

1. Cervical traction	❐ Yes	❐ No	__________
2. General anesthesia	❐ Yes	❐ No	__________
3. Trauma to head or neck	❐ Yes	❐ No	__________
4. Oral or facial surgery	❐ Yes	❐ No	__________
5. Chiropractic treatment	❐ Yes	❐ No	__________
6. Osteopathic treatment	❐ Yes	❐ No	__________

13) What kind of sports do (or did) you practice?

1. ____________________ Date: __________
2. ____________________ Date: __________
3. ____________________ Date: __________
4. ____________________ Date: __________

14) Did you participate in any of the following in the last five years? If so, give date.

1. Recreational parks: Date: __________
2. Dancing parties: Date: __________
3. Homecoming events: Date: __________
4. Singing parties: Date: __________

15) For Women:

1. Are you pregnant? ☐ Yes ☐ No
   Expected delivery date: __________
2. Any history of previous miscarriages? ☐ Yes ☐ No
3. Ovulate regularly? ☐ Yes ☐ No
4. Do you menstrate regularly? ☐ Yes ☐ No
5. Have you reached menopause? ☐ Yes ☐ No

List supportive medication taken:

1. ____________________
2. ____________________
3. ____________________

6. Have you had a hysterectomy? ☐ Yes ☐ No
7. Have you been diagnosed as having PMS? ☐ Yes ☐ No
8. Do your nails break easily? ☐ Yes ☐ No
9. Does cold weather bother you? ☐ Yes ☐ No
10. Do you take birth control pills? ☐ Yes ☐ No

INDICATE LOCATIONS OF PAIN ON THE FOLLOWING DRAWINGS.

Please mark on the drawings the exact spot(s) where your pain starts with a solid dot (•). Also mark what type of pain it is (Moderate pain, Severe Pain, Internal, etc.).

• .... Pain
EP .... External Pain
IP .... Internal Pain
MP ...... Moderate Pain
SP .... Severe Pain
› .... Shooting Pain
NN .... Numbness

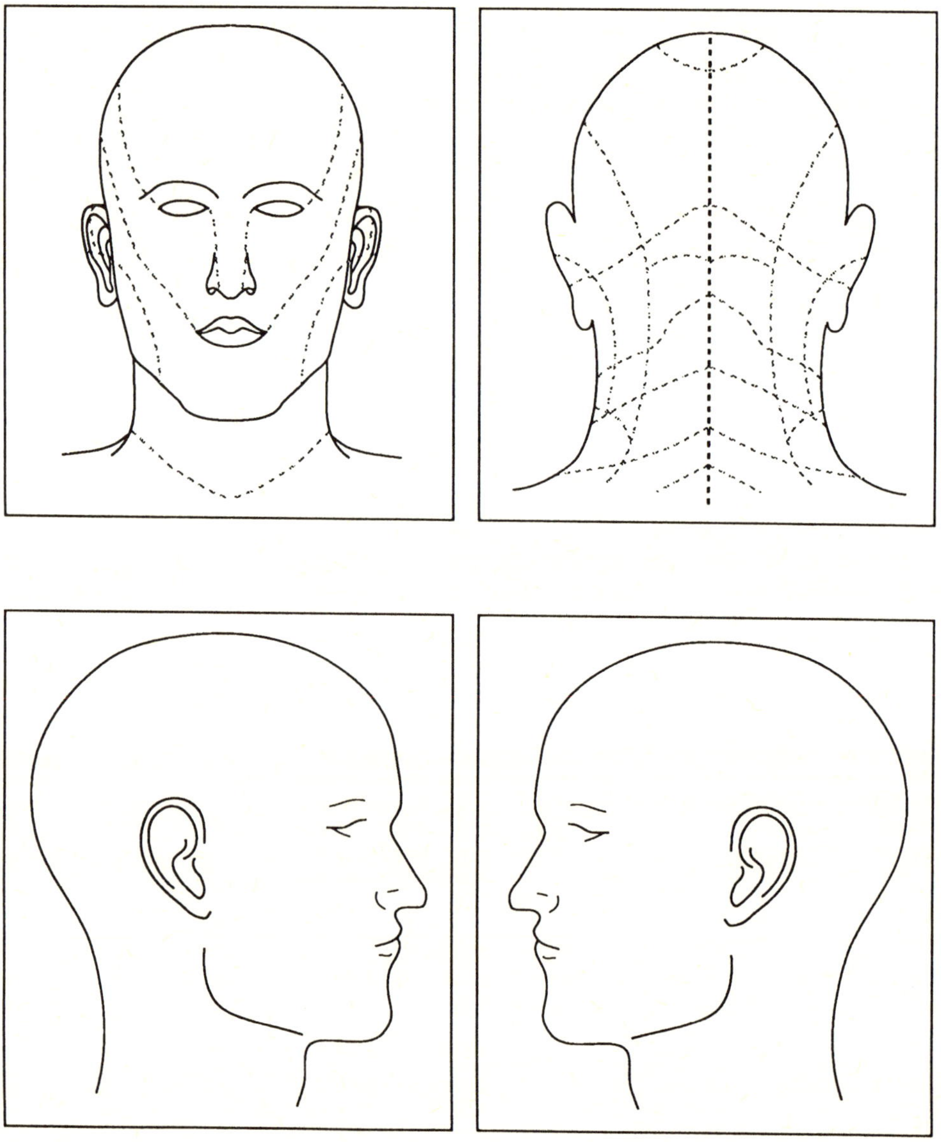

INDICATE LOCATIONS OF PAIN ON THE FOLLOWING DRAWINGS.

Please mark on the drawings the exact spot(s) where your pain starts with a solid dot (•). Also mark what type of pain it is (Moderate pain, Severe Pain, Internal, etc.).

• .... Pain
EP .... External Pain
IP .... Internal Pain
MP ...... Moderate Pain
SP .... Severe Pain
› .... Shooting Pain
NN .... Numbness

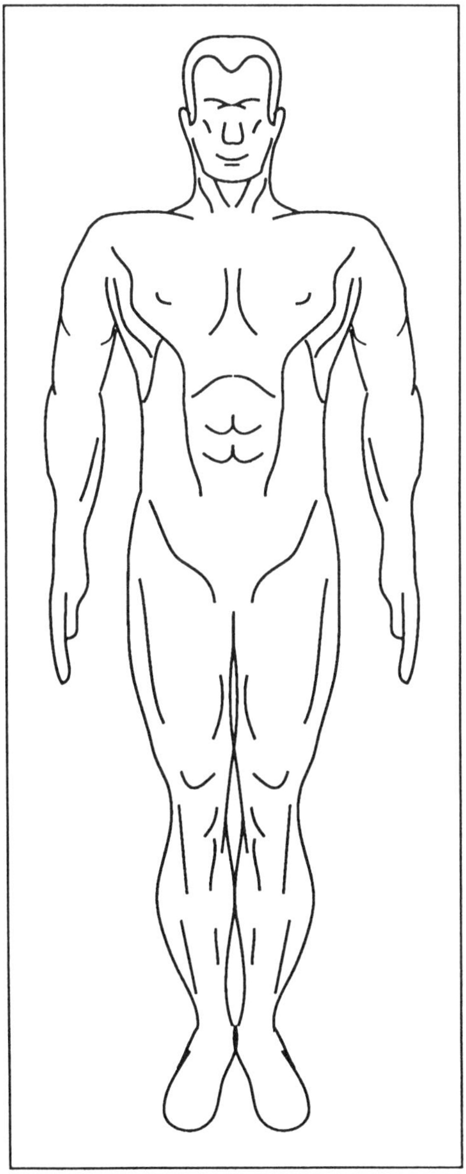

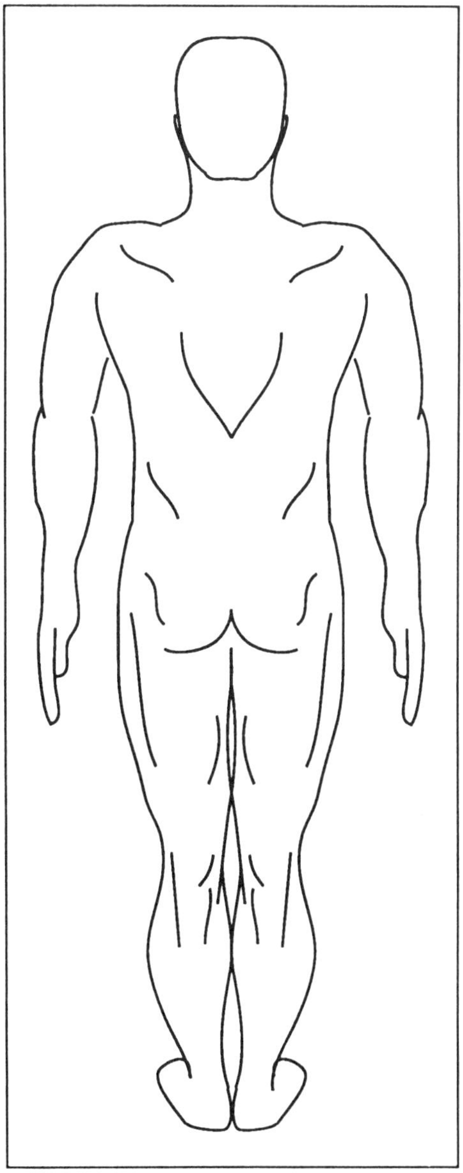

APPENDIX B

SAMPLE OF CLINICAL EXAMINATION

FACE:

Symmetrical	______	Deviated chin to R-L	______
Asymmetrical	______	Elevated R-L eye	______
Retrognathia	______	Deviated nose R-L	______
Shorter lower third	______	Prominent R-L cheekbone	______

OCCLUSION:

Midline shift to L R mm	______	Broken teeth #	______
Overbite mm	______	Interference #	______
Overjet mm	______	Cuspid guidance L R	______
Class I II III L R	______	Group function L R	______
Missing teeth #	______		

RANGE OF MANDIBULAR MOTION:

Active: ______mm vertical, ______mm to right, ______mm to left

Passive: ______mm vertical, ______mm to right, ______mm to left

MUSCLE EXAMINATION — TENDERNESS TO PALPATION:

	Right	Left
Temporalis	______	______
Masseter	______	______
Lateral Pterygoid	______	______
Medial Pterygoid	______	______
Suprahyoids	______	______
Temporalis Insertion	______	______
Sternocleidomastoid	______	______
Trapezius	______	______
Posterior Cervicals	______	______
Splenius Capitus	______	______
Suboccipital area	______	______

TEMPOROMANDIBULAR JOINT FINDINGS:

	Right	Left
Normal function	______	______
Deviation on opening to	______	______
Deviation on closing to	______	______
Tenderness in TMJ on palpation:	______	______
Lateral Wall	______	______
Posterior Wall	______	______
Swelling	______	
Pain on opening/closing	______	______
Crepitation	______	______
Clicking - opening	______	______
Clicking - closing	______	______
______	______	______
______	______	______
______	______	______

POSTURE EVALUATION:

Forward head posture	❒ Mild	❒ Mod	❒ Sev.
Forward shoulders	❒ Mild	❒ Mod	❒ Sev.
Head tilt to	❒ R		❒ L
Shoulder High	❒ R		❒ L
Iliac Crest High	❒ R		❒ L

DECOMPRESSION TEST: ______________________________

VAPOCOOLANT TEST: ______________________________

RADIOGRAPHIC FINDINGS:

Panoramic: ______________________________
Submental vertex: ______________________________
Transcranial: ______________________________
Tomograph: ______________________________

MRI:

____
____
____
____
____
____

DIAGNOSTIC IMPRESSION:

____
____
____
____
____

RECOMMENDATIONS:

____
____
____
____
____
____
____

PROGNOSIS:

____
____
____
____
____
____

APPENDIX C

SAMPLE OF DIRECT EXAMINATION OF PLAINTIFF'S EXPERT BY PLAINTIFF'S LAWYER

Q. Please state your name.
A. My name is Dr. T.M.J.
Q. Doctor, what is you profession?
A. I am a dentist.
Q. How old are you?
A. 40
Q. Doctor, where do you practice?
A. I practice at street, city, state.
Q. Doctor, would you be kind enough to tell us about your professional background?
A. Yes sir. I practice dentistry with an emphasis on diagnosis, prevention, and treatment of oral, facial pain, and TMJ disorders. I graduated from (state university) in (year). I have done one year internship at (dental school), I have earned a master degree in (subject), at (university).
Q. Doctor, do you belong to any professional association?
A. Yes, I do. I belong to the American Dental Association, State Dental Association, Central State Dental Association, County Dental Society, Academy of General Dentistry, American Academy of Head, Neck, Facial Pain, and TMJ Orthopedics, International College of Craniomandibular Orthopedics, International Association of Orthodontics, American Association for Functional Orthodontics.
Q. Doctor, can you tell us how long you have been practicing as a dentist?
A. I have been a dentist for the last seventeen years.

Q. Doctor, do you have a license in the state of (state)?
A. Yes, I do.
Q. Are you licensed to practice in any other state?
A. No
Q. Doctor, do you happen to have any other professional activities you can mention to the jury?
A. Yes, I do.
Q. What are they?
A. I am presently involved in lecturing on the subject of temporomandibular joint disorder and oral facial pain to professionals such as, lawyers, physicians, dentists, and other health care providers.
Q. Doctor, have you been invited to any dental societies or any organizations?
A. Yes, I have.
Q. What are these organizations or societies?
A. The State Dental Society, The County Dental Society, and The County Dental Hygiene Society.
Q. Doctor, what other activities are you involved in?
A. I have written several articles in the field of oral, facial pain and TMJ disorders.
Q. Doctor, can you mention the name of these articles and where can we find them?
A. TMJ Disorders and Overview in the State Dental Journal, Diagnosis and Treatment of TMJ in the National Dental Journal, January 1981.
Q. Doctor, are you an affiliate with any schools, hospitals, or any institutes?
A. Yes, I am. I am affiliated with (dental school) and (city hospital).
Q. Doctor, will you give the jury an estimate of the number of patients you have treated for temporomandibular joint disorder?
A. Yes sir, about a thousand cases.
Q. Doctor, how many of these cases are as a result of traumatic injury?
A. About 400. I don't count, but I can guess that one out of three patients is a traumatic injury individual.
Q. Doctor, where do you get your referrals?
A. I get refferals from physicians, dentists, chiropractors, and other health care providers in the area and nationwide.
Q. Doctor, would you describe what you mean by temporomandibular joint?

A. Temporomandibular joint or T.M.J. is the jaw joint found in front of each ear on the side of the face.

Q. Doctor, what studies have you read concerning the incidence of the temporomandibular joint problems?

A. Several, listed in scientific journals and books.

Q. Doctor, how are the differences between male and female, different age groups in prevalence of temporomandibular joint disease?

A. T.M.J. disorder is predominant in women 3 to 1 or 9 to 1 and can be mostly in people between 20-40. However, you cannot rely totaly on this because we see different ratios in different practices and locations.

Q. Doctor, what are the classic symptoms of TMJ disorder?

A. Jaw pain, jaw clicking when opening and closing, tension, headaches, earaches, inability to open mouth all the way, inability to eat hard food, and many others.

Q. Doctor, how common is a TMJ disorder?

A. T.M.J. disorder is very common.

Q. Doctor, would you please mention the probable causes of TMJ disorder?

A. T.M.J. disorder can be caused by mechanical traumas, emotional traumas, iatrogenic factors, malocclusion. It can be predisposed by systemic, nutritional, or chemical factors.

Q. Doctor, when was the first time you saw the plaintiff?

A. (date)

Q. Doctor, where was that examination held?

A. In my office.

Q. Doctor, how did the plaintiff enter you office?

A. She was referred by Dr. "Orthopedic Surgeon".

Q. Doctor, what was the chief complaint of the "plaintiff"?

A. Jaw pain, jaw clicking, difficulty chewing hard food, and headaches.

Q. Doctor, when did the plaintiff tell you that she first experienced the problems for which she was complaining?

A. (date)

Q. Doctor, did you take a history from this plaintiff?

A. Yes, I did.

Q. Can you tell us why you took a history?

A. History is a very important part of assessment of patient's condition and is an essential part before examining him or her.

Q. What did the history reveal?

A. Chief complaints of jaw pain, jaw clicking, difficulty chewing hard food, and headaches.

Q. What else did the history reveal?

A. The patient denied any of these symptoms before (date) when she was involved in an auto accident and her face hit the steering wheel.

Q. Do you have an opinion if this direct trauma is the cause of her symptoms?

A. Yes, I do.

Q. What is your opinion?

A. This direct trauma can be the cause of Mrs. Plaintiff's symptoms.

Q. Is this opinion within reasonable degree of medical and dental probability?

A. Yes, sir.

Q. What else did you find through the history?

A. The past medical history was unremarkable.

Q. Doctor, what do you mean by unremarkable?

A. Unremarkable means, that none of her past medical history can be related to this accident. There was no history of mechanical trauma. There was no history of previous illness or disease. There was no history of previous surgeries. There was no history of improper dental work.

Q. Did you do any physical examination on the plaintiff at that time?

A. Yes, I did.

Q. What kind of physical examination did you perform?

A. I performed facial analysis, occlusal analysis, range of motion, muscle palpation, decompression test, vapocoolant test.

Q. Doctor, what do you mean by facial analysis?

A. Facial analysis is analysis of the face looking for symmetry or asymmetry, deviations or any descrepancies.

Q. What is the value of this facial analysis?

A. It can indicate the pattern of facial growth and/or deformity in the face.

Q. Did you find deformity in my client's face?

A. Not really.

Q. What did you find?

A. I found some asymmetry. It is slight, but could be due to slight disturbed growth.

Q. What else did you find in your examination?

A. The occlusion seemed normal.

Q. What do you mean by normal occlusion?
A. Occlusion means the bite or the way the teeth mesh together and I did not find any real deviations from normal bite.
Q. You also measured the range of motion.
A. Yes, I did.
Q. What do you mean by range of motion?
A. It is the distance traveled by the lower incisor teeth away from their maximum biting position to the maximum opening position.
Q. How did you measure it?
A. I used a regular millimeter ruler placed between the upper and lower jaws and asked the patient to open wide as much as she could.
Q. And how much was it?
A. It was 38mm. She also moved her jaw 7mm to the right, and 9mm to the left.
Q. Would these measurements be considered normal or abnormal?
A. These are abnormal.
Q. What is normal?
A. 46mm-56mm vertical and 8-12mm to each side and this of course depends on the height and size of the person.
Q. Doctor, did you examine the facial muscles?
A. Yes, I did.
Q. What is your findings?
A. I found several muscles are in spasm.
Q. What are these muscles?
A. The right and left Masseters
The right and left Lateral Pterygoid
The right and left Temporalis
The right and left Medial Pterygoid
The right and left S.C.M.'s
The right and left Suboccipital
Q. Was that all what you did for your examination?
A. No, sir.
Q. So, what else did you do?
A. I examined the T.M.J.'s
Q. How did you do it?
A. I inspected the joint visually, I palpated the joint digitally, and I listened to the joint.
Q. What did you find when you examined the T.M.J.?

A. Visually the skin was with normal appearance, pulpating the joint indicated tenderness an evidence of capsulitis.
Q. What do you mean by capsulitis?
A. Capsulitis is an inflammation in the capsule surrounding the T.M.J..
Q. What else did you find in the T.M.J. exam?
A. I listened to the joint using a stethoscope and found loud distinct noises or snapping on the left side when opening and closing.
Q. What does this indicate?
A. It indicates a displacement of the cartilaginous disc in between the ball and socket of the jaw joint.
Q. Did you do any of the dianostic aids?
A. Yes, I did.
Q. What did you do?
A. I measured the joint sound, took x-rays, measured electrical muscle activities, recorded the mandibular pattern of motion, took impressions of the teeth, and took photographs.
Q. Doctor, what kind of x-rays did you take?
A. I took panoramic x-rays, I took transcranial x-rays and/or tomographic x-rays.
Q. Doctor, what are your findings in those radiographs?
A. Panoramic views were essentially normal. The tomographic views showed backward displaced condyles.
Q. Doctor, did you do electromyography?
A. Yes, I did.
Q. What was your findings?
A. Increased muscle activities.
Q. What does this mean?
A. It means that the muscles are in a state of hyperactivity which may be due to overwork.
Q. Did you take computerized mandibular scan?
A. Yes, I did.
Q. What was your findings?
A. Abnormal irregular pattern of mandibular motion.
Q. Doctor, would you explain why you had irregular abnormal pattern of mandibular motion?
A. Probably due to muscles and/or ligaments incoordination.
Q. Is that a disease?
A. It is a dysfunction called dyskenesia.
Q. What is dyskenesia?

A. Abnormal muscle movement.
Q. Did you do Sonography?
A. Yes, I did.
Q. What is your findings?
A. Abnormal noises in the joint.
Q. What does it mean abnormal noises?
A. It means that the mechanics of the joint are not adequate and a significant disturbance in the joint balance resulting in vibrations, frictions, or snapping which can be recorded by a computer.
Q. Did you order an M.R.I.?
A. Yes, I did.
Q. What is an M.R.I.?
A. M.R.I. is a magnetic resonance imaging where the use of a state of the art medical machine is used to measure the different magnetic energy of the body tissues to show the soft and hard tissues as well.
Q. What was your findings?
A. Anterior disc displacement in closed mouth position.
Q. Is this pathology?
A. Yes it is in some cases.
Q. How could this happen?
A. Probably due to trauma.
Q. What kind of trauma?
A. Mechanical trauma.
Q. Doctor, what was your diagnostic impression at that time?
A. Anterior disc displacement with reduction and myofacial pain dysfunction.
Q. Did you plan any treatment for the plaintiff at that time?
A. Yes, I did.
Q. What was your plan?
A. #1 Continue medical supervision
#2 Mandibular orthopedic repositioning appliances
#3 Physical therapy
Q. Doctor, did you determine a prognosis at that time?
A. Yes, I did.
Q. What was your prognosis?
A. Guarded.
Q. Why was your prognosis guarded?
A. I was not sure in the beginning.

Q. Doctor, do you have an opinion of what could be the cause of the injury sustained by my client?
A. I believe that the plaintiff was injured in the accident in question.
Q. Doctor, do you have any objective findings about my client's symptoms?
A. Yes, I do.
Q. What are your objective findings about my client's symptoms?
A. The range of motion was restricted. The muscle palpation was painful, the sonography was abnormal, the E.M.G. was with higher electrical activities, the M.R.I. showed displaced disc.
Q. Did you see this patient for a follow up visit?
A. Yes, I did.
Q. What was that date?
A. (date)
Q. What did you do on that visit?
A. I inserted a mouth piece or what we call a splint, and gave the patient instructions of how to use the splint and some restrictions.
Q. Doctor, can you explain to the jury what you mean by a mouth piece or splint?
A. It is a piece or plastic placed on the teeth, to prevent overclosure of the lower jaw and decreases the stress on joint and relaxes the facial muscles.
Q. Doctor, what kind of restrictions and/or instructions did you give to the plaintiff?
A. The patient was instructed to use the appliance or splint 24 hours a day, use heat/cold applications, eat soft diet, rest her jaw, avoid any vigorous oral activities such as excessive talking, chewing gum, singing, kissing, etc.
Q. Doctor, did you see the patient after this visit?
A. Yes, I did.
Q. How many times did you see the patient after this visit?
A. About 18 times.
Q. Doctor, was my client cooperative?
A. Yes, she was.
Q. Doctor, did my client show up to your office on time every visit?
A. Yes, she did.
Q. Doctor, did my client follow the instructions?
A. Yes, she did.
Q. Did my client reach maximum medical improvement?

A. Yes, she did.
Q. Doctor, what is you future plan for my client?
A. I am planning light orthodontic treatment to increase the height of her back teeth to support the mandible in the new position.
Q. Doctor, how much did you charge my client for the treatment you rendered?
A. About $3,500.00
Q. Doctor, how much will it cost for the future treatment?
A. About $3,200.00
Q. Doctor, were these costs reasonable and necessary in the treatment of my client for the injuries she sustained from this accident?
A. Yes, sir.
Q. Did you arrive at an opinion on whether my client has a permanent impairment or not?
A. Yes, I did.
Q. What is your opinion?
A. The plaintiff suffered a permanent impairment.
Q. Doctor, do you have a percentage rating of permanent impairment for my client?
A. Yes, I do.
Q. What is the percentage rating of permanent impairment for my client?
A. About 3% of the body as a whole.
Q. Is this based on any kind of rating?
A. Yes.
Q. What is the rating based on?
A. I based it on a modified version of a combination of the American Medical Association and the American Academy of Head, Neck, Facial Pain, and TMJ Orthopedic Guidelines.
Q. Doctor, do you think that this is a reasonable rating?
A. Yes, I do.

Thank you, I have no further questions.

APPENDIX D

CROSS-EXAMINATION OF PLAINTIFF'S EXPERT BY DEFENDANT'S LAWYER

Q. Doctor, would you state your name, profession, and professional address?
A. My name is Dr. T.M.J. and I am a dentist and my address is street, city, state.
Q. Doctor, did you have a chance to see the past medical records and other medical records of the plaintiff?
A. No, sir.
Q. No, you didn't?
A. I was not provided with the past medical history.
Q. Did you request the past medical records?
A. No, sir.
Q. Did you ask the patient about her past medical history?
A. Briefly.
Q. What did she tell you?
A. She told me what was written in the records here.
Q. Doctor, did you know that this plaintiff had an auto accident six months prior to this accident in question?
A. No, sir.
Q. Doctor, did you know that this accident was a severe accident and could have been the reason for all of her complaints?
A. No, sir.
Q. Doctor, did you ask her about previous injuries?
A. I'm not sure.
Q. Doctor, don't you think that it is important to ask about previous injuries, previous accidents, or trauma?
A. Probably, yes.

Q. But you didn't ask her about that?
A. Probably not.
Q. Doctor, don't you think it is important to ask about previous traumas to reach a fair opinion?
A. Probably, yes.
Q. Doctor, what are the causes for temporomandibular joint disorder?
A. Mechanical, emotional, chemical, thermal traumas
Q. Doctor, did you know that the plaintiff had a fist fight with an injury to the face a year ago?
A. No, I didn't.
Q. Doctor, don't you think it is important to know about it as a part of the history?
A. Probably, yes.
Q. But you didn't ask the patient about this?
A. No, sir.
Q. Doctor, did you know the medication that was taken by this plaintiff?
A. I am not aware of any.
Q. Doctor, did the plaintiff tell you that she was taking birth control pills for the last five years?
A. No, I did not.
Q. Don't you think that this could cause some headaches?
A. I'm not sure.
Q. You are not sure?
Q. Did you look to the P.D.R. (Physicians Desk Reference)?
A. I don't recall.
Q. Do you review the medications taken by the patient and the side effects?
A. I usually do.
Q. Did you do this in this case?
A. No, I didn't.
Q. Doctor, don't you think that it was important to see the side effects of taking medications before concluding an opinion?
A. Probably, yes.
Q. Doctor, can you tell me all the courses that you have taken for temporomandibular joint in the last year?
A. (explanation)
Q. How many hours of continuing education are these?
A. Fifteen.

Q. Doctor, do think fifteen hours are adequate for you to keep updated with the progress in the field of temporomandibular joint disorder?
A. Probably, yes.
Q. Doctor, don't you think that with the advancement of temporomandibular joint field that you need more hours?
A. Maybe.
Q. Doctor, would you tell us how many books you read in the last year about temporomandibular joint disorder?
A. (explanation)
Q. What are the authors of these books?
A. (explanation)
Q. What did you learn from these books?
A. (explanation)
Q. Doctor, have you testified before on the plaintiff's side?
A. Yes.
Q. What are the percentages of your practice from patients who came to you as the result of traumatic injury?
A. (explanation)
Q. What are the percentages of patients in your office involved with litigation?
A. (explanation)
Q. Doctor, did you happen to get referrals from the plaintiffs counsel's office, other than this patient?
A. (explanation)
Q. So you have a large number of patients coming from the same law firm?
A. (explanation)
Q. So your opinion might affect future referrals?
A. (explanation)
A. I have written several articles in the field of the oral, facial pain and TMJ disorder.
Q. Doctor, can you mention the name of these articles, and where can we find them?
A. Yes, sir. These articles are on an overview of the TMJ disorders in the State Dental Journal and the diagnosis and treatment of TMJ disorder in a National Dental Journal.
Q. Doctor, are you an affiliate with any schools, hospitals, or institutions?
A. Yes, I am. I am affiliated with (hospital) and (institute).
Q. Doctor, would you give the jury an estimate of the number of patients you have treated for temporomandibular joint disorder?

A. Yes, sir. Over a thousand cases.
Q. Doctor, how many of these are related to traumatic injuries or auto accidents?
A. About 30%.
Q. Doctor, do you get referrals from other professionals?
A. Yes, I do.
Q. Who refers patients to you?
A. Doctors, physicians, chiropractors, physical therapists, and patients.
Q. Doctor, would you list the last ten continuing education courses you have taken?
A. Yes, sir.
Q. Doctor, within reasonable degree of medical probability do you have an opinion on what was the cause for the plaintiff's complaint?
A. Yes, I do.
Q. What is your opinion?
A. (explanation)
Q. Doctor, can you tell me how much you charged this plaintiff for the services rendered?
A. About $3,500.00.
Q. How much of this was paid by the patient?
A. None.
Q. How much was paid by other parties?
A. About $1,500.00.
Q. How much is the balance?
A. About $2,000.00.
Q. Doctor, do you think that Mrs. Plaintiff has to win this case in order for you to get paid?
A. It does not make a difference. I charged her and she is responsible for the balance.
Q. Doctor, what will happen if the plaintiff loses this case?
A. I cannot predict that sir.
Q. Doctor, have you done independent medical examinations?
A. Yes, I have.
Q. Doctor, have you found any patient with a traumatic experience but did not suffer from temporomandibular joint disorder?
A. Yes, I have.
Q. Do you treat patients with TMJ disorders from other reasons than mechanical traumas?
A. Yes, I do.

Q. What are the other reasons?
A. Stress, malocclusion, normal disturbances, and others.
Q. Doctor, can you compare the temporomandibular joint patients in litigation to patients who are not in litigation?
A. Yes, I can.
Q. In what aspect are they different?
A. Maybe the severity of the condition, maybe motivational factors.
Q. Can you tell me the length of treatment, does it vary in patients involved in litigation and patients not in litigation?
A. Yes, patients in litigation take a longer time to treat.
Q. When did you see this patient first?
A. (date)
Q. What were the chief complaints?
A. Headaches, neckaches, jaw pain, and earaches.
Q. Doctor, these symptoms are what the plaintiff told you?
A. Yes, sir.
Q. Are these subjective or objectives?
A. Subjective.
Q. Doctor, what does subjective mean?
A. Means given by the patient.
Q. Did you do an exam?
A. Yes, I did.
Q. What are your findings?
A. Anterior disc displacement and myofacial pain dysfunction.
Q. Was the EMG result significant? How significant?
A. It showed muscle spasm.
Q. Was CMS result significant and how significant?
A. It showed deviated mandibular pattern of motion.
Q. Can the patient voluntarily deviate her mandible?
A. Yes, she can, but we advise to open and close naturally.
Q. Was sonography result significant and how significant?
A. It showed abnormal noises.
Q. Do normal joints have noises?
A. Yes, mild noises can be acceptable as normal.
Q. What did you see in the x-ray films and how significant?
A. It showed displacement of the condyles backwards.
Q. What type of x-ray technique?
A. Tomographic technique.

Q. Doctor, how much are you paid for this deposition or (court appearance)?
A. I am not paid.
Q. Is it for free?
A. No, sir.
Q. You mean you do not get any money for this appearance?
A. I get compensation for the time lost from patient's care.
Q. So you get $500.00 an hour compensation?
A. Yes, sir.
Q. Did you write that many people go undiagnosed with T.M.J. disorder?
A. Yes, sir.
Q. So doctor, based on your articles is it possible within a reasonable degree of medical/dental probability that the disc displacement as well as symptoms can be pre-existing in Mrs. Plaintiff.
A. Disc displacement maybe but the symptoms I don't have evidence of it.
Q. Could Ms. Plaintiff have had symptoms but never reported to any dentist or physician?
A. Everything is possible.
Q. Doctor, you testified earlier today that the plaintiff suffered an injury from the auto accident in question, now after you knew the history of the previous auto accident and the fist fight, do you still have the same opinion?
A. I am not sure.
Q. Doctor, you testified before that trauma can be a cause for T.M.J. disorder, didn't you?
A. Yes, I did.
Q. Now comparing the accident of (date), the previous accident of (date) and the fist fight, do you think this could have done any change to the T.M.J.?
A. Probably, yes.
Q. What can happen to T.M.J. from a direct fist fight?
A. Well, it depends on the force, the position, and the health of the host.
Q. Doctor, listen carefully we are talking about the same person and almost the same age as the 3 incidents that happened within a year period. Would you say that T.M.J. disorder caused by the first accident, the fist fight, or the accident we are here for today?
A. Probably initiated by the first accident, maybe aggravated by the fist fight, and reaggravated by the second accident.

Q. O.K. doctor, and when you know that the plaintiff had severe jaw pain and her jaw was locked before the accident for which we are here today would this change your opinion?
A. I don't have a record of this.
Q. Doctor, let us assume that this was true, would it change your opinion as to what the probable cause of her T.M.J. disorder?
A. Yes, sir.
Q. How would it change it?
A. It could be the previous auto accident or the fist fight.
Q. Doctor, you testified that if there were symptoms of that nature, this means a pre-existing disorder?
A. Yes, sir.
Q. Doctor, have you seen these hospital records?
A. No, sir.
Q. Would you read it?
A. It says patient reported locked jaw after receiving trauma through a fist fight from her husband while roughhousing.
Q. Was patient cooperative in the course of her treatment?
A. Yes, sir.
Q. Would you read in your records the dates you have seen this patient after (date)?
A. It is (date)?
Q. How far apart?
A. 3 months.
Q. Would this delay affect the course of treatment?
A. Somewhat.
Q. When was the last visit you saw the plaintiff?
A. (date)
Q. Is she scheduled for another appointment?
A. No, sir.
Q. Did you release her?
A. Yes, sir.
Q. What was her complaints at the last appointment?
A. Headaches, jaw pain, earaches, difficulty chewing hard food, and talking.
Q. Are these subjective or objective?
A. Subjective.
Q. Did you consider these symptoms in your rating of her permanent impairment?

A. Yes, sir.
Q. Sir, let us assume for a moment that this patient was able to speak for a long time, eat hard food, would this change your permanent impairment rating?
A. Yes, sir.
Q. In what way?
A. Decrease it.
Q. Sir, let us again assume that this patient never complained of headaches during her work or home, would it change your permanent impairment rating?
A. Yes, sir.
Q. In what way.
A. Decrease it.
Q. Sir, if there are neither motor nor sensory dysfunctions would you give this patient any impairment rating?
A. Probably, no.

Thank you doctor, I have no further questions.

APPENDIX E

SAMPLE OF REDIRECT EXAMINATION OF PLAINTIFF'S EXPERT BY PLAINTIFF'S LAWYER

Q. Doctor, did you believe Ms. Plaintiff when she told you about her symptoms?
A. Yes, I did.
Q. Do you think she was honest?
A. Yes, I do.
Q. Doctor, do you have patients who receive trauma, and recover.
A. Yes, sir.
Q. Then another trauma could cause reoccurrence of the disorder?
A. Yes, sir.
Q. Do you think this was the case with my client?
A. Could be.
Q. Doctor, do you know that my client had no residuals from this small incident of the fist fight and required no further treatment?
A. No, I did not.
Q. Now doctor, my client has a small auto accident in which there was no direct trauma to her face or head, and had a fist fight touching her face during a friendly roughhousing with no subsequent treatment or medical or dental care. Then she received a major accident in which she had direct trauma to her face. Does this within a reasonable degree of medical and dental probability tell you something?
A. Yes, sir.
Q. What does it tell you?

A. There was a recovery from the previous incident and reoccurrence caused by this accident.

Q. What was the reason for my client's interruption of treatment for 3 months?

A. I do not know.

Q. Doctor, did you know that she was using the T.E.N.S. unit at home and she could not miss any other time from her work?

A. I am not sure.

Q. Is it reasonable that some patients disappear for 3 months during which they are self treating themselves?

A. Could be.

Thank you, I have no further questions.

APPENDIX F

SAMPLE OF DIRECT EXAMINATION OF DEFENDANT'S EXPERT BY DEFENDANT'S LAWYER

Q. Please state your name.
A. My name is Dr. I.M.E.
Q. Doctor, what is your profession?
A. I am a dentist.
Q. How old are you?
A. 40.
Q. Where do you practice?
A. I practice at street, city, state.
Q. Do you have a specialty or special interest in any field? or subject of dentistry?
A. Yes, I have.
Q. What is that?
A. I have a special interest in the field of oral, facial pain and T.M.J. disorder.
Q. Could you give us a summary of your professional background?
A. Yes, sir. I practice dentistry with an emphasis on diagnosis and treatment of oral, facial pain and TMJ disorders. I graduated from (university) in (state) in (year). I have done an internship at (dental school). I have earned a master degree in (subject) at (university).
Q. Doctor, do you belong to any professional associations?
A. Yes, I do. I belong to the American Dental Association, State Dental Association, Central State Dental Association, County Dental Association, Academy of General Dentistry, American Academy of Head, Neck, Facial Pain, and TMJ Orthopedics, International Col-

lege of Craniomandibular Orthopedics, International Association of Orthodontics, American Association for Functional Orthodontics.

Q. Doctor, can you tell us how long you have been practicing as a dentist?

A. I have been practicing dentistry for the last (# of years).

Q. Doctor, do you have a license to practice dentistry in the state of (state)?

A. Yes, I do.

Q. Are you licensed to practice in any other state?

A. No.

Q. Doctor, do you happen to have any other professional activities you can mention to the jury?

A. Yes, I do.

Q. What are they?

A. I am presently involved in a series of lectures to physicians, dentists, and lawyers in the field of T.M.J.

Q. Have you been invited to any dental associations or societies to lecture?

A. Yes, I have.

Q. What are these organizations or societies?

A. State Dental Society, County Dental Hygiene Society.

Q. What other activities are you involved in?

A. I have written several articles in the field of the oral, facial pain and TMJ disorder.

Q. Doctor, can you mention the name of these articles, and where can we find them?

A. Yes, sir. These articles are on an overview of the TMJ disorders in the State Dental Journal and the diagnosis and treatment of TMJ disorder in a National Dental Journal.

Q. Doctor, are you an affiliate with any schools, hospitals, or institutions?

A. Yes, I am. I am affiliated with (hospital) and (institute).

Q. Doctor, would you give the jury an estimate of the number of patients you have treated for temporomandibular joint disorder?

A. Yes, sir. Over a thousand cases.

Q. Doctor, how many of these are related to traumatic injuries or auto accidents?

A. About 30%.

Q. Doctor, do you get referrals from other professionals?

A. Yes, I do.

Q. Who refers patients to you?
A. Doctors, physicians, chiropractors, physical therapists, and patients.
Q. Doctor, would you list the last ten continuing education courses you have taken?
A. Yes, sir.
Q. What are they?
A. I have taken a course on the Anatomy of the Temporomandibular Joint, Radiology of the Temporomandibular Joint Disorder, Diagnosis of the TMJ Disorders, Imaging Technique of Temporomandibular Joint Disorders. I have attended the National Conference of the American Academy of the Head, Neck, Facial Pain and TMJ Orthopedic. I have attended the National Conference of the American Academy of the Head, Neck, Facial Pain and TMJ Orthopedic. I have attended the National Conference of the International College of Craniomandibular Orthopedics. I have attended state dental meetings. I have attended an update seminar on Medicolegal Aspects of the Temporomandibular Joint.
Q. Doctor, would you list the last ten books you have read?
A. Yes, sir. I have read Fundamentals of Occlusion and Temporomandibular Joint Disorders by Okeson, Temporomandibular Joint Disorders, Diagnosis, and Treatment by Sigmond and Wiesberg, The Stomatognathic System by Franco Mongini, Occlusion and Malocclusion by Howat, Abnormal Jaw Mechanics by Solberg and Clark, The Physiology of Oral Reconstruction by Dubrul and Menekratis, TMJ and Cranio-Facial Pain by Fricton, et al, Temporomandibular Joint by Norman and Bramley, Neuromuscular Dental Diagnosis and Treatment by Robert Jenkelson, Myofacial Pain Dysfunction by Travel and Simon, Facial Pain by Mahan and Alling, Temporomandibular Joint Problems by Solberg and Clark, Bone Remodeling by Qussizk, The Clinical Management of the Maxillo Facial Orthopedic Appliances by Dr. Witzig and Spahl (part one and two).
Q. Doctor, would you explain by what you mean by temporomandibular joint disorder?
A. Temporomandibular joint disorder means a problem in the jaw joint. That is the hinge joint which is found on each side of the face just in front of the ear and it moves when you open and close your mouth. Temporomandibular joint disorder means that there is a problem in that jaw joint.

Q. Doctor, would you please mention the probable causes of temporomandibular joint disorder?

A. Temporomandibular joint disorders can be caused by many factors such as anxiety, anger, depression, sadness, worry, fear, frustration, and irritability. These can cause muscle spasms and subsequently problems in the jaw joint. Some bad habits or parafunctions such as bruxism (grinding of the teeth) and clenching. This is putting to much pressure on the muscles or mastication causing overloading of the temporomandibular jaw joint and spasm of the Lateral Pterygoid muscle which is attached to the joint and causing a disorder. Also malocclusion or poor bite such as overbite, crossbite, increased overjet, shifting of the midline, teeth crowding, open bite, or if we have premature contact of the teeth. These can cause too much stress in the joint and can cause increase pressure on the TMJ and can cause a problem. Also, mechanical trauma such as sports events, auto accidents, falling on the floor, or going on simulated speed rides, like recreational parks and carnivals. Also it can be caused due to administration of medical or dental treatment such as improper forcible extractions, improper and forcible pressure during delivering of general anesthesia, improper traction when you put the parts of the traction device on the chin.

Q. What other causes or factors can weaken or predispose the TMJ?

A. Predisposing factors or weakening factors are like nutritional deficiencies such as calcium deficiencies, additives to the food, hormonal disturbances, vascular problems, systemic problems such as diabetes, lupus. All these factors can weaken the tissue when a regular will be received by this. These weakened tissues the reaction will be as overloading the joint and problems can arise.

Q. What other factors can cause similar conditions?

A. Medications can cause some side effects such as facial pain.

Q. What are these medications?

A. Many medications can cause those problems such as anti-psychotic tranquilizers, oral contraceptives (birth control pills), diatritics, digitals. Some drugs such as phenergan, haldol, mellaril, thorazin can cause the muscles to be rigid. They can cause something called dysponia and also tardine dyskenesia which means the patient will do unusual movements or ticks.

Q. Doctor, do you think there is other several causes other than traumatic incidences to cause temporomandibular joint disorders?

A. Yes, sir.
Q. Doctor, did you happen to examine the plaintiff?
A. Yes, I did.
Q. When did you examine the plaintiff?
A. (Date)
Q. Who requested this examination?
A. Your partner Mr. Defense lawyer, sir.
Q. How long did this exam take?
A. About an hour.
Q. Doctor, what did you do during the exam?
A. I took an extensive history from the patient and performed a clinical examination.
Q. Doctor, what where your questions in the history and you may use your report which was written on that date if you like?
A. I took her chief complaints.
Q. What were these chief complaints?
A. It was headaches, jaw pain, jaw clicking, earaches, and neckaches.
Q. Did she relate these to any incidents.
A. Yes, sir. She claimed that she had these symptoms as the result of an auto accident on (date).
Q. Did you ask her about prior accidents?
A. Yes, sir.
Q. What did she say?
A. She said that she did not have any other accidents.
Q. Did you ask her about other traumas she might have received?
A. Yes, sir.
Q. What did she say?
A. That she did not mention receiving any other traumas other than the accident in question.
Q. Doctor, did you take a past medical history?
A. Yes, sir.
Q. What was it?
A. According to the patient it was not significant.
Q. Did she tell you how the accident happened?
A. Yes, sir.
Q. What did she say?
A. She said that she was driving with a seat belt on and she was rear ended by another vehicle driven at 45mph.
Q. Did she tell you how her body moved during this accident?

A. Yes, sir. She claimed that she hit the steering wheel with her face which caused bruises.
Q. Did she tell you how she sought medical attention?
A. She was referred by her lawyer to Dr. Orthopedic Surgeon who referred her to Dr. T.M.J..
Q. When did she start seeing Dr. T.M.J.?
A. She started seeing Dr. T.M.J. on (date).
Q. What did Dr. T.M.J. do for her?
A. He fabricated a splint after doing a preliminary examination. He also told her that she had permanent impairment and she might have to live with this or she might need surgery.
Q. Doctor, is it the usual manner to tell the patient that he/she needs surgery and has a permanent impairment in the first visit?
A. No, sir.
Q. What is the usual way?
A. The usual way is to exam the patient after taking the history, start formulating the treatment plan, and treating the patient the best way you can. Then your goals should be a total elimination of problems, signs, and symptoms, then if you fail in total elimination of symptoms you may decide if the patient needs surgery or has permanent impairment in his body.
Q. Doctor, do you refer for surgery?
A. Yes, when it is indicated.
Q. What are the criterias for referring a patient to surgical intervention?
A. Actually surgery is not indicated in many cases.
Q. Why, sir.
A. Surgery has a lot of complications and is not guaranteed. Many patient have gone for surgery and the symptoms are still persistent.
Q. So what are your guidelines for referring a patient for surgery?
A. The guidelines are that the patient must have disc or structural disorder which is documented by an appropriate imaging technique such as arthrograph or M.R.I.. Also the patient must have a severe problem which could not be eliminated or reduced by the non-surgical techniques. The non-surgical therapy should be delivered adequately for an adequate time. i.e. the patient had at least six months (for a moderate to severe case) of non-surgical treatment which can include properly fabricated mandibular splints, physical therapy, and behavioral therapy. In addition we have to remove all kinds of parafunctions, such as bad habits and rehabilitate the dental

occlusion temporarily in order to see the affect on the joint symptoms. Furthermore the patient must consent to this kind of treatment with the knowledge that there is no guarantee of the surgery and knowledge of alternative approaches such as living with the conditions without treatment.

Q. Doctor, you mean that surgery is needed only for very, very rare cases.

A. Yes, sir, it is not needed in most of these disorder cases.

Q. Doctor, after you have taken the history of the patient did you do a physical examination?

A. Yes, sir.

Q. What does your physical examination consist of?

A. The physical examination consists of facial analysis, muscle palpation, occlusal analysis, measure the range of motion, listening or auscultation of the temporomandibular joint.

Q. Doctor, would you explain what is the significance of facial analysis?

A. Facial analysis is analysing or looking to the face looking for any deformity or asymmetry.

Q. Doctor, what is the significance of deformity or asymmetry?

A. Well, deformity could be due to the fracture of the mandible or maxilla from any severe traumatic problems which has healed with disfigurment. Asymmetry could be in cases where the eyebrows are on different levels, the nose is deviated to one side, or even the chin may be deviated to the other side. Sometimes we see the reduction of the lower third of the face height. These are indications of the lack of adequate growth of the mandible and/or maxilla.

Q. Doctor, what does this mean to you in lay terminology?

A. It means there is a disturbance in the growth and development during the childhood or teenage years. Also it can indicate a previous mandibular displacement.

Q. Doctor, what else have you done?

A. I did occlusal analysis.

Q. Sir, what do you mean by occlusal analysis?

A. It means looking to the bite and checking for any deviation from normal.

Q. How did you do this?

A. By looking and analyzing the bite in three dimensions. For example, vertical dimension (upward and downward) I looked to the overlapping of the upper teeth and the lower teeth, this was 5mm overlap. There was horizontal difference between the upper and lower teeth about 7mm. There was also deviation of the midline to the right about 3mm.

Q. What does this deviation mean?
A. This deviation means that there is a misplacement and displacement of the mandible.
Q. What else did you see in the bite.
A. I saw a crossbite.
Q. What do you mean by crossbite?
A. It means that the lower teeth are meshing with the upper teeth opposite of the normal way of biting.
Q. What does this indicate?
A. This indicates too much stress on the TMJ and can cause overloading or overstretching of the ligaments.
Q. What else did you find during your physical examination?
A. I found the range of motion to be 35mm, this is when the patient opened on her own. However, when I overextended the mandibular opening I found it to be 50mm.
Q. How did you do that?
A. Well, there is an active range of motion this is what is given by the patient and the patient has control over it, and there is a passive range of motion where the therapist is opening the mandible to the full extent and that was 50mm.
Q. Was her active and passive range of motion within the normal range?
A. Yes, sir.
Q. What else did you find in your physical examination?
A. I palpated the muscle.
Q. What do you mean by palpating the muscle?
A. I used my two hands and pressed the muscles gently and firmly and checked the consistency of the muscles and looked for a response by the patient.
Q. What was your findings?
A. I found no change in the consistency of the muscles. However, the patient showed verbal responses when I touched the Masseter muscles and the Temporalis muscles.
Q. Doctor, would that depend on the patient's response.
A. Yes, sir.
Q. Was that a subjective response?
A. Yes, sir.

Q. Do you have any objective findings from that muscle palpation?
A. Yes, sir.
Q. What was it?
A. There was no change in the consistency of the muscles.
Q. What does that mean?
A. It means that there is no pathology or that there is no muscle spasm.
Q. What else have you done for this examination?
A. Observing the patient while talking.
Q. Why is this observation?
A. To see if she is opening wider in other occasions or if there are disturbed mandibular movement.
Q. Did she open wider or did you see a disturbed mandible?
A. No sir, she seemed normal.
Q. Did you listen to the joint?
A. Yes, sir.
Q. How did you do that?
A. I used a stethoscope.
Q. Did you see any movement or any abnormal signs?
A. Yes, sir. I found some small clicking on the left side.
Q. Is the click a pathology by itself?
A. Yes and no. Let me explain that. Some clicks are incipient and they are not harmful when it is compensated. However, when this click is increased it becomes louder and occurs with an interference or deviation of the mandible in opening that can be of harm to the patient.
Q. Doctor, after examining the patient and taking the history do you have an opinion of what are the causes for her symptoms?
A. Yes, sir.
Q. What is your opinion?
A. My opinion is that she had pre-existing problems which could cause TMJ symptoms.
Q. Is that opinion based on a reasonable degree of medical probability?
A. Yes, sir.
Q. Therefore, how do you explain that the disc displacement was pre-existing in Ms. Plaintiff?
A. Sir, if we are looking to this (using a model) you can see here the position of the teeth and the position of the condyle. The teeth are meshing together in a normal fashion like gears and the condyles is rested against the posterior slope of the articulating eminence with

a cartilaginous disc interposed. If for some reason we move a part of the teeth enamel or grind part of the teeth or the teeth did not erupt or grow in the normal position, then the condyle and the mandible as a whole will be pushed or displaced backward. Due to the fact that the fossa cannot stretch the disc which is soft tissue will be pushed or forced to be displaced anteriorly. Therefore, I have seen the wear facets in the teeth. This seemed like it happened long before the accident in question. Therefore, in my opinion the disc displaced prior to the accident.

Q. Doctor, how many times did I ask you to appear in court on my behalf?

A. This is the first time.

Q. Doctor, are you being paid whether we win or lose this case?

A. Yes, sir.

Q. So you opinion is independent?

A. Yes, sir.

APPENDIX G

CROSS-EXAMINATION OF DEFENDANT'S EXPERT BY PLAINTIFF'S LAWYER

Q. Doctor, you just said that the disc was displaced anteriorly, do you have any proof of that?
A. Yes, sir.
Q. What is your proof?
A. My proof is the condyle is displaced backward which I can see on the x-ray film through flattening of the posterior surface of the condyle. I can also see the lack of complete eruption of growth of teeth to the proper height. I can see the deep bite which means the supporting height is not adequate enough to support the mandible. Therefore, from these objective findings I can conclude that the mandible as well as the condyle were displaced backward. This can cause within a reasonable degree of medical probability the disc to be displaced forward.
Q. Doctor, did you know that the patient did not feel any clicking prior to the accident?
A. It is possible.
Q. Doctor, so could it be that the patient has all of these malocclusion and the theory that you are talking about on the x-ray that the disc is not displaced?
A. No, sir.
Q. Can you explain that?
A. Within a reasonable degree of medical probability 51% of the cases, if we have a malocclusion deep bite and remodeled condyle such as we find in Ms. Plaintiff it's most likely that the disc will be displaced anteriorly. The question that the patient does not feel it doesn't mean it is not existing, it is just simply that the patient was not aware of it.

Q. Doctor, are you aware that my client has been to five dentists since her childhood and none of them diagnosed her as having temporomandibular joint disorder or disc displacement?
A. Well, many dentists don't pay attention to examining the temporomandibular joint. Being not recorded on the record does not mean it did not exist. It could be pre-existed and misdiagnosed or overlooked by other professionals.
Q. Doctor, do you know that Dr. General Dentist is a very competent dentist and Dr. Prothodontist who is board certified prothodontist have seen this patient and never noted in the record that she had disc displacement?
A. Well sir, I can't comment on another experts level of expertise however, generally speaking in the dental community we have very little information about temporomandibular joint disorders. Fortunately it is increasing with time.
Q. Doctor, are you saying that those doctors are neglient in recognizing the temporomandibular joint?
A. Sir, I am not saying that. I'm just saying it must have been overlooked.
Q. Doctor, you testified earlier that you took an hour examining the patient. I don't see it recorded in your report.
A. Well sir, I don't record that on the report.
Q. How did you monitor your timing?
A. Well the appointment book indicated that I saw this patient between 11 and 12am on that date.
Q. Doctor, so you took one hour examining that patient?
A. I took one hour taking the history from the patient and examining her.
Q. So how long was the history?
A. About 25 to 30 minutes.
Q. How long was the examination?
A. About the same.
Q. Did the patient tell you that she had headaches, jaw pain, jaw clicking, and earaches?
A. Yes, sir.
Q. Do you have a doubt about what she was telling you?
A. I'm not sure.
Q. Do you think that she was lying when she was telling you her symptoms?

A. Well I'm not saying that, but it could be imaginary or psychosamatic or pre-existing or a compensation neurosis.

Q. Compensation neurosis, what do you mean by that? You mean my patient is crazy?

A. No, sir. I am saying that due to the fact that this case is in litigation the patient is getting psychological conditioning that she is going to get some money if she does have pain and permanent impairment.

Q. Doctor, did you review any of her medical records prior to the appointment?

A. Yes, sir.

Q. What records did you review?

A. I reviewed the emergency room records, I reviewed the medical doctor's records, Dr. Internist, Dr. GYN, Dr. Neurologist, Dr. Orthopedic Surgeon, the physical therapy records, and Dr. TMJ records.

Q. Doctor, did you take an x-ray on this patient?

A. No, sir, but I used the x-ray taken by Dr. TMJ.

Q. What kind of x-ray did he take or did you read?

A. I have a transcranial x-ray and panoramic x-ray.

Q. From these x-rays you can tell that the patient had a pre-existing condition?

A. No, sir.

Q. So why do you say that she has a pre-existing condition?

A. The x-rays or radiographic testing is one part of the whole deal. It is like one piece of the puzzle. The history of the patient, review of the previous records, clinical examination, and x-rays and other testing forms pieces in order to solve the puzzle and see the whole picture.

Q. But, you didn't take x-rays?

A. No, I didn't. Neither did Dr. TMJ, his assistant did and if this patient was in my office I would do the same. My assistant would take the x-rays and I will read it.

Q. Sir, now how did you measure the range of motion?

A. I used a ruler.

Q. Is this a cheap ruler you used and you are concluding your opinion?

A. No, sir, I am concluding my opinion of the range of motion based on my measurements as well as assessment of the patient's condition. I also read the conclusion of the sonography taken by Dr. TMJ.

Q. What did it show?

A. Well my findings were consistant with the sonography studies found by Dr. TMJ.

Q. Doctor, don't you see that many people with malocclusion don't have TMJ symptoms.
A. Yes, sir.
Q. Don't you see some people with remodeled condyle and don't have TMJ symptoms?
A. Yes, sir.
Q. So if you have seen this how can you conclude that a patient had pre-existing symptoms.
A. Sir again like what I explained to you before that every factor and every finding form a piece in solving the big puzzle. So by putting pieces together we can see the whole picture. So my conclusion is based on the history, the clinical examination, review of previous records, review of x-rays films and review of other testing.
Q. Doctor, how much are you being paid to testify for the defendant today?
A. I am not paid, sir.
Q. Are you telling me that you are coming for free and you don't get any money?
A. Sir, I get compensation for the time lost from the patients care.
Q. How much is that compensation?
A. $500.00 an hour.
Q. $500.00 an hour, is that reasonable?
A. Yes, sir.
Q. How do you reach that figure?
A. Well based on my gross income and the amount of hours I am working every year, the amount of overhead, the rent in my office, the salaries for the employees, the expenses for supplies, I concluded this figure to be reasonable.
Q. You mean to tell me that you spend $500.00 an hour for that office?
A. Sir, this is a very stressful time and it will take some time for me to recover afterward. Therefore one hour of being in the deposition or court appearance might need me a half a day to relax or rest and in addition I have to be prepared for this too. So if you calculate the amount of time consumed for a deposition and a court appearance and the time needed before and after you will see that my compensation rate will be far less than what you are trying to make a big deal of.
Q. Doctor, how many depositions have you done?
A. Dozens

Q. How many times have you appeared in court?
A. Several
Q. Are you testifying mainly on the defendants behalf?
A. No, sir.
Q. What is your defendant to plaintiff ratio in testifying?
A. I don't calculate exactly how much, but I try to be balanced to testify on both sides.

Thank you doctor I have no further questions.

INDEX